Falling In Love

OTHER BOOKS BY AYALA MALACH PINES

Couple Burnout: Causes and Cures
(Routledge)

Career Burnout: Causes and Cures

Experiencing Social Psychology: Readings and Projects
(with Christina Maslach)

The Juggler: A Working Woman: Problems and Solutions
(available in Hebrew)

Psychology of Gender
(available in Hebrew)

Romantic Jealousy
(Routledge)

Falling In Love

WHY WE CHOOSE THE LOVERS WE CHOOSE

AYALA MALACH PINES

ROUTLEDGE
New York London

Published in 1999 by
Routledge
29 West 35th Street
New York, NY 10001

Published in Great Britain by
Routledge
11 New Fetter Lane
London EC4P 4EE

Library of Congress Cataloging-in-Publication Data

Pines, Ayala Malach
    Falling in love: why we choose the lovers we choose / by Ayala Malach Pines.
       p. cm.
    Includes bibliographical references.
    ISBN 0-415-92046-9 hb
      1. Man-woman relationships. 2. Love. 3. Mate selection.
  I. Title
  HQ801.M366 1999
  306.7—dc21
                                       99-22987
                                           CIP

For the people I love most,
My children Itai and Shani
My husband Israel
My parents Judith and Zeev.

Contents

ACKNOWLEDGMENTS

I am a very fortunate woman to be surrounded by brilliant, loving, and generous colleagues who are also my dear and cherished friends. All of them are extremely busy professionals who, nonetheless, found the time to read an early version of this book and improve it immensely with their profound feedback. Dr. Anya Lane, my dear friend for many many years, has contributed to the book her deep knowledge of psychoanalytic theory. Her insights were so profound that, generally, I simply quoted her. Dr. Lillian Rubin, my dear friend and admired role model, has helped make the book more concise and my voice in it clearer. Dr. Carole Pettiet, my spiritual and clear-thinking soul sister, read every word of the book and gave me priceless feedback that helped improve both its organization and style. Dr. Orenya Yanai helped clarify my thinking about the irrationality of falling in love.

This book has been brought to print by a young and dynamic team at Routledge. The team is headed by my wise and energetic publishing director, Heidi Freund; her hard-working assistant, Shea Settimi; the highly skilled managing editor, Anthony Mancini; publicists Ron Longe and Katharine Smalley; product manager Amy Lee and intern Joshua Feldman. Another invaluable member of the team is Abigail Baxter—the best, most intelligent copy editor an author can wish for. They are a wonderful team and a joy to work with.

But my deepest gratitude is reserved for the hundreds of people who took part in my research and clinical work, who shared with me their moving, exciting, poetic, better-than-fiction, love stories.

Introduction

ABOUT FALLING IN LOVE
AND ABOUT THIS BOOK

Love to faults is always blind,
always to joy inclin'd,
lawless, wing'd, and unconfin'd,
and breaks all chains from every mind.
—William Blake, "Poems,"
William Blake's Notebook

Love blinds the eyes from seeing faults.
—Moshe Ben Ezra,
"The Song of Israel"

"*From the first time I met him, there was something that attracted me to him. I was actually going out with someone else, but there was something about the way he conducted himself that attracted me . . . . With the couple of people I really, really liked, it's been the same thing. Right off I knew. But it wasn't lust. There are definitely better looking people out there. But there's something about them . . . the combination of things . . . the look in their eyes . . . the way they hold themselves . . . there's this kind of animal thing.*"

"*This is really funny. When I first saw her, I got the wrong impression. She was the good-looking blond chick that lived next to my friend Bob. I had the impression that she was the party type. This turned out to be totally wrong when I got to know her better. Since I spent a great deal of time with Bob, I saw a lot of her too. Once I helped her with her Italian. Later it turned out that her Italian is far better than mine.*"

A NOTE. The quoted remarks throughout the book have been modified to protect the anonymity of the people interviewed. Primarily, I modified any references to culture, race, or geographic location, or references likely to identify the person speaking.

"A friend of mine wanted me to meet him because she was madly in love with him. When I first met him, I didn't understand what she saw in him. The next time I met him we had a chance to talk and then I found out what was so wonderful about him. He was interesting, and it was really pleasant to talk with him. He made me laugh, and I fell in love with him. I thought he was adorable, funny, warm . . . I had a boyfriend at that time, but I lost interest in him real quick. I did everything I could to see more of him . . . I changed my bike route so I would go past his house. But he didn't seem to notice. Later I discovered that he is very shy. He thought I was dating the other guy and didn't want to make waves. So it took him a very long time to get it. Finally, after about six months, we started dating. I think I said something like 'That guy is history.' Then he said 'So, let's go out.' From then on, our relationship took off. Now it's really hot. We are together all the time."

"She was a student in a class I taught. She was very interested in the class, and spent a lot of time with me. With time we became good friends. At first I wasn't attracted to her. Now it's so obvious. . . . I feel sorry for people who don't have this kind of relationship. She makes me feel complete. The best thing is the actual living together . . . the simple things. We love each other and we love the relationship. She once said to me on the phone, 'I'm in love with being in love with you.'"

THE MAGIC OF LOVE

What sparks it? Why does one particular person ignite it, while another person, who seems so much more appropriate, does not? Throughout history people have tried to understand and control the mysteries of love with magic potions, spells, prayers, and the powers of witches and sorcerers. This is not surprising, given the fact that, for most people, falling in love constitutes one of the most emotionally intense, exhilarating, exciting, and significant of life's experiences. Alan Watts (1985) describes falling in love as a "divine madness" that is akin to the experience of mystical vision.

Falling in love is a thing that strikes like lightning and is, therefore, extremely analogous to the mystical vision . . . We do not really know how people obtain [these experiences], and there is not as yet a very clear rationale as to why it happens. If you should be so fortunate as to encounter either of these experiences, it seems to me to be a total denial of life to refuse it (p. 23).

Even after many years, couples can describe in great detail how they fell in love with each other. Occasionally, but it's rare, their love is at first sight; a little more frequently it springs from a long friendship. At times it's the beloved's look that sparks the romantic attraction, at other times it's a wonderful and endearing quality, or a deeply moving, shared experience. The infatuation may evolve into a rewarding, committed love, or end in a destructive and painful relationship, or, it may just fizzle out. These last cases make us wonder. Since there was obviously nothing there to love, what was it that made me fall in love with this person? The inevitable conclusion is, I was blinded by love. Like the Romans who believed that Cupid, the naughty angel, arbitrarily shot his love arrows at his unsuspecting victims, so too do many of us believe in the arbitrariness of love. (See Figure 1.)

We *fall* into love, it seems, both literally and figuratively. Infatuation commonly determines the final choice from a broad field of potential candidates, and some researchers claim that infatuation is "inherently random" (Lykken & Tellegen, 1993). Thus many people, both lay and professional, do not believe that falling in love is a good enough reason for getting married. After all, love is blind, irrational, and temporary, while choosing a marriage partner is serious business. Because it is expected to last forever, marriage is, and should be, given careful thought and consideration.

FIGURE 1. In Roman mythology, Cupid is the god of love and passion; in Latin, *cupido* means passion. He is the son of Venus, the goddess of love and beauty. Naughty Cupid has no respect for age or social rank. He flies here and there shooting his arrows arbitrarily at his victims—gods and mortals alike. Instantly, they fall in love and burn with boundless passion. (Cupid is identified with the Greek god *Eros*.)

IS LOVE REALLY BLIND?

A large body of theory and research, as well as my own research and many years of clinical work, have convinced me that the answer to this question is a firm no! In this book I will try to show that we fall in love neither by chance or accident. Rather, we choose those with whom we fall in love very carefully in both conscious and unconscious ways. I will try to show how we choose the lovers we choose. From the discussion of this question it will become apparent why it is that people so often make what seem to them "errors in judgment." I will suggest steps for turning such "errors" into opportunities for individual and couple growth. For people who are looking for love relationships, each chapter of the book offers concrete tips for finding romantic love.

This book represents the two hats I wear as a psychologist. One is the hat of a social psychologist and researcher who, for many years, has studied various aspects of couple relationships. The other is the hat of a clinical psychologist who has worked for many years with individuals and couples on relationship issues. While I am very comfortable wearing both of these hats, scholars in these two branches of psychology tend to be rather dismissive of each other. Social psychologists like to conduct controlled studies involving large numbers of subjects. They regard clinical psychologists' data, which is based on clinical work with a small number of subjects who are often patients, as non-scientific at best. Clinical psychologists find social psychologists' obsession with statistics boring and their findings very often trivial.

I, myself, find the contributions of both approaches valuable and complementary (Pines, 1999). The social psychological approach focuses on the question of how people fall in love. What are the conditions that increase the likelihood that romantic love will happen? The clinical approach focuses on the question of why people fall in love with particular persons. Using social psychological research, it is possible to arrive at very specific and concrete recommendations that tell people what they should do to find a romantic partner. Using theories in clinical psychology, people can figure out why they fall in love with particular persons or a particular category of people. While researchers find clinicians' preoccupation with such questions unscientific and their conclusions unfounded, clinicians often find researchers' conclusions simplistic and insignificant. I value both approaches and do not hesitate to present in this book, a) concrete, simple suggestions on how to find a romantic partner, and b) guidelines for discovering why we choose the lovers we choose. The first part of the book presents the social psychological perspective, the second and third parts present the clinical perspective. Researchers, students, and general readers who are interested in the details of a particular study, theory, or issue can find them in the endnotes.

In addition to an extensive review of the research done by others, this book is based on different studies in which I took part. In particular, three clinical studies will be mentioned prominently throughout the book. The first study involved close to one hundred young men and women who were interviewed about their most significant romantic relationships.[1] The second is a cross-cultural study that compared American and Israeli accounts of falling in love.[2] The third study, using one hundred couples, compared the reason each partner gave for why he or she had fallen in love with the reason behind the greatest stress that each later experienced in the relationship.[3] The interviews were recorded and transcribed.

If you had been a subject in one of these studies, you would have been asked the following series of questions. (It's a good idea to think about these questions before reading the book.)

Are you in a romantic relationship? If your answer is no, think about the most important relationship you have ever been in.

What was happening in your life at that time?

How did you meet your partner?

What was your first impression?

What attracted you to your partner?

At what point, if any, did you fall in love?

How did the relationship evolve?

What was, or is, the relationship like?

Is your partner similar to either one of your parents?

What were, or are, the areas of conflict in the relationship? How are they resolved?

What was, or is, the most stressful aspect of your partner or of the relationship?

In analyzing the transcribed interviews I examined the different aspects of falling in love that previous studies and relevant theories had pointed out as critical. Do situational variables such as proximity and arousal really have an effect? Are characteristics of the beloved such as beauty and personality what make us fall in love? What about the effect of such things as similarity and a feeling of being desired? What is the level of commitment in the romantic relationship? What is the level of intimacy?[4]

The analysis of the interviews enabled me to examine different theories that explain how people fall in love and whom they choose as romantic partners. The first part of the book presents the most noteworthy of these theories. Most of the research studies have focused on one aspect of falling in love. The romantic attachment interviews, and an analysis of them, enabled me to examine simultaneously all the different aspects of falling in love.

The first two chapters discuss variables that have nothing to do with the beloved. These are *situational variables* that encourage and enhance falling in love. The first chapter presents studies documenting the power of *proximity* as a hidden matchmaker. We feel more comfortable with and prefer familiar people. The second chapter focuses on the role played by *arousal* in falling in love. People who are aroused, because of a painful loss, an unexpected success, or an exciting experience, are sitting ducks for Cupid's arrows. A woman in one of the romantic attraction studies described the arousing effect of an anticipated trip abroad:

> *"Our first date was unbelievable. We talked the whole night. We came home at 2 A.M., talked the whole night, and then collapsed. He was very interesting. There was some magic in the fact that we got along so well. He had to leave for Europe in two months. During these two months we spent every moment together. Everything went so well that we were a bit suspicious. In the past we had both had short-term relationships, after which we were happy to be alone. All of a sudden we discovered each other. He was supposed to be away for six months and was thinking about canceling the whole trip. In those two months we got out of the relationship what you get out of a three-year relationship. When he was away he wrote and called. A phone bill of close to a thousand dollars waited for him when he returned."*

Suppose I were to ask you, "What made *you* fall in love?" Chances are that in at least a part of your answer, you would mention some endearing personality *traits of the beloved* that captured your heart. In another part of your answer you would most likely mention some attractive feature in the beloved's look. *Beauty and character,* and the role they play in falling in love, are the subjects of the third chapter.

A woman says: "He was open and friendly and looked cute." A man says: "She looked very good, attractive, with her feet on the ground, and she was easy to talk to." She mentions his cute looks at the end, he mentions her good looks first. A coincidence? No, say evolutionary psychologists, whose theory is presented in chapter seven.

In addition to situational variables and beloved variables, there are *relationship variables* that have to do with different aspects of the interaction with the beloved. One such variable—*similarity*—is the matchmaker's rule of thumb. Chapter four analyzes the role of similarity in romantic attraction, including similarity in interests, values, background, attractiveness, intelligence, and even in such things as genetic makeup and psychological health. Hundreds of studies from all over the world suggest that we love our reflection in the other. A young woman describes the effect.

> *"He is similar to me in many things, even though there are also many things in which we are different. We have many things in common. For example we are both first-born children in our families and as a result we had similar childhood experiences, and we play similar roles in our families. We had a special kind of closeness because of our personality. We had similar insecurities about things."*

The other relationship variables, which are discussed in chapter five, are *reciprocity in attraction*, meaning the knowledge that the other is attracted to us, and *need satisfaction*, the fact that the other satisfies an important need or provides something of value. The man who laughingly said, "The thing that I found most attractive about her was the fact that she was attracted to me" gives an example of reciprocity. The man who said, "She needed me, she needed someone who will respect her and I needed her" describes the positive effect of need satisfaction.

After discussing the seven variables that influence when and how people fall in love—each chapter ending with tips for seekers of love—chapter six describes the different roles these variables play at different stages of the falling-in-love *process*. At the beginning, during the getting-acquainted stage, physical appearance is an important selection criterion; a person whose appearance repulses us is, in most cases, rejected outright. In later stages, personality traits become important, and even later than that, similarities in attitudes, values, and interests. Only a person who has successfully passed the selection criteria of stage one, can proceed to stage two, where other selection criteria need to be passed in order to proceed to stage three. A man describes this process, "What attracted me most was her looks, at first. Later, that she's great. She's nice. There was something about her, she would put my mind at ease."

The subject of chapter seven is *gender differences* in love. Is it true that different selection criteria direct the romantic choices of men and women? Do women really prefer men who are rich and successful whereas men prefer women who are young and beautiful? Some, much debated evidence suggests that the answer is yes. A woman describes the attraction of an older, well-to-do man. "He was older than me. There was a difference between him and the boys my age. . . . He could go out and spend money . . . the maturity . . . I don't know." A man describes the appeal of beauty. "She totally dazzled me. . . . She is very beautiful, a natural beauty, and quiet. There was something mysterious about her that charmed me."

The first part of the book deals with variables that are largely known and conscious and, thus, the subject of a huge number of studies. Social psychologists are primarily interested in how the environment, both physical and social, affects the individual. Consequently, this part of the book focuses on external variables that are observable and enhance the chance of falling in love.

While the first part of the book is based primarily on research, the second and third parts are based primarily on clinical experience—others' and mine—and on psychodynamic theory. While social psychology emphasizes the role of the external environment, psychodynamic theory emphasizes the role played by internal images and unconscious forces. Chapter eight addresses the question of why some people seek and find intimate relationships easily and feel secure in them; while others avoid love, either because they are not interested or because they are "simply" too busy; and yet others cling to it so desperately that they scare off potential partners. Chapter nine discusses Freud's well known dictum that a woman falls in love with a man who reminds her of her father, and a man falls in love with a woman who reminds him of his mother. Chapter ten focuses on the *internal romantic image* that determines those with whom we choose to fall in love, and explains why.

Chapter eleven demonstrates the operation of the internal romantic image in four stories told by two men and two women: a man and a woman who describe very intimate and satisfying relationships, and a man and a woman who, at the same age, have never been in intimate relationships.

The third part of the book answers the question why people so often believe that they have made mistakes in their romantic choices, and how such seeming errors can be turned into opportunities for growth. This part is based almost entirely on my experience as a clinical psychologist and couple therapist, and on the writings of other couple therapists. It represents my conviction that the best place for us to grow as individuals is in the context of an intimate relationship. It is far more challenging, and thus better, than individual therapy, which takes place only one or a few hours a week in the security and comfort of a therapist's office.

Chapter twelve is based on an analysis of the relationships of one hundred couples. A few of these couples are described in detail. In each case, the problem that brought the couple for treatment is presented, followed by key points in the personal history of each partner, and finally, their history as a couple, from their first encounter, through falling in love, deciding to form a committed relationship, to their problems becoming serious enough to seek help. In each case it is clear that the traits and behaviors that made the couple fall in love with each other continue to play a significant role in their relationship later on. This connection has very practical implications that are translated into *step-by-step instructions for couples on how to turn their relationship problems into opportunities for growth.*

A caveat. The last two parts of the book present falling in love from a psychodynamic perspective. This perspective has been criticized for putting too much emphasis on childhood experiences and unconscious forces and not enough emphasis on people's conscious goals, hopes, aspirations, and spiritual quests. This is an important point to address because people today, more so than in other periods of history, have very high hopes when they fall in love. Despite the subjective feeling of lovers that love is timeless and boundless, it is nonetheless true that romantic love exists within a particular cultural context (Lindholm, 1998). While romantic love has reigned supreme among other forms of love since time immemorial, it is only in recent years that it has been promoted as the basis for marriage. There is an almost universally shared desire to believe that the emotional bond of love is strong enough to sustain a long-term intimate relationship. Many people today even try to derive a sense of meaning and significance for their entire lives from their love relationships.[5] Thus, it is extremely important that people's ideals, goals, hopes, and spiritual journeys be given as much acknowledgment as their past.

The research appendix, the last part of the book, presents the categories used to analyze the romantic attraction interviews. It makes it possible for interested readers to analyze their own relationships according to these categories. The appendix also presents research data on different aspects of falling in love. It enables those readers who graded their relationship to compare it to the data generated in the different studies. Students and researchers can find in the appendix the kind of "hard" data that they need but that most readers can do without.

All in all, the book addresses the following fascinating questions about falling in love:

- What situations increase the likelihood of falling in love?
- What traits and behaviors make some people easier to love?
- What selection process precedes and later underlies falling in love?
- What is the role of beauty in falling in love?
- Are the things that make men and women fall in love similar or different?
- Is it true that men fall in love with women who remind them of their mothers and women fall in love with men who remind them of their fathers?
- Why do some people fall in love easily and find happiness in their relationships, some want desperately to be in a relationship but are not, and some avoid love altogether?
- How do we choose our lovers?
- Why do some people fall in love repeatedly with people who are bad for them?
- What is the dynamic of obsessive love?
- Where in the brain does falling in love happens?
- What brain chemistry is responsible for the elation associated with falling in love?
- Why can we fall in love with only one person at a time?
- What is it about certain men and women that makes many people fall madly in love with them?

After describing what the book contains, I need to address some of the many fascinating and important things that have been written about love that the book does not address.

WHAT THE BOOK IS NOT ABOUT:
ON THE STYLES, COMPONENTS, AND FORMS OF LOVE

> Love is such a tissue of paradoxes, and exists in such an
> endless variety of forms and shades, that you may say
> almost anything about it that you please and it is likely
> to be correct.
> —Finck, *Romantic Love and Personal Beauty,* 1891

A huge number of books and articles describe the different styles, components, faces, and forms of love. Greek philosophers distinguished among six *styles of love*; they were the love between best friends, unselfish love, posses-sive love, practical love, playful love, and romantic love called *eros*. Contem-porary scientists, in large-scale studies, found confirming evidence for the existence of these very styles of love (Lasswell & Lobsenz, 1980; Lee, 1998).[6]

While love styles point to the consistent differences in the way people experience and express romantic love, this book assumes that each experi-ence of falling in love is unique because it is determined by both conscious and unconscious elements in *both* partners. The same person, whether pas-sionate, game playing, logical, or selfless, will be somewhat different in each romantic relationship because the lover is different and brings unique ele-ments to the interaction between them.

A well known "triangular model of love" describes three *basic components of love*: intimacy, passion, and commitment. The presence or absence of any of these components explains the different faces of love. For example, a rela-tionship with intimacy only is liking. A relationship with passion only is in-fatuation. A relationship with commitment only is empty love. According to the model, romantic love has passion and intimacy but not commitment, whereas the perfect love, the love that includes intimacy, commitment and passion is consummate love[7] (Sternberg, 1986). This book examines only romantic love, but analyzes many more than these three components.

Love can take different forms not only because of the different compo-nents that define it but also because of the different objects to which it is di-rected. Among the *different forms of love* are love between parent and child, brotherly love, motherly love, erotic love, self-love, and love of God (Fromm, 1956). Psychoanalyst Theodore Reik (1957) complains that,

> Love is one of the most overworked words in our vocabulary. There
> is hardly a field of human activity in which the word is not worked
> to death. It is not restricted to expressing an emotion between the
> sexes, but also expresses the emotion between members of a family. It
> signifies the feelings for your neighbor, for your friend, and even for
> your foe, for the whole of mankind, for the home, social or racial
> group, nation, for all that is beautiful and good, and for God Himself.
> It is almost incredible that it can be equal to its many tasks (9).

From all these wonderful forms of love, this book focuses only on ro-mantic, erotic, love—the hunting grounds of Eros. Psychoanalyst Rollo May (1969) explains the significance of Eros.

Eros is the drive toward union with what we belong to—union with our own possibilities, union with significant other persons in our world in relation to whom we discover our own self fulfillment. Eros is the yearning in man which leads him to dedicate himself to seek *arate,* the noble and good life. . . . The ancients made Eros a god, or more specifically a daimon. This is a symbolic way of communicating a basic truth of human experience, that eros always drives us to transcend ourselves (72–73).

Rollo May makes a distinction between romantic love—eros—and sex. "Sex is a need," he writes, "but eros is a desire." Eros is a mode of relating to others; in eros, we don't seek the release of sex, but seek rather "to cultivate, procreate, and form the world." Studies show, however, that people view sexual desire as an important feature of romantic love. Its presence or absence in a dating relationship is believed to have implications for the emotional tenor and interpersonal dynamics of that relationship (Regan, 1996).

Besides psychologists, whose interest in love is not always appreciated—Senator Proxmire once awarded the Golden Fleece Award, for stupid and insignificant research that wasted taxpayers' money, to social psychologists who attempted to measure and study love—there are many others who write about romantic love. Poets and writers have written wonderful poems, stories, and books about romantic love. Philosophers, historians, sociologists, anthropologists, and, more recently, biologists and biochemists who describe the chemistry of love, have investigated and written about romantic love. Despite the richness and beauty of the poets' descriptions, and despite the depth and sophistication of the scholars' analyses, this book focuses on the contribution of just one field of scientific endeavor—psychology.

In addition to this limited, and by definition, limiting, point of view, this book also narrows its frame. It does not address any other stage in the life of a love relationship besides that of falling in love. This is the stage that was described by Italian sociologist Francesco Alberoni as the "flower," the "nascent state," from which can evolve a fruit that is marriage (1983).

Not only is falling in love a unique stage in a love relationship—a stage that is significantly more intense than other stages—but some psychotherapists view it as a rather insignificant stage. Scott Peck (1978), for example, defines love as an "effortful act of will." It is "the will to extend one's self for the purpose of nurturing one's own and another's spiritual growth." According to this definition, falling in love is not real love because it is not an act of will: it is effortless. Peck suggests that the clearest proof lies in the annoying observation that "lazy and undisciplined individuals are as likely to fall in love as energetic and dedicated ones." Furthermore, falling in love cannot be true love because it is "specifically a sex-linked erotic experience." And the final proof, "the experience of falling in love is invariably temporary" (81–84).

I believe that falling in love is one of the most wonderful, most exciting and significant experiences in life, most definitely so in my life. Furthermore, I believe that falling in love is one of the most significant stages in a love relationship. As I will attempt to show in the third part of this book, falling in love explains not only the best and most positive aspects of a love relationship, but also its most challenging problems,[8] and the path to healing those problems.

The last boundaries of the book that I want to acknowledge are the time in history for which it is appropriate and the Western audience for which it is intended. *Our definition of romantic love reflects a particular time period and a particular culture.* Love is a social construction. Societies differ in their understanding of the nature of love; cultures in different time periods define love differently. In some time periods, for example, we see a belief that love includes a sexual component, whereas in other eras, love described a lofty, asexual experience (Beall & Sternberg, 1995).

ROMANTIC LOVE
AND THE SEARCH FOR EXISTENTIAL SIGNIFICANCE

According to Greek mythology Eros is a god (see Bouguereau's *Cupidon* in Figure 2). And romantic love has been described as divine by contemporaty psychologists as well. The Pulitzer prize winner, psychologist Ernest Becker (1973), describes romantic love as one of the ways we satisfy our need to feel "heroic," to know that our life matters in the larger "cosmic" scheme of things, to "merge with something higher" than ourselves, something "totally absorbing." The "urge to cosmic heroism" is fixed on the beloved who becomes the "divine ideal" within which life can be fulfilled, the one person in whom all spiritual needs become focused (p. 160).

I am well aware that one of the reasons why I and so many others are attributing such great importance to romantic love is that we are living at the end of the twentieth century in a Western, secular society. In such a society, as Otto Rank (1945) noted, people are looking for romantic love to serve the function that religion served for their predecessors—to give life a sense of meaning and purpose. Romantic love is an interpersonal experience through which we make a connection with something larger than ourselves. For people who are not religious and have no other ideology or calling in which they strongly believe, romantic love can be the only such "divine" experience. The unparalleled importance given to romantic love in modern Western society was noted by Denis de Rougemont (1940) who wrote: "No other civilization, in the 7,000 years that one civilization has been succeed-

ing another, has bestowed on love known as romance anything like the same amount of daily publicity" (291–292).

In summary, this book deals with the falling-in-love stage, only, of romantic love relationships, only, from a psychological perspective, only, as it applies to people living in Western secular society at the end of the twentieth century.

AND ON A PERSONAL NOTE

I started this introduction by saying that throughout history people have tried to understand the mysteries of love and control it with magic potions and spells. Psychologists have joined this quest with their tools of the trade—research and clinical work. I remember myself as a young girl wishing I would decipher the secret that makes people fall in love. When I grew up, instead of learning how to brew magic potions or cast magic spells, I developed the skills of a researcher and a

FIGURE 2. *Cupidon* by William-Adolphe Bouguereau. *Eros,* the god of love according to Greek mythology (Cupid in Roman mythology) is the son of the goddess of love and beauty, Aphrodite (the Roman Venus), and is portrayed as a winged naked youth. Gods represent the totality of experiences that humans can experience only in moderation. Only when they are struck by Eros' arrow, can mortals experience the totality of falling in love.

couple therapist. But even today, I find people's stories about how they fell in love the most enchanting and fascinating of all. In every workshop that is even remotely related to couple issues, I ask participants to describe how they met their partners and what made them fall in love. I ask these questions of every person I see in individual therapy on relationship issues and of every couple in couple therapy. I find that this is a very good way to start, even when people come to talk about relationship problems.

This is my tenth book, and the book I have enjoyed writing the most. As I write these words I can hear my close friend saying, "Yes, yes, we know, this is what you say about every book you write." These are the same friends who have heard me say about every period in the lives of my children, "Forget everything I said before, *this* is the most wonderful age." So forget everything I said before, because the question of how we fall in love is the most exciting question I have ever dealt with. I hope that after reading this book you will agree with me.

Part One

CONSCIOUS CHOICES

Increasing The Likelihood Of Falling In Love

HIS PART OF THE BOOK DEALS WITH THOSE ASPECTS OF FALLING in love that are familiar to matchmakers and serve as their major criteria for identifying potential marriage partners. As the following story suggests, matchmakers are not the only ones who are in on these secrets.

Some years ago, in a workshop I led in Big Sur, California, a man in his early forties described how he had found his "true love." After a long series of stormy, unsatisfying, and destructive relationships, he decided to let go of the dictates of his heart and choose a partner according to strictly logical considerations. His previous relationships having helped him define what he could not accept, he spent many long weeks preparing a list of traits he was looking for in a mate. The result was a list of 68 traits!

Lest we conclude that whoever makes such a list must be a demanding and unreasonable person, I hasten to add that most of the items on his list were rather reasonable. For example, he wanted his partner to be close to him in age and in height, preferably a little shorter. It was important to him that she not be too fat or too skinny and that she be reasonably attractive. He wanted her to be an independent woman who could support herself, enjoyed her work, had her own interests, but was also open to exploring new things. And he thought it important that she be able and willing to discuss problems as they arose.

The best proof that these were not unreasonable demands is the fact that not long after making the list, he found, through a group at his church, a woman who answered every single one of his criteria. It is true, he admitted, that their relationship lacked some of the incredibly intense, verging on the insane, highs that characterized his previous relationships, but it didn't have the horrible devastating lows either. The relationship was good, warm and close, and, with time, love grew in it too.

Orthodox Jewish couples who marry through a matchmaker also report that love frequently grows in the marriage that took place between people who hardly knew each other. While this kind of love relationship seems very different from "love at first sight"—a love that is closer to our prototype of romantic love—the people in these relationships, and the studies about them, indicate that their love tends to be warm, stable, and satisfying.

This part of the book deals with the kind of reasonable variables the man in my workshop had on his list. This is not to say that these variables are always obvious. As we will see, some of them are not obvious at all. What they are, however, is observable, and thus can be the subject of research. As a result, the evidence for the roles these variables play in romantic attraction is documented in a huge number of studies. The more interesting and significant of these studies will be presented in the following seven chapters. Finally, based on this research, each chapter ends with concrete suggestions on how to increase the likelihood of falling in love.

1

PROXIMITY,
THE HIDDEN MATCHMAKER

When I'm not near the one I love,
I love the one I'm near.
  —E. Y. Harburg, *Finian's Rainbow*

Advice for good love: Don't love
those from far away. Take yourself one
from nearby.
The way a sensible house will take
local stones for its building,
stones which have suffered in the same cold
and were scorched by the same sun."
  —Yehuda Amichai,
   "Advice for Good Love," *Love Poems*

"*We were friends as soon as we met at school. I was actually going out with his roommate so I spent a lot of time in their house and we became really close friends. And then we started falling in love.*"

"*We both used to work in the same coffee shop. We just started hanging around together after work. I don't know, we just got to be good friends. He is my best friend.*"

"*We sat next to each other in class, and with time, after several months, we became good friends. I don't recall who it was that pushed for it to become an intimate relationship, whether it was she or I, but it moved in that direction.*"

"*I started working at his office. Actually, he was my boss's boss, so we would see each other often and we would always make fun of each other. Then we started flirting with each other. First it was only with words. Things would get really hot between us just talking. Then he asked me out.*"

"*She was in class with me. One evening we did our homework together,*

then we continued talking the whole night. Then we did it again and
again. I never spent so much time with anyone except my parents and my
closest friends, and I loved every moment."

These quotes are from in-depth interviews with young men and women
who talked about their most significant romantic relationships. An analysis
of the interviews suggests that in well over half of the cases, the romance
started between two people who had known each other previously.[1] More
often than not the initial acquaintance was through work —"we worked at
the same coffee shop," through school —"we sat next to each other in
class," or through the place of residence—"we lived on the same floor."

Obviously, in order to fall in love, people first have to meet. While love
relationships can and do start in other ways, such as correspondence—in-
ternet romances are becoming increasingly popular—usually, the relationships either take off or die out after the couples have met face-to-face. As we
will see shortly however, there are other, perhaps less obvious, reasons for
the power that physical proximity exerts over romance.

THE EVIDENCE FOR THE EFFECT OF PROXIMITY
ON ATTRACTION

A number of classical studies demonstrate that as the geographic distance
separating potential couples decreases, the probability of their marrying
each other increases. In one of these studies, conducted in Philadelphia in
the 1930s, some 5,000 marriage licenses were examined. The research
showed that 12 percent of the potential couples lived in the same building,
as evidenced by the same address, when they applied for a marriage license.
An additional 33 percent lived a distance of five or less blocks from each
other. The percentage of marriages decreased significantly as the geographic
distance between the potential couples increased (Bossard, 1932).

In another study, conducted in Columbus, Ohio, in the 1950s, 431
couples who applied for marriage licenses were interviewed. It turned out
that 54 percent of the potential couples were separated by a distance of 16
blocks or less when they first went out together, and 37 percent were separated by a distance of five blocks or less. The number of marriages decreased
as the distance increased between the potential couples' places of residence
(Clarke, 1952).

The two most famous studies documenting the relationship between
proximity and attraction were conducted in college dormitories. Since most

of the students who live in dormitories haven't known each other previously, a dormitory provides a good setting for the study of how close relationships develop.

Leon Festinger (1951) conducted a study of the residents of married student housing on the campus of the Massachusetts Institute of Technology. The MIT dormitories were built in a U-shape around a central court covered with grass. The exterior sides of the buildings faced the street, while the central section faced the inner courtyard. Festinger's famous conclusion was that the architect had inadvertently determined the patterns of relationships among the dwellers of the two buildings.

Two factors appeared to exercise the greatest influence on personal relationships: the location of the apartments and the distances between them. The most important factor in determining who would be emotionally close to whom was the distance between their apartments. The closer people lived to each other, the more likely they were to become friends. Next-door neighbors were far more likely to become friends with each other than with people who lived in adjacent buildings. As a matter of fact, it was difficult to find close friendships between people who lived more than five apartments away from each other. In over two-thirds of the cases, close friendships were between next-door neighbors.

In addition, the location of some of the apartments created more opportunities for their residents. Those residents who lived near staircases or mailboxes met more of their fellow residents and met them more often. The frequent encounters increased the chances that these well-placed people would talk to others, get to know them, form friendships, and increase their own popularity. On the other hand, people who lived in apartments that faced the street had no next-door neighbors. As a result, these residents made half the number of friends made by those who lived facing the inner court.

The second study was conducted in a student dormitory at the University of Michigan in Ann Arbor. Once again, the results of the study showed that what most influenced the formation of close personal ties between the students was not their compatibility, but their physical proximity. Roommates were far more likely to become close friends than people were who lived several doors down from each other (Newcomb, 1961).

In yet another study, using a group of new recruits to a police academy, most of the police trainees described their best friend as a person whose last name started with the same letter as theirs. The reason? Assignments to rooms and classroom chairs were made according to last names. This meant that the trainee's roommate and neighbor in class was someone whose last name started with the same letter as the trainee. This constant physical proximity was found to better predict the development of close ties than did similarity in age, religion, marital status, ethnic background, level of education, membership in organizations, and even leisure time activities (Segal, 1974).

Seventy years of research on attraction between neighbors, roommates, classmates, coworkers, and members of organizations testifies to the effect of physical proximity on attraction. Students tend to develop closer friendships with other students who take the same courses, sit next to them in class, live with them, or live next to them in dorm rooms. Sales people in department stores form closer friendships with people who work right next to them than with people who work just several yards away. And most important, the likelihood of individuals marrying increases as the physical distance between them decreases (Berscheid & Hartfield–Walster, 1978).

What can explain this strong positive effect of physical proximity? One of the main reasons, claims Robert Zajonc (1968), is that physical proximity makes "repeated exposure" possible. Repeated exposure, it turns out, increases our liking for practically everything, from the routine features of our lives to decorating materials, exotic foods, or music.

REPEATED EXPOSURE

During his military service, a friend of mine who grew up in a home where classical music was the only kind of music he heard, was assigned to a unit whose heroine happened to be the Egyptian singer, Omm Kolthum. At first her seemingly endless, wailing songs were a torture. He would shut his ears and cover his head with a pillow to escape the never-ending torment. But with time the torment decreased, and he got used to the songs. One day he discovered that he was nuts about Omm Kolthum. Then he started torturing his family and friends in an effort to get them to appreciate the wonders of her incredible voice.

Robert Zajonc showed that repeated exposure to practically everything we encounter, from Chinese characters all the way to the faces of unfamiliar people, increases our tendency to like them. In all his studies, a relationship was found between the frequency of repeated exposure and the level of liking. In one of these studies, Zajonc invited subjects to participate in what they thought was a test of their visual memory. He presented them with 12 pictures of people. Each picture was shown for 35 seconds, but some pictures were shown only once, while others were shown 2, 5, 10, or even 25 times. Results of the study showed that the subjects' positive feelings toward the individuals pictured increased with the frequency that their pictures were shown. In other words, even when the exposure was a very brief, and silent, 35 seconds, the more often people saw a picture, the more positively they felt toward the person in it (Zajonc, 1968).

A more recent study on the effect of repeated exposure was conducted in a large lecture hall on a university campus. Four women, confederates of the researchers, pretended to be students in a particular class. Avoiding contact with the other students in the class, the first woman attended one lecture, the second one attended ten lectures, and the third attended fifteen. The fourth woman didn't attend any of the lectures. At the end of the course, students were shown slides of the four women and asked about their feelings and attitudes towards them. Despite the fact that the students had had no personal contact with the women, the liking they reported toward them was inversely related to the number of times that they had seen them in class. The woman who didn't attend any lectures was liked the least, and the woman who attended all the lectures was liked the most. In addition, the more lectures a woman attended, the more likely she was to be perceived by the students as attractive, intelligent, interesting, and similar to themselves (Moreland & Beach, 1992).

In a study specifically related to romantic attraction, men and women who didn't know each other were asked to look in each other's eyes for two minutes, a very long time when you look into the eyes of someone you don't know. The results? Both men and the women reported an increase in their romantic attraction to the other person (Kellerman et al., 1989).

The positive effect of repeated exposure seems to arise out of an inborn discomfort that we all feel around strange and unfamiliar things, an inner programming that warns us that the strange can be dangerous and should be avoided. As children, we are taught not to talk to strangers, and even as adults we are not likely to respond positively to a stranger who, approaching us on the street and introducing himself, says that he would like to get acquainted. Most of us are likely to assume that the stranger is crazy, drunk, trying to sell us something, convince us of something, or even hurt us. If however, we have seen the same stranger every day in the supermarket, on the bus, or in the elevator, we are likely to respond very differently. After a number of such casual encounters, if the person were to ask our opinion on the weather or the political situation, chances are that we would respond positively and willingly continue the conversation, possibly the acquaintance. Repeated exposure tells us that the person, or thing, is not dangerous, so we can relax and enjoy the encounter.

Repeated exposure makes us respond positively to strangers who just look familiar to us (White & Shapiro, 1989). The mere fact that a person looks like someone we know is enough to make him or her seem familiar and thus less threatening. This positive influence remains even when we are not consciously aware of the exposure.

In a study demonstrating this point, subjects were asked to talk about some neutral topic with two different people who were, in fact, confederates of the experimenter. Before the conversation, a photograph of one of the confederates was flashed on a screen so quickly that the subjects were unaware of it. Despite the subjects' lack of awareness of this subliminal exposure, they still responded more favorably toward the familiar person, than they did toward the person whose photograph was not flashed on the screen (Bornstein et al., 1987).

The attraction to the familiar may have a greater effect on romantic attraction than a certain physical look. This provocative conclusion is based on the results of a study in which men and women were asked to choose from groups of photographs the person they could possibly marry. Next, some of the photographs were projected on a screen several times. At the end, the subjects were asked to note their romantic preferences a second time. In many of the cases, both men and women changed their original preferences and chose someone whose photograph they had seen several times (Thelen, 1988).

As the interviews at the beginning of this chapter illustrate, the effect of repeated exposure can also explain romantic relationships in the work place (Pierce et al., 1996). "We both used to work in the same coffee shop. . . . I don't know, we just got to be good friends." "I started working at his office . . . then we started flirting with each other." "We worked at the same place and that made things go faster."

We may not be aware of our preference for familiar faces, but this preference seems to play an important role in our attraction to certain faces. Actually, our preference for familiar faces includes even certain aspects of our own faces. This was demonstrated in an original study that investigated the effect of repeated exposure on the way we view ourselves. In the study, female subjects were asked to arrive with a close friend. The researchers proceeded to take two pictures of each subject. One was a regular picture, the other a mirror picture that showed how the woman looked when she saw herself in the mirror. The women and their friends were asked which picture they liked more and which one they thought flattered them more. Results showed that the women preferred the mirror pictures while their friends preferred the regular pictures. The reason is obvious: since the women most often saw themselves in the mirror, this is the view of themselves that they liked. Their friends, who more often saw them straight, rather than left-side-right as is the case in a mirror picture, preferred the regular pictures (Mita et al., 1977).

The preference for familiar faces can explain people's tendency to fall in love with, and marry, people who look like them and like members of their family. Since they often see their own faces in the mirror, and see the faces of their family members around them, people with similar characteristics seem familiar and attractive.

Contrary to the poet's view, familiarity breeds content. We prefer the faces of people we see often on television, the music we hear often on the radio, and the foods we grow accustomed to. Advertisers know that the more contact we have with a certain brand name, or a new product, the more we are likely to prefer them. Similarly, repeated exposure to a person who lives, works, studies, or spends leisure time near us is likely to increase our comfort with, our liking for, and, at times, our romantic attraction to that person.

Could this process also work in reverse? Could we develop liking, attraction, and comfort because we know we are going to spend time with a certain person? If we know that we are going to meet a certain person often—because he is going to work next to us, study in the same class, or live next door—don't we have a vested interest in seeing him as warm, pleasant, and friendly? After all, who wants daily contact with someone who is cold, nasty, and uncooperative? Once we convince ourselves that a person is warm, friendly, and pleasant, we treat him as such, which makes him respond in a way that confirms our expectations.

This proposition received support in a study conducted in the 1960s. Female students were told that as part of a psychology department survey of sexual habits among college students, they would have to meet other students, whom they didn't know, and discuss their sexual habits. Every subject received two very similar descriptions: one, of the student each was going to meet, the other, of a student another subject would meet. Results of the study showed a clear tendency for each subject to like more, and attribute more positive traits to, the student she was going to meet (Darley & Berscheid, 1967). Clearly, the students preferred to talk about an issue as intimate and private as their sexual habits with someone they considered pleasant and likable.

There are two final points that need to be made about the effects of proximity and repeated exposure. One point addresses an on-going argument about the effect of separation on romantic attraction. That is, does geographic distance enhance or diminish love? The other point concerns the negative effects of proximity and repeated arousal. That is, does proximity increase hostility and dislike as well as attraction?

DOES TEMPORARY SEPARATION
INCREASE OR DECREASE ROMANTIC LOVE?

According to one view, separation causes longing that enhances romantic love. From afar, people can see clearly, and appreciate, the wonderful qualities of a partner, qualities that daily proximity may prevent them from seeing. Indeed, my studies of marriage burnout suggest that a temporary separation, especially one that involves some danger and worry, such as a husband's army reserve duty, increases the romantic spark in the marriage (Pines, 1996).

According to the other view, "what is far from the eye is far from the heart." Just as physical proximity enhances emotional closeness, physical distance reduces it. Indeed, it was shown that married couples who don't live together are significantly more likely to divorce than couples living together (Rindfuss & Stephen, 1990). The problem with reaching a conclusion based on these findings is that couples who don't live together may have problems in their relationship. It is possible that these problems—and not the physical distance in and of itself—are what eventually cause the divorce.

What then can we conclude about the effect of separation on lovers? While there are wonderfully romantic stories of mythological loves, such as the one between Odysseus and Penelope that remained intense despite long years of separation, for most couples a long separation may not be too beneficial. When the relationship is close and loving, however, a separation—especially when short—may help intensify the romantic spark. But when the relationship is not good, and the separation long, it is easy to get used to life without the partner and come to prefer it.

PROXIMITY AND REPEATED EXPOSURE
INTENSIFY ALL FEELINGS, POSITIVE AND NEGATIVE.

When someone annoys us, repeated exposure, rather than making us like that person more, will intensify our negative feelings. This is why police records show that most acts of violence do not happen between strangers but between people who are very close, such as husband and wife, family members, friends, and neighbors. In other words, repeated exposure intensifies the dominant emotion in the relationship. When the dominant emotion is anger, repeated exposure enhances the anger. When the dominant emotion is attraction, repeated exposure enhances the attraction.

This conclusion is supported by the findings of a study in which subjects were shown twenty different pictures and were asked how much they liked each one of them. In the second stage of the study they were shown some of the pictures one more time, and other pictures five or ten times. In the results, those pictures that the subjects either liked or felt neutral toward were rated more positively after subjects were exposed to them several times. On the other hand, repeated exposure to those pictures that subjects disliked served only to increase the dislike (Brickman et al., 1972).

SUGGESTIONS FOR PEOPLE SEEKING LOVE

An opportunity to meet and get acquainted in person is almost a prerequisite for the development of a romantic relationship. While platonic love relationships do develop by means of letters, telephone, and more recently electronic mail, and can be extremely exciting and rewarding as such, most people need to meet in person before they allow themselves to fall in love. And when people live, work, or play in close proximity, their likelihood of meeting increases.

But meeting once is not enough. The results of the analysis of the romantic attachment interviews suggest that in only 11 percent of the cases, the love described in the interview was at first sight. Repeated exposure is yet another requirement for a romantic spark to turn into the steady flame of a love relationship.

Meeting repeatedly, however, does not guarantee love. If the first impression is negative, it is best to cut contact, let the first impression dissipate, and then give the relationship another chance. In such a case, repeated exposure will not change the initial dislike or disdain into love, but will increase them.

The conclusion for people who are seeking romantic love is obvious. Try to arrange your life in such a way that you have many opportunities to meet people through your work, place of residence, or recreational activities. It is important that your close physical environment include the kinds of people you want to engage in a relationship, be it a friendship or a romantic attach-

ment. Being involved in activities you love, or could love, is important not
only because such activities offer the most likely meeting grounds in the
search for a romantic partner, but they also assure living genuinely and,
therefore, more happily.

When seeking candidates for romantic love, the encounters should offer
not one-shot opportunities, the kind that take place on a busy street or in a
crowded bar, but instead, time together and repetition. The meetings
should either take a while—such as a week-long ski or mountain hiking
trip—or be repeated regularly as daily encounters at the cafeteria at work,
next to the elevator or the mailboxes at the apartment, during a year-long
class, or a regularly scheduled, athletic activity.

2

AROUSAL, THE ELIXIR OF LOVE

To start love like this: with a cannon shot
. . . That's a religion! That's a love!
—Yehuda Amichai, "Ideal Love,"
from *Love Poems*

"*To both of us everything seemed too much. All the people around, the madness, and the whole college experience. Both of us wanted at least one good friend. I came into the class and she was the first person I noticed. She looked at me that very moment, and both of us said 'wawoo.'*"

"*Our relationship started in such a romantic way that neither of us wanted to accept the fact that we had nothing in common. We were at a party out of town. I was drunk and the guy who drove the car was drunk. He hit the side of the road and it was a miracle that we didn't get killed. She was in a car right behind us and they stopped when they saw the accident. She got out of the car and I got out of the car. We ran toward each other and hugged. That's how the relationship started.*"

"*I met him a couple of months after my divorce. I initiated the divorce, but it struck me hard afterwards. . . . He was there for me after the divorce and it just went on from there.*"

"*We both took the same summer class. I decided earlier on that I wasn't interested in a romantic involvement with anyone. He was one of the only people who knew about my father's death. He and another friend invited me over and we started talking. . . . I was so comfortable with him that it seemed weird. . . . He was supportive and understanding about my father, and always interested in me and in being with me.*"

"*We met when my mother died and my whole world fell apart. I was new in town and he was the caring and considerate person who couldn't hurt another person's feelings. I needed stability and he is very different from those guys who can leave someone for another. I was very depressed about my mother. . . . We took care of each other.*"

In one-fifth of the romantic attraction interviews, the relationships described started during stormy periods in the lives of the men and women interviewed.[1] Sometimes the heightened emotional sensitivity followed an experience of loss, such as the death of a parent, or a painful breakup. And at other times, the heightened emotions followed an exciting adventure, such as a trip abroad, leaving home for college, or a particularly dramatic event, such as miraculously surviving an accident.

THE TWO-FACTOR THEORY OF LOVE

A terrified person is potentially a person in love, as is an angry person, a jealous person, a rejected person, and a happy person. Actually, every person who experiences the physiological arousal that accompanies strong emotions is potentially a person in love. This is the basic proposition of the two-factor theory of love first articulated by Elaine Walster and Ellen Berscheid (1971).

A man or woman who meets a potential partner after the excitement of winning a great promotion is more likely to fall in love than he or she would be on a routine day. Likewise, a man or woman is more likely to fall in love when mourning a terrible loss. The reason, in both cases, has to do with the two components of love: *arousal* and *label*.

The two-factor theory of love is a derivation of a more general theory of emotions (Schachter, 1964). According to this theory, all strong emotions have two components, one is physiological and has to do with the body, the other is cognitive and has to do with the mind. The physiological component is a state of arousal. The cognitive component is a label that explains the arousal. In order for us to identify a particular emotion, we first need to experience a general state of physiological arousal that goes with all strong emotions, that is, rapid heartbeat, fast breathing, and so on. Then we need to put an emotional label on the physical arousal—a label that will give it a particular characteristic—love, anger, pain, fear, envy. We learn the appropriate labels for different states of arousal. In other words, we learn what we are supposed to be feeling in different situations from the society in which we live, from our parents, teachers, friends, and from personal experience. For example, even when the physiological experiences are the same, we know that we are expected to feel delighted when a dear friend comes for a visit, but anxious when being followed on a dark street. And what we are expected to feel has a major influence on what we actually feel.

Walster and Berscheid explain the combined effect of physiological arousal and a romantic label on the experience of romantic love:

> To love passionately, a person must first be physically aroused, a condition manifested by palpitations of the heart, nervous tremor, flushing, and accelerated breathing. Once he is so aroused, all that remains is for him to identify this complex of feelings as passionate love, and he will have experienced authentic love. Even if the initial physical arousal is the result of an irrelevant experience . . . once he has met the person, been drawn to the person, and identified the experience as love, it is love (47).

We all know the phenomenon of love on the rebound, when someone who has just come out of a long or significant relationship jumps immediately into another one. Feeling vulnerable and lonesome, the person has a difficult time being alone and is desperate to be coupled again. Folk wisdom warns against love on the rebound because it is seen as fragile and temporary.

The threat of death precipitates the phenomenon of war love. In Israel during the Gulf War, this phenomenon affected couples who had just met, couples of long-standing whose relationships were cemented by the war, and divorced or separated couples who reunited after spending long hours in shelters.

Stories of hostages who fall in love with their captors never fail to amaze us, and stories about hot romances that started during exciting vacations and unusual adventures delight us. Cruise love even received the recognition of a weekly, comedy show on television. Every week, viewers of *The Love Boat* tuned in to watch the exciting affairs of the cruise travelers, affairs that, in the main, were far more exciting than they would have been on land.

Many people are personally acquainted with the phenomenon of spring fever. This wonderful love ailment strikes during the early days of spring, arriving with the sun, the blossom, and the fresh air after the long gloom of winter. But as the personal experiences that opened this chapter suggest, every major life change causes arousal. From the exciting yet anxiety-provoking change of starting school or a new job, to a change in residence, to the painful loss of a significant person, major life changes can increase the likelihood of falling in love.

Cindy, a professional woman in her early forties, had decided that she was no longer interested in a committed relationship with a man. "Men are too much trouble" she explained. "You get much more from investing your energy in your career." Yet when her sister, the sole surviving member of her family, died of cancer, Cindy fell in love. She fell in love with a man very different from the kind of men she usually dated and to whom she always deferred. He was a simple, unsophisticated man from an Italian background. He was warm and affectionate, supportive during the last stages of her sister's illness and after her sister's death. The relationship lasted for about a year, the customary period of mourning in Judaism, and was Cindy's most significant romantic relationship as an adult.

STUDYING THE EFFECTS OF AROUSAL ON ROMANTIC ATTRACTION

In the last thirty years a number of fascinating studies have documented the impact of arousal on romantic attraction. Several of these studies were conducted by researcher Arthur Aron. Art became interested in the topic of romantic attraction when he fell in love with Elaine, then his girlfriend, now his wife. He conducted an extensive literature search and discovered a number of relevant theories and studies. In one of these studies, two college classes were tested for sexual arousal and aggressive feelings. One class included students who were angered by a professor who had berated them viciously for having done poorly on a recent test. The second class served as a control. Both groups were asked to write stories in response to a projective test. Results showed that the angered group, as evidenced by the explicit sexual content of their stories, was significantly more sexually aroused than the control group (Barclay & Haber, 1965).

Art concluded that people are more likely to be attracted to those they meet during an unusual and exciting experience, an experience that involves the use of force, mystery, loneliness, or powerful emotions. The question he wrestled with was how to create such an experience in the laboratory. The solution he chose was role-play.

In his study, the male students who served as subjects assumed the role of a soldier who was captured behind enemy lines. The soldier was to be tortured by an interrogator, played by an attractive female research assistant, trying to force him to reveal army secrets. The interrogator "tortured" the soldier by dropping "acid" (actually water) into his eye. Each subject was instructed to imagine that the acid caused him unbearable pain, that it burned his eye, that if the torture continued, it would burn his brain and, eventually, cause a horrible death. The subject was encouraged to scream every time the "acid" touched his eye.

The students really got into the role. They shook and sweated, later reporting that they had felt terrible fear. Even the female assistant had to be comforted and calmed after going through the difficult experience of "torturing" six "soldiers" every day. A control group, also playing captured soldiers, had water dropped into their eyes, but were told that the water represented the first, easy stages of interrogation.

The results? The young men who went through the hair-raising experience of being "tortured" were far more attracted to their "interrogator" than were the control "soldiers". They expressed a greater desire to kiss her and be close to her. In addition, there were more erotic and romantic themes in the stories they wrote afterwards (Aron & Aron, 1989).

Another study used two bridges over the Capilano river in Vancouver (Dutton & Aron, 1974). The "experimental" bridge was the Capilano Canyon Suspension Bridge (see Figure 3). The bridge is 5 feet wide, 450 feet long, and is constructed of wood boards attached to wire cables that run from one side to the other of the Capilano Canyon. It has many arousal-inducing features: a tendency to tilt, sway, and wobble, creating the impression that one is about to fall over the side; very low handrails of wire cable, which contribute to this impression; and a 230-foot drop to rocks and shallow rapids below. The "control" bridge was a solid wood bridge further upriver. It is only 10 feet above a small, shallow rivulet, has high handrails, and does not tilt or sway.

When potential male subjects had crossed one of the bridges, an attractive young woman intercepted them. The woman was a research assistant

FIGURE 3. The Capilano Canyon Suspension Bridge

and unaware of the study's hypothesis. The woman explained that she was doing a project for her psychology class on the effects of attractive scenery on creative expression. She then asked if the subject would fill out a short questionnaire, one part of which asked the subject to write a brief dramatic story based on a picture of a woman (see Figure 4 for a picture inspired by the TAT card).

This picture is part of a projective test called the TAT, Thematic Apperception Test. The assumption is that every person sees the picture differently, according to his or her own psychological screens, and projects onto the figure in the picture his or her own self-perception in relation to others (Murray, 1943). For example, one person may see the woman pictured as sexual: "She is madly in love with a man and just got out of bed after spending a whole night making love to him;" or, "She's a whore, the place is a whore house, and she has just risen from giving pleasure to her tenth customer of the day." In another person's description, the woman's sexuality may not be mentioned: "She just woke up from a terrible nightmare and is trying to shake it off;" or, "She has just come home from the fields after working hard all day and is about to lie down and rest."

In the Capilano Bridge study, stories were scored for sexual content. Scores ranged from 1 for no sexual content, to 5 for high sexual content, according to how many and what kind of sexual references appeared in the story. A story that mentioned sexual intercourse received five points; but if the strongest sexual reference was "girlfriend," it received a score of two; "kiss" counted three and "lover" four.

After the subject had completed the questionnaire, the research assistant thanked him and offered to explain the experiment in more detail when she had more time. She tore off a

Figure 4. A picture inspired by the Thematic Apperception Test (TAT) card. What is the story in this picture?

corner of a sheet of paper, wrote down her name and phone number, and invited the subject to call if he wanted to talk further. In order to more easily classify the callers, men who had crossed the suspension bridge were told that the interviewer's name was Gloria; control subjects who had crossed the safer, wooden bridge were told that her name was Donna.

Results showed that the stories written by the men who went through the heart- and leg-shaking experience of crossing the suspension bridge had significantly more sexual and romantic themes than did the stories of the men who crossed on the safer wood bridge. The aroused men were also more likely to be romantically attracted to, and show an interest in, the woman who interviewed them on the wobbly bridge. This was evident in the fact that many more—eight times more!—of the subjects called Gloria "to find out more about the study." How do we know that it was she they were interested in, and not the study? We know because in a control study done on the same two bridges with a male experimenter, almost none of the male subjects called the experimenter.

Since researchers in field studies don't have complete control, another study was done in the laboratory with male students. As each subject entered a room containing an array of electrical equipment, the experimenter welcomed him and asked him if he had seen another person who was searching for the laboratory. The experimenter then excused himself "to look for the other person," and left the subject a copy of an article reporting "previous studies in the area we are investigating." The article discussed the effect of electric shock on pain and learning.

The experimenter reentered the room with the "other subject," an attractive female confederate who knew that the study involved sexual attraction but didn't know the experimental hypothesis. The experimenter explained that the study focused on the effects of electric shocks on learning, and emphasized the value and importance of this research. He then asked if either subject chose not to continue. As expected, no subject requested to leave. The experimenter then said that two levels of shock would be used in the experiment. One shock level was quite painful while the other was "a mere tingle" that some people even described as enjoyable. To be "completely random," the allocation of shock level was to be determined by the couple's flip of a coin. After the subject and the confederate had flipped a coin and learned the level of shock each could anticipate, the experimenter described the procedure, the way the shock series would take place, the method used for hooking them up to electrodes, and so on.

At this point the experimenter said that it would take him a few minutes to set up the equipment. While doing so he said, "I would like to get some information about your feelings and reactions, since these often influence performance." He assigned subject and confederate to separate cubicles, and handed each a questionnaire to complete. The questionnaire included the same TAT picture used in the Capilano Bridge study and two questions which assessed the male subject's attraction to the female confederate: a) How much would you like to ask her out on a date? b) How much would you like to kiss her?

Results showed that the students who anticipated getting severe shocks were significantly more attracted to the female confederate than were subjects who expected weak shocks. More of them had a greater desire to ask her on a date and kiss her, and their TAT stories held far more romantic and sexual themes (Dutton & Aron, 1974).

The arousal that causes romantic attraction does not have to be fear or anxiety. Sexual arousal can work just as well. This was demonstrated when male students were invited to take part in a study on university dating. While waiting for their assigned dates, half of them were given an erotic story to read, while the other half were given a boring story about the life of seagulls. Both groups were then given the same description and picture of the woman each subject was about to date. The woman was described as active, smart, easy-going, and liberal; her picture showed an attractive blond. After they read their stories, the men were asked for their opinions of their prospective dates. Results showed that the men who were sexually aroused described the woman as more attractive and sexier than did the men who were not sexually aroused. Furthermore, and I really like this next finding, the men who were sexually aroused described themselves as more attracted to their own girlfriends (Stephan et al., 1971).

Many of us get regular infusions of arousal by going to the movies; some of us translate the arousal into love. In a recent field study, expressions of love and affection, in words and physical gestures, were recorded between couples on their way in and out of movie theaters. Some of the couples watched an action movie, others watched a movie that was less emotionally arousing. Findings of the study showed that the couples who watched the emotionally arousing action movie expressed more affection toward each other after the movie than they did before seeing it. The non-action movie had no effect on the amount of affection expressed by the couples who watched it (Cohen et al., 1989).

Even when we mistakenly believe that we find someone sexually arousing, the person seems more attractive to us. Male subjects were told that their heartbeats would be amplified and recorded while they looked at ten slides of half-nude Playboy Bunnies. But, in fact, the subject heard not his own heartbeat, but prerecorded heartbeats arranged to beat faster when various, randomly chosen, photographs were projected. In other words, the men believed that their hearts were beating faster in response to certain photographs, when in fact they were not. Then, they were asked to rate the attractiveness of the ten Playboy Bunnies. Results showed that the men rated those women who supposedly made their hearts beat faster as significantly more attractive, and chose their pictures when offered a poster of a Bunny as a token of appreciation for taking part in the study. Even a month later, in a totally unrelated situation, when asked to rate the same ten pictures, they again rated the same women as more attractive (Valins, 1966).

AROUSAL IS NOT ENOUGH

Obviously, arousal is not enough to make us fall in love. As noted in the two-factor theory of love, after being aroused we still need to meet the right person. The woman whose father had died a short time before she met her boyfriend described the many reasons that made her fall in love with him:

> "He looked very nice [attraction to good looks] and after talking to him I discovered that he is a good thinker as well [attraction to similar intelligence and interests]. When I went to his place for dinner, I really liked his room and his apartment [attraction to similar tastes]. I was so comfortable with him that it seemed weird. He is a very good listener. He really understood me. He understood right away what I meant and this was new to me. I think I am a complicated person, but he understood me. His comments were always right on target. And he was very supportive and understanding about my father and always interested in me and in being with me. He was always interested in what was best for me [attraction to someone who fills important needs]. From the very first moment, I was myself with him because I didn't have the energy to be something else. Our relationship was based on honesty and this was new for me. [The vulnerability caused by the father's death created a greater openness to intimacy.] We're different, but we complement each other. Whatever is lacking in me he has [attraction to the complementary]."

Arousal enhances romantic attraction when a potential candidate is attractive. When the potential candidate is not attractive, the result can be very different. To create either high or low arousal, men were asked to run in place for either two minutes, creating high arousal, or fifteen seconds, creating low arousal. After running, they watched a short video in which they saw a young woman they were going to meet later. By using professional makeup, the researchers made the woman look either very attractive or very unattractive. Results showed that when the woman looked attractive, the arousal caused an increase in the men's attraction to her. But when she looked unattractive, the arousal actually decreased their attraction to her, meaning that the aroused men were even less attracted to her (White et al., 1981).

It is interesting that the nature of an emotional arousal—happiness because of a wonderful victory or sadness about a painful loss—doesn't have an effect, but the attractiveness of the potential partner does. This was demonstrated in a study in which subjects listened to one of three tapes. One-third of the subjects listened to a tape that described the brutal murder of a missionary in front of his family. A second third of the subjects heard one of Steve Martin's funniest comedy routines, and the final third listened to a tape recording of a very boring lecture on the physiology of the frog. Each subject then watched a video clip that showed either a very attractive or a very unattractive woman whom he was going to meet. Once again, results showed that both the arousal and the woman's attractiveness had an effect. The men who were aroused by either the funny tape or the horrible tape found the attractive woman more attractive than did the men who were not aroused by the boring tape. Furthermore, the aroused men found the unattractive woman even less attractive than did the men who were not aroused (White et al., 1981).

WHY DOES AROUSAL INFLUENCE ROMANTIC ATTRACTION?

What causes the aphrodisiac effects of arousal? One explanation is known as *misattribution*: the arousal is attributed, incorrectly, to sexual arousal, when in fact something else causes the arousal—such as fear, as was the case in the Capilano Bridge study.[2] Alternatively, *excitation transfer* is operating: the arousal caused by one thing, such as an expected electric shock, is added to the arousal caused by another, an attractive woman. A third explanation is known as *response facilitation*: the state of arousal resulting from running in place, for example, enhances every other reaction we have, be it attraction or repulsion.

When we are aroused, the origin of the arousal doesn't matter and it doesn't matter whether or not we are aware of the reason. Arousal automatically reinforces our natural response to any situation, including romantic attraction (Allen et al., 1989). This helps explain the phenomenon of folk-dancing love, well-known among people who are hooked on this kind of leisure-time activity. Some such addicts dance four and five days a week. The physical arousal, caused by the dancing, and the emotional arousal, inspired by the music and/or the words of the song, reinforce the dancer's natural response of attraction to the partner. When people are in the midst of the ecstasy of performing a dance they love, to the sound of a song they love, do they say to themselves that the strong excitement they feel toward their dance partner is the result of "misattribution" or "excitation transfer"? Probably not. Neither, in all probability, do they dismiss the excitement they feel as merely resulting from the arousal of the dance rather than the irresistible charm of their partner. Instead they get excited, attracted, sexually turned on, and, at times, fall madly in love. They don't always fall in love, however. They also need to feel that their partner is an appropriate mate in terms of such things as appearance, age, education, and social class. If these prerequisites are satisfied *and* they are aroused, then they are far more likely to misattribute their arousal and think they are in love (Walster–Hartfield & Walster, 1981).

OBSTACLES ENHANCE LOVE

> Some obstacle is necessary to swell the tide of libido to its height; and at all periods of history whenever natural barriers in the way of satisfaction have not sufficed, mankind has erected conventional ones in order to enjoy love.
> —Sigmund Freud, "The Most Prevalent Form of Degradation in Erotic Life"

> "The less my hope, the hotter my love."
> —Terence. Eunuchus, I. 160 B. C.

One of the best sources of folk wisdom about strong emotions such as romantic love is folk songs. "The jukebox, a particularly American institution, has long been a rich source of social psychological truths" wrote James Pennebaker and his colleagues (1979).

According to Mickey Gilley's country western song, "all the girls get prettier at closing time." Is it true that when the time for closing the bar draws near, and with it the painful thought of going home alone, the standards go down and the attractions of the available people in the vicinity go up? To test this hypothesis, Pennebaker and his colleagues conducted a study that sounds like it was a lot of fun.

They approached men and women in one of three "drinking establishments within walking distance of a respectable Southern University." Subjects were selected randomly, with the restriction that they not be in conversation with a member of the opposite sex. They were approached by a same sex experimenter and asked to rate the attractiveness of members of the opposite sex present that night. This was repeated three times: At 9:00 p.m., 10:30 p.m., and midnight, a half-hour before the bars closed. Findings showed a linear increase in attractiveness rating of both men and women. As the hour grew later, the opposite sex in the bar appeared more attractive. The data also showed that men tended to rate women as more attractive than women rated men. A later study showed that this effect was not the result of alcohol consumption.

Why do girls get prettier at closing time? One explanation is offered by reactance theory: when our freedom to act, think, or feel is threatened, we are motivated to try and get it back. Reactance theory explains why people want more the things they have lost, and why, in the case of romantic love, they desire more those people whom they feel they have lost. The theory also explains why obstacles enhance love (Brehm & Brehm, 1981).

To enhance love, says reactance theory, the obstacles need to be outside the relationship, for example an enforced separation or a parental objection. The most famous case of such obstacles to love is, no doubt, the tragic story of Romeo and Juliet.

Does parental interference really enhance love? Researchers who investigated the "Romeo and Juliet Effect" found that for both married and unmarried couples there was indeed a positive correlation between romantic love and parental interference. The greater the interference, the greater the love (Driscoll et al., 1971).

Obstacles also increase attraction. One of the best known studies in social psychology showed that we tend to love more the people for whom we had to work or suffer. In the study, young women had to go through an embarrassing initiation, which included reading aloud very explicit pornographic material, to be accepted to a discussion group. These women liked and appreciated the group significantly more than did women who did not have to make such a big effort to join the group (Aronson & Mills, 1972).

Is it true then, that people who play hard-to-get win in the game of love?

Playing hard-to-get means creating challenges, putting up obstacles against being easily won. Despite the wide acceptance of this assumption, five different studies failed to find any evidence for the "hard-to-get-effect." It turns out that people like choosy partners, but only those who are choosy toward others, not toward them (Walster et al., 1973).

This conclusion was criticized on the grounds that there is a big difference between choosiness and rejection. A person who is choosy about the people he or she will go out with is different from a person who won't go out with us, which is to say a person who rejects us personally. In a study that proved this point, subjects, all single, received information about members of the opposite sex that differed in their levels of choosiness. The "very choosy" were described as ready to go out only with people of "exceptional" quality. The "choosy," selective about their friends, were not willing to go out with just anyone. The "not choosy" were willing to go out with practically anyone. Findings showed that subjects were most attracted to the people who were described as choosy, and were not attracted to the very choosy people, who were perceived to be snobs. Women were even more likely than men to respond negatively to "very choosy" potential dates (Wright & Contrada, 1986). These results, partially confirming folk wisdom, suggest that women, but not men, should play hard-to-get.

MOOD AND LOVE

When we are in a good mood we tend to feel good about the people around us. When we feel happy, satisfied, excited, interested, curious, we show greater interest in people and are friendlier and more open than when we are sad, depressed, or despairing (Clark & Watson, 1988). Our mood also influences our romantic attraction (Kaplan, 1981).

Music is one of the things known to influence mood. It was shown that with pleasant music in the background, women looking at photographs of men they didn't know, rated their attractiveness higher than women did who rated the photographs with no music in the background. The former women liked the men more and found them more physically attractive. On the other hand, women who listened to unpleasant music liked the men less and found them less attractive. In other words, the mood evoked by the music influenced the women's willingness to be attracted to men as well as the women's judgments of the men's attractiveness (May & Hamilton, 1980).

Hearing good or bad news also has an effect on our moods and consequently on our feelings toward other people. People who hear good news that lifts their spirits respond to strangers more than those who hear news that depresses them (Veitch & Griffitt, 1976). The same effect on attraction can be seen when people watch happy or sad movies. Once again, a good mood enhances attraction (Gouaux, 1971). When people are depressed or nervous, regardless of the reason for these feelings, they like less the people they meet and evaluate them more negatively (Shapiro, 1988).

Our mood influences our feelings as well as our behavior toward people. Men who received a good-mood treatment—watching a funny movie and receiving a positive evaluation of themselves—or the bad-mood treatment—watching a depressing movie and receiving a negative evaluation—responded very differently to a young and attractive woman who started talking to them. The men in the "good mood" group responded to her much more positively than did the men in the "bad mood" group. The former were friendlier, more open, and more ready to talk to her (Cunningham, 1988).

What is the reason for the influence of mood on attraction? At the most basic, most simplistic level, we love everyone and everything that makes us feel good, and we dislike everyone and everything that makes us feel bad. Our attraction and repulsion are based on the feelings, either good or bad, that are generated in us.

At a more complex level, we not only respond to the person, object, or event that is directly responsible for our emotional reaction, but also to every unknown person or neutral object that was present when our strong emotions were aroused. The stranger or the neutral object becomes related in our minds with the good or bad feeling. This connection is called conditioning. After conditioning has occurred, the person or the object continues to generate the same emotion in us (Clore & Byrne, 1974). This is why we like a stranger who just happens to be around when we hear good news. The person is not responsible for our good mood, the good news is. Nevertheless, we make a connection between the person and the good feeling we have while hearing the news, and our feelings toward the person change accordingly.

The conditioning effect is so powerful that even a washed and pressed shirt worn by a despised person ranked as far less desirable than a washed and pressed shirt that was worn by a person who was loved and admired. In other words, a contact between a neutral object and a person who generates in us either very good or very bad feelings is enough for the feeling to be transferred to an object as neutral even as a clean shirt (Rozin et al., 1986).

THE AROUSAL CAUSED BY EXPECTING ROMANTIC LOVE

We live in a culture that builds in us great expectations for, and from, romantic love. Expressions such as "love at first sight," "a match made in heaven," and "made for each other," are familiar to all of us and generate high expectations of romantic love and falling in love. A recent poll showed that over 56 percent of the people polled believed in love at first sight; my analysis of the romantic attraction interviews showed that only 11 percent actually experienced it.[3] Most people growing up in a Western culture know what romantic love is and have experienced it at one time or another in their lives. For many people, romantic love is one of the most powerful positive emotions ever felt. Some believe that love can answer the question of human existence, celebrate the freedom of choice and pursuit of happiness, and provide the best basis for marriage (Pines, 1996).

In the early part of this chapter I presented the two-factor theory of love. Let me end the chapter with a three-factor theory of love. The third factor is the role of *social expectations.* According to the theory, the three requirements for falling in love are: 1) a social-cultural background that builds the expectation to fall in love; 2) an appropriate candidate in terms of such things as appearance, personality, background, and values; and, 3) arousal that gets the label romantic love (Hartfield & Rapson, 1993).

Since we live in a culture that builds high expectations of romantic love, we clearly fulfill the first condition. After reading this chapter we know the importance of arousal and have some idea how to create such a state or else make use of an existing one. All that is left is the small matter of finding the right person. According to the above theory of love, two of the most important features identifying a potential partner as appropriate are his or her appearance and personality. These are the subject of the next chapter.

SUGGESTIONS FOR PEOPLE SEEKING LOVE

Take advantage of times in which you are emotionally aroused by either positive or negative events in your life. These are times when you are likely to be more open to love. Look for situations of high physical and emotional arousal: folk dancing, hiking, aerobics, jogging, trips abroad, stimulating classes, action movies, exciting concerts, and spiritual journeys. Choose activities that you really enjoy and find exciting. Make sure they are favored by people of the sex and age you are looking for, who are open and free to have an intimate relationship, and are likely to be appropriate romantic partners. Try to be in a good mood when you meet new people. If need be, don't hesitate to put yourself in a good mood by listening to music with a beat, a funny tape, or watching an uplifting movie. And remember that external obstacles enhance attraction.

3

BEAUTY AND CHARACTER

The most poetic love depends not on moral qualities
but . . . on the way of doing up the hair, the complex-
ion, the cut of the gown.
    —Leo Tolstoy, "The Kreutzer Sonata"

All the beauty of the world. 'Tis but skin deep.
    —Ralph Venning, *Orthodox Paradoxes*, 1650

Grace is deceitful and beauty is vain.
    —Proverbs, 31, 30

"*She was very attractive, very beautiful. Appearance is more important to me than to most people. . . . She is attractive, quiet, knows she is attractive. She has a presence and she's aware of it. She is sure of herself and very aware. Not a woman for a flirt only, but a . . . serious person.*"

"*He is an all-around nice person, really nice, friendly, warm. He had a friendly presence, a warm presence, and was full of life, with a good sense of humor. And I thought he was cute, not stunning. With two feet on the ground.*"

"*I thought she was very beautiful, very striking, long dark hair. The first night we met, we talked the whole night—we had a lot in common.*"

"*What attracted me most at first was his personality. I also thought he was very sexy. He carried himself well, and dressed nicely. He's a very real and honest person. . . . He comes off as being very confident, almost cocky. That's what attracted me to him.*"

"*My first impression was that she is beautiful and quiet and insecure. When I started talking to her I discovered that she is very sweet . . . wonderful. What attracted me most was that I could talk to her about everything. She is very understanding.*"

"*He's sort of handsome, and he's very nice, very laid back. He made me feel good.*"

"She's a knock-out, long hair, blue eyes. . . . She seemed very nice, really sweet."
"From the beginning he was really cute, really nice, real sensitive."

From these remarks it is apparent that the young men and women interviewed were attracted to endearing personality traits in the beloved: "very sweet," "friendly," "good sense of humor." But they also mentioned attraction to the beloved's appearance: "he's handsome," "she's a knock-out."

Which attracts us more, personality or appearance? Analysis of the romantic attraction interviews reveals that over 90 percent of all the men and women interviewed mentioned some aspect of a partner's character when they tried to explain why they fell in love. Women mentioned personality traits more often than men, but the gender difference was small and insignificant. A smaller portion of the interviewees, about two-thirds, mentioned the beloved's appearance. But here the gender difference was very large. Significantly more men, 81 percent, than women, 44 percent, were attracted to the physical appearance of the beloved. In other words, personality traits play a more important role in falling in love than physical appearance, and appearance plays a far more important role for men than it does for women.[1] This last finding was replicated in many other studies (Feingold, 1990).

Is physical attractiveness really less important than character? And are women really less influenced by it? Or is this finding an artifact, the result of people's tendency to underreport the impact of physical attractiveness on their dating preferences? A recent study attempted to find out.

Women were shown profiles containing photographs and information about the personalities of potential, male, dating partners. When the women thought they were connected to a lie detector, they admitted being more influenced by the physical attractiveness of the men, and described physically attractive men as more desirable. When they were not connected to the apparatus, the women tended to underreport the impact of the men's physical attractiveness on their preferences (Hadjistavropoulos & Genest, 1994).

Apparently, a social norm tends to inhibit us, especially women, from admitting the importance of physical attraction. In addition, it is possible that people, especially men, assess first a potential candidate's appearance. Only after the candidate passes this initial screening, does the appraiser notice the personality traits that lead to a perception of something deeper and more significant than beauty alone.

Because it serves as a screen in our selection of a mate, physical appearance plays a crucial role in the beginning of a romantic relationship. If someone's appearance is repulsive, the chances for a romantic involvement are slim. But as the lovely story "Beauty and the Beast" suggests, on those rare occasions when people are forced to spend time with an unattractive person and get to know that person well, they may discover that under the repulsive appearance lies a hidden treasure of wonderful traits. In such a case they may fall in love with the person despite the initial disdain. The following example is a case in point.

An attractive widow in her early forties wanted to build a new, and significant, intimate relationship. She had met many men, but didn't like any of them, especially when she compared them to her late husband and recalled the depth of the emotional bond she had had with him. Then her close friends arranged a blind date with a "charming man" whose company they were convinced she would enjoy. When he rang the doorbell and she first saw him, she couldn't believe that her friends, who knew how sensitive she was to people's appearances, could have introduced her to such a funny-looking man. Her late husband had been a very handsome man and the men she had dated after his death were also attractive. But this man was short, possibly even shorter than she, chubby, balding, and wore glasses. She saw no chance of a romantic involvement with so unbecoming a man. Within the first seconds of meeting him, she made up her mind that at the end of the evening, she would gently dismiss him and never agree to another date. But since she was stuck with "chubby" for the night, and they had a reservation to a wonderful restaurant that was one of her favorites, she decided to spend the evening with him. While driving to the restaurant in his elegant car, she discovered that he was a very pleasant and entertaining man. At the restaurant, she learned that he was a connoisseur of wines and enjoyed good food as much as she did. She also discovered that he was a successful lawyer who loved his work. Moreover, he was a fascinating conversationalist with a great sense of humor, and when she talked, he listened attentively. He was a marvelous, sensitive man.

Among the last to leave the restaurant, she realized that hours had gone by without her noticing and that she had enjoyed every minute. Furthermore, it had been years since she had enjoyed herself so much. So despite her earlier decision, she responded happily when the misnamed "chubby" invited her out again.

Unfortunately, most of us reject outright those whose appearances we don't like, and we don't give unattractive people a chance to reveal their personalities. A woman who had gone on a blind date once told me, "When I saw him at the café and saw how he looked I decided not to go in. Why bother? There was no way I was going to go out with a man who looked like that." Beauty may be skin deep, but the role it plays as an initial screen gives it enormous power in romantic relationships. Through this *attractiveness screen* many a person who might have made a wonderful lover and mate is discarded. The reason for our prejudice against unattractive people is, at least in part, the result of a connection we make between beauty and love.

BEAUTY AND LOVE

In Roman mythology, Venus is the goddess of both beauty *and* love (see Figure 5). And in modern times, a large number of studies in social psychology demonstrate the connection between beauty and love (Hartfield &

FIGURE 5. *Venus Awaits the Return of Mars* by Lamert Sustris, c. 1560. Venus, the Roman goddess of love and beauty (the Greek Aphrodite), reclines with her winged son Cupid (Eros). Venus, the magnificent golden goddess, carried beauty around her. Flowers sprang up wherever her feet touched the earth. Her single divine duty was to make love and to inspire others to make love as well. She was desired by all. Gods and mortals alike lost their heads when they heard her voice. There was neither happiness nor beauty without her.

Sprecher, 1986). When we meet new people, we tend to be far more attracted to beautiful people than we are to the less attractive.

Of course, what is considered beautiful is different for different people, in different periods of history, and in different cultures (Hartz, 1996). Nevertheless, studies repeatedly show a relationship between finding people attractive and evaluating them positively. We tend to believe that attractive people possess positive personality traits. We want to meet and get to know them, and we want them as friends and romantic partners. We view attractive men as more masculine, and beautiful women as more feminine (Gillen, 1981). And we see beautiful people as more desirable partners for sex, romance, and marriage.

One of the earliest investigations into the influence of beauty on romantic attraction studied 752 students who participated in a university dance. Researchers began with a lot of information about the participating students—personality traits, attitudes toward a variety of topics, intelligence scores, and so on. With the help of a computer, the researchers paired the students according to these characteristics. Then, as the students entered the dance hall, a team of judges, themselves students, scored each participant for attractiveness. During a break, the reseachers asked the students how satisfied they were with their partners, and if they were interested in meeting their dates again. Results showed that the level of satisfaction with the blind date, the desire to meet again, and the probability of meeting again, were all a function of only one thing—the physical attractiveness rating! Personality traits, intelligence, and similar attitudes had very little effect (Walster et al., 1966).

People assume that what is beautiful is good. When men and women were shown photographs of very attractive, very unattractive, and average looking people, they attributed many more positive personality traits to the more attractive men and women (Dion et al., 1972). We tend to view highly attractive people as exciting, sexual, romantic partners, interesting, secure, relaxed, warm, intelligent, strong, generous, open, giving, pleasant, polite, modest, successful, sensitive, friendly, independent, psychologically healthy, socially skilled, and poised (e.g., Calvert, 1988). We expect them to be famous and successful both socially and professionally. We expect their marriages to be happy and their lives to be full and exciting (Dion et al., 1972). When things don't work out for them, we are surprised and disappointed.

This positive bias toward beauty can even be found in people's attitudes toward beautiful babies (Karraker et al., 1987) and young children

(Berkowitz & Frodi, 1982). Beautiful children are not only more popular among their peers, but they tend to be treated more kindly, blamed and punished less by their kindergarten teachers as well (Dion, 1972).

This prejudice toward beauty was found in young children as well as people over sixty (Johnson & Pittenger, 1984). It was found in men as well as in women, even though the gender difference may be larger when men and women talk about what attracts them to a potential partner rather than when one examines what really attracts them (Feingold, 1990). And it was found to be more important than other qualities, including, for example, quality of communication (Sprecher & Duck, 1994).

Beautiful people have a great influence on us, both negative and positive. This fact was nicely demonstrated in a classic study by Herold Sigall and Elliot Aronson (1969). Because men are supposed to be more influenced by physical appearance than women, the subjects in the study were young men. The researchers chose a beautiful woman as a confederate. In half of the cases, she was made to look extremely unattractive. She wore ill-fitting and unattractive clothes, a badly cut blond wig that didn't suit her skin color, and makeup that made her skin look oily and unappealing. The woman pretended that she was a doctoral student interviewing psychology students for her dissertation research. At the end of a given interview she gave each subject her personal, clinical evaluation of him. Half of the men received a very positive evaluation, the other half, a very negative evaluation.

Results of the study showed that when the woman looked ugly, it didn't matter to the men whether her evaluation of them was positive or negative. In both cases they didn't like her. When the woman looked beautiful, they liked her very much—but only when she gave them a positive evaluation. When she gave them a negative evaluation, they disliked her even more than they had when she looked ugly. And yet, the men who received negative evaluations from the beautiful woman were anxious to be given another chance to interact with her in other studies. It seems that her evaluation of them was so important that they desperately wanted a chance to try and change her opinion of them.

WHAT IS BEAUTIFUL?

While beauty may be "in the eye of the beholder," to a large extent, social norms and fashions determine what is considered beautiful (Banner, 1983).

The athletic look that characterizes attractive women at the end of the twentieth century is very different from the voluptuous look that characterized beautiful women in previous eras (Silverstein et al., 1990). Despite the general agreement among people in a particular culture about what is attractive, most of us find it difficult to describe exactly what makes certain people attractive to us.

A researcher who tried to find out used pictures of women from college yearbooks and beauty pageants and asked men to rank them according to their beauty. He found that the men ranked two types of faces as most attractive: the "baby face"—a childish face with big eyes, a little nose, and a little chin—and the "sexy woman"—high cheekbones, high brows, wide pupils, and a big smile. The same features were ranked as attractive for white, black, and oriental women (Cunningham, 1986). Another cross-cultural study showed that 17- to 60-year-old men and women in five different cultures show attraction to large eyes, small noses, and full lips (Jones, 1995).

Besides a beautiful face, a beautiful body is obviously very important for the general attractiveness of men and women. Actually, a woman with a very pretty face and an unattractive body gets a lower attractiveness score than a woman with a very attractive body and an unattractive face (Alicke et al., 1986). The most attractive body type for women is of normal weight, rather than skinny or fat (Singh, 1994). An important contributor to the attractiveness of a woman's body is her bust size. The most attractive bust is medium size, not too big and not too small (Kleinke & Staneski, 1980).

An interesting feature, related to the physical attractiveness of women is the waist-to-hip ratio. It turns out that men, from young adults to 85-year-olds, find women with a low waist-to-hip ratio more attractive (Singh, 1993). A low waist-to-hip ratio means a narrow waist and wide hips, an impossible physical ideal that causes women to do unhealthy things, from wearing corsets to cosmetic surgery, to their bodies. An examination of the winners over the last thirty-to-sixty years of the Miss America contest and *Playboy's* "Bunny of the Month," shows very few changes in the waist-to-hip ratio of these declared beauties. Narrow waist and wide hips are important contributors to a woman's sex appeal. (Marilyn Monroe is a famous example. See her perfect waist-to-hip ratio in Figure 6.)

The most important contributors to the attractiveness of a man's body are narrow legs and hips, wide shoulders, and small buttocks (Lavrakas, 1975). Height is another contributor. An analysis of eight different studies published between 1954 and 1989 supports "the male-taller norm" in romantic attraction (Pierce, 1996). Responses to lonely-hearts advertisements show that men who mention the fact that they are tall get more letters from interested women than men who don't mention their height (Lynn & Shurgot, 1984).

When 594 students completed a questionnaire that asked about height, preference in an ideal partner, and whether they were currently in relationships, results showed that tall men enjoy a noticeable dating advantage. The height advantage seemed to diminish for men taller than 6 feet, and height had no dating consequence for women (Hensley, 1994). Another study showed that 95 percent of the women interviewed preferred to date a man taller than they were, whereas 80 percent of men interviewed preferred to date a woman shorter than they were. Shorter women had more dates, men described them as more attractive and preferred to go out with them (Sheppard & Strathman, 1989).

WHY ARE WE PREJUDICED TOWARD BEAUTY?

One explanation is that we enjoy the company of attractive people because their appearances give us aesthetic pleasure. Just as we enjoy a beautiful art object, we enjoy beautiful people.

A second explanation derives from an assumption about appearance and personality, namely, that whatever looks good on the outside is also good inside. This assumption can influence attraction in one of two

FIGURE 6. Marilyn Monroe, the mythical image of feminine sex appeal.

ways. First, if what is beautiful is also good, then we not only double our reward from an attractive person, but a person who can give us greater rewards seems more attractive to us. Second, it is possible that our belief creates reality. If we believe that beauty implies goodness, and we behave accordingly, our actions can encourage attractive people to develop the positive traits we expect from them.

A third explanation is that attractive people have more social skills. Since they have long histories of rewarding relationships, they develop social skills that, in themselves, attract people around them. Studies show that attractive people indeed have better communication skills (Brehm, 1992).

A fourth explanation points to the social benefit we get from associating with attractive people, the reflected glory that shines on us. A person of average attractiveness is perceived as more attractive when in the company of a highly attractive person of the same sex. The same person looks less attractive when in the company of a highly unattractive person (Geiselman et al., 1984).[2]

Yet another explanation rests on our need to believe in a just world, a world in which people get what they deserve and deserve what they get. In a just world, good things happen to good people and bad things happen to bad people. Therefore, we want to believe that people of unusual good looks deserve them because of their wonderful personality traits. Indeed, it was found that the more people believed that the world was just, the more likely they were to attribute positive personality traits to beautiful people and assume that they were going to be successful in their lives (Dion & Dion, 1987).

Finally, the explanation offered by evolutionary psychologists. According to this explanation, cultural stereotypes of beauty are the result of evolutionary processes and are based on requirements for breeding and survival. Romantic attraction plays an important role in the development of the human race (e.g., Buss, 1994). During the thousands of years of evolution, physically attractive men and women had a higher probability of finding a mate, reproducing, and raising their offspring to maturity. In this way they ensured that their genes—including the genes responsible for their good looks—were passed on to future generations. Why are large breasts and a low waist-to-hip ratio considered attractive in a woman? Because, argue evolutionary psychologists, there is an assumed connection between big breasts and the ability to nurse a baby. Babies of women with breasts full of milk had a higher chance of survival. A narrow waist and wide hips create the assumption that a woman is healthier and more able to bear children.

Good skin and rosy cheeks are evidence of good health and youth that are also related to fertility. Why are height and an athletic body considered attractive in a man? Because, in the far away past, these features marked an ability to function well as a hunter, protector, and provider. Offspring of men who were good hunters had a higher probability of survival and thus passed on the genes responsible for their height and athletic build to future generations.

Are attractive people really better? The answer, overall, is no. Attractive people do not seem to have more positive traits, skills, or abilities than unattractive people (Hartfield & Sprecher, 1986). Nevertheless, attractive people have several important advantages. They tend to have better social skills and are correspondingly more popular (Feingold, 1990). Attractive people, women especially, have more friends and pursuers; they communicate with members of the opposite sex better than unattractive people do (Reis et al., 1980); and they have more active sex lives (Curran & Lippold, 1975). In addition, attractive people are less at risk for emotional disturbances than unattractive people are (Archer & Cash, 1985). They tend to work in better jobs, make more money, and, in general, report more satisfaction from their lives than unattractive people do (Umberson & Houghs, 1987). In one study, 737 yearbook pictures of business school graduates were given attractiveness ratings. Results showed a correlation between the attractiveness rating and level of earnings. The more attractive the graduate, the higher his or her future earnings (Frieze et al., 1991).

THE COST OF ATTRACTIVENESS

Despite the importance of beauty and despite the positive stereotypes we associate with beautiful people, beauty does not guarantee happiness, and does not ensure success in love. It may even be the case that the positive effects of our prejudice toward beauty and the negative effects associated with it, such as envy, hostility, harassment, and distrust of people's evaluations, cancel each other.

Unusually beautiful women tend to be viewed as snobs, insolent, materialistic, and unfaithful (Cash & Duncan, 1984). I have often heard such women complain that their beauty scares men away. At parties, men whom the beautiful woman would like to have gotten to know don't dare approach her. In addition, attractiveness can cause envy and hostility in members of one's own sex and constant harassment by members of the other sex. And since beauty tends to fade with time, its loss can be devastating. A woman who was exceptionally beautiful in her youth grew up to be a merely beautiful woman. When people see her they often gasp and say, "You were soooo beautiful." It doesn't comfort her when they continue, "Now you are a 10, but then you were a 12!"

While good looks may be good for future earnings, they are not always good for self-esteem. Actually, the opposite may be true. While attractive people may feel more comfortable in their interactions with the opposite sex, they are not more self-confident. The reason is their concern that they are liked and sought after because of their looks, and not because of who they really are (Major et al., 1984). A beautiful young woman, currently in therapy with me, is an example. Her problem is a severe lack of confidence, because all her life people only saw her pretty face, and didn't see her obvious intelligence. "And what will happen to me when I am old and no longer beautiful?" she asks with real pain and anxiety.

SIMILARITY IN ATTRACTIVENESS

There is extensive evidence that the lovers we choose share with us a similar level of attractiveness. While we may have preferred to get involved with the most attractive person we knew, most of us eventually have to compromise and accept someone who is neither more attractive nor less attractive than we are.

It is possible that this similarity results not from an active selection process, but rather from a screening process that operates in the following manner. The first to find love are the most attractive people, leaving in the pool the people who are second in their level of attractiveness. Once these people are picked, those below them in attractiveness are taken. The process continues until only the most unattractive people remain in the pool, and those are forced to choose from whoever is left (Kalick & Hamilton, 1986).

Those dreaming of a romantic relationship with a movie star or a famous beauty, and unwilling to get involved with the less attractive mortals they meet in their everyday lives, should be aware of the advantages of choosing a lover who is similar to oneself in attractiveness. It turns out that similarity in attractiveness ensures greater satisfaction in a relationship—and greater success *for* the relationship—than does involvement with a person of unusual beauty. Furthermore, involvement with a partner of unusual beauty, unless one is also exceptionally attractive, can cause serious romantic jealousy (Pines, 1998). The unattractive partner feels threatened by the people who surround the beautiful partner like bees around honey, admiring, desiring, coveting, and flirting.

BEAUTY IS SUBJECTIVE

There are those more beautiful than her,
But no one as beautiful.
—Natan Alterman, *Love Poems*

Even while some men's and women's beauty is uncontested, they can look more beautiful to some people than to others. As we go down the scale to the average levels of attractiveness, where most people are, the role played by subjective perception increases. The following story demonstrates just how subjective can be the perception of attractiveness. A young man met a woman while traveling in the Far East and fell madly in love with her, sure that in addition to all her other virtues, his beloved was a stunning beauty. He couldn't wait to introduce her to his friends. But when he returned home, he was shocked to discover that his friends not only did not see her as beautiful, but actually considered her rather homely.

A woman, convinced that her best friend is extremely beautiful, can similarly discover, to her great dismay, that men find her friend totally lacking in any kind of appeal. On the other hand, she can watch with amazement as the same men flock to a woman that she herself finds totally unappealing. Not only can someone who appears very attractive to us, appear very unattractive to others, but our perceptions can change in reaction to things that have nothing to do with appearance. People we learn to love look more attractive to us than they did initially, whereas people we learn to despise can come to look ugly.

For unattractive people, disheartened by the unfairness of the bias toward beauty, there is the comforting evidence that beauty doesn't guarantee finding the best marriage partner or succeeding in romantic relationships. Indeed one of the most unattractive girls who studied with me in elementary school was the first one to get married, and is still happily married today. On the other hand, the most beautiful girl in high school married very late and is twice-divorced.

When people calculate their own overall levels of attractiveness, and the levels of attractiveness of their partners or potential partners, physical appearance is just one of the components in the formula—and its importance is different for different people. Many other traits, including intelligence, sense of humor, social and economic status, interests, and, of course, character, can enhance or diminish one's overall attractiveness.

CHARACTER

What are the traits of the people you like and the traits of the people you dislike? Almost forty years ago, when social psychologists asked people this question, they discovered that at the top of the list of traits that people liked were honesty, competence, ability, intelligence, and energy (Lot et al., 1960). Thirty years later the desired traits were sociability, high activity, and low emotionality (Krueger & Caspi, 1993). The problem with studies of this kind is that it is not clear whether the people we like really have these traits, or whether we convince ourselves that they have these traits because we like them. Probably both are true to some extent.

Is it possible to put the different ingredients of attraction into a formula and calculate the overall attraction? A mathematical model attempted to do just that. According to this model, attraction is in direct proportion to the value given to personality traits. The model assumes that every trait can be given a numerical value, and that the value of a certain trait can be different for different people. The more positive the traits, the greater the attraction. The more negative the traits, the greater the disdain. A trait such as "intelligent" is likely to be rated very positively (+4) and a trait such as "hesitant" as somewhat negative (-1). The overall attraction score is a summary calculated from the values of all the traits that were put into the formula. In the end, the higher the overall evaluation, the higher the attraction (Anderson, 1981).

One could assume that the more able, talented, and competent a person is, the more attractive he or she will be to us. Elliot Aronson (1992), who studied this issue during the presidency of John F. Kennedy, discovered that the relationship between abilities and attraction is not so simple. Aronson was intrigued by the finding that Kennedy's popularity went up after the Bay of Pigs fiasco. The explanation he offered was that Kennedy had been simply too perfect. He was young, handsome, bright, witty, charming, athletic, a voracious reader, and a war hero who had endured great pain. In addition, he had a beautiful and talented wife who spoke several foreign languages, two lovely children, a boy and a girl, and a rich, close-knit family. The testimony to a human weakness that was offered by being responsible for a humiliating national blunder, could have made him appear more human and, hence, more likable.

In order to test this explanation, Aronson and his colleagues conducted the following experiment. Using audio tapes, they asked subjects to evaluate the attractives of four candidates being interviewed for a famous quiz show. The first interviewee was nearly perfect; he answered 92 percent of the questions correctly, had been an honors student in high school, the editor of the yearbook, and a member of the track team. The second interviewee was nearly perfect as well, but committed the blunder of spilling coffee on himself during the interview. The third interviewee was mediocre; he answered only 30 percent of the questions correctly, had received average grades in high school, had been a proofreader on the yearbook, and had failed to make the track team. The fourth interviewee was also mediocre and committed the spilled-coffee blunder.

Results showed that the superior person who committed the blunder was rated most attractive; the average person who committed the same blunder was rated least attractive. The perfect person, who made no blunder, was second in attractiveness; the mediocre person who made no blunder finished third. "Clearly, there was nothing inherently attractive about the simple act of spilling a cup of coffee" writes Aronson, "although it did serve to add an endearing dimension to the perfect person, making him more attractive. The same action served to make the mediocre person appear that much more mediocre and, hence, less attractive" (356).

Are ability and competence important factors in romantic attraction? Let us examine some of the traits men and women mentioned during the romantic attraction interviews when they talked about the reasons they fell in love.

> "The first thing that attracted me was the smile on his face. He looked so happy. . . . He was just smiling at me. And he had the nicest smile. He's like that all the time. It's nice to be around someone who is like this. You can just forget everything that bothers you. And I tend to carry that kind of stuff with me. . . . He's a lot different from anyone else. He's real. . . . He's really calm and he's funny. . . . He's really outdoorsy. He does what he wants. He's also independent which is the way I am, which makes me happy."
>
> "She is smart and dynamic and sensitive and nice. It is easy to trust her. . . . People like her. She gets along well with people. She's easy to like."

"He's kind of crazy [laughs] and wild. I was attracted to his craziness, his loudness. He's really playful and can be very outgoing."

"He is very funny and witty. . . . I don't know what attracted me, but I know I immediately felt comfortable . . . just his conversation and he is so outgoing. He is one of those people that you immediately feel comfortable with. He is interesting, funny, witty. . . . It's fun. . . . He's outgoing and not shy, sort of opposite than me."

In none of these examples, nor in any of the quotes at the beginning of the chapter, are abilities or competence mentioned directly. Of the traits mentioned, intelligence and wit come the closest to competence.

What, then, are the personality traits that attract us to a romantic partner? The traits that were mentioned most often by both men and women were nice, friendly, and a sense of humor. The traits that were mentioned several times by the men were easy-to-talk-to, understanding, warm, sweet, smart, energetic, funny, self-confident, quiet. The traits that were mentioned several times by women were easy-going, sensitive, and intelligent.

The picture that emerges is of attraction to people who make us feel good, people who are warm, sensitive, and funny. In studies that examine what men and women look for in a marriage partner, a similar list of traits emerges. At the top of the list—for both men and women—are warmth and consideration (Goodwin, 1990). An analysis of personal ads in papers also shows that at the top of the list of desirable traits in a romantic partner, both men and women put understanding and a sense of humor (Smith et al., 1990).

The importance of warmth and sensitivity can explain the interesting findings of a recent study in which young college women read various descriptions of men. Women were found to prefer feminine men over masculine men, both as friends and as romantic partners. When rating the attractiveness of the men described, the women gave greater weight to personality factors than they did to success factors. They found the feminine men to be most attractive and the masculine men most repulsive. A man's belief in gender equality had the greatest influence on both the women's platonic and romantic attraction to him (Desrochers, 1995).

Some of the desirable traits in a mate that people mention today are similar to the traits mentioned by people in previous generations, and some are different. A comparison study that examined the desirable traits in the 1930s and in the 1980s shows, for example, that while emotional stability and trustworthiness remain as important today as they were fifty years ago, mutual attraction became more important and sexual purity decreased in importance (Hoyt & Hudson, 1981).

Warmth, sensitivity, and sense of humor are not the first traits that leap to mind when we imagine a wild love affair. Why, then, do they come up again and again in people's descriptions of the kind of person they are attracted to and would like to have as a romantic partner? One obvious explanation is that these traits are more closely related to intimate relationships than they are to wild sexual affairs. Even if the popular portrayal of falling in love is of blind physical passion, the people most of us are attracted to as lovers are people with whom we can be intimate, people with whom we are comfortable and easy.

Warmth and sensitivity are also important because people who like themselves prefer the company of people who like them and make them feel good. Warm, sensitive, considerate people make those around them feel good. And as we know, when people feel good they are more open to love.

BEAUTY AND CHARACTER

When you think about your most significant romantic relationship, what was it that most attracted you? Arthur Aron and his colleagues (1989) wanted to know what made people fall in love. So they asked fifty men and women who had fallen in love within the previous eight months to think about the experience for a few minutes and then describe it in as much detail as possible. Analysis of their stories revealed that the variable that was mentioned most often was either physical attractiveness or personality traits; they did not differentiate between the two.

Beauty and character influence each other, and both influence us. A warm, sensitive person with a good sense of humor tends to look more attractive. And a highly attractive person tends to look warmer, nicer, wiser, and more exciting. The *halo effect* refers to our tendency to perceive people consistently. If we see a person as attractive, we will attribute to that person other positive traits that are associated in our minds with attractiveness—whether these traits are there or not. The best example of the halo effect is falling in love, which makes us see our beloved with starry eyes blinded by love, passion, and admiration.

In addition, all of us are influenced by the norms and values related to attractiveness in the society in which we live. In dating games and personal ads of the 1990s, for example, many more men describe themselves as "sensitive" than did men in the 1970s or 1980s. Admiring the personality traits of the beloved is part of the romantic ideal on which we are raised. It is possible that, because of this enculturation, people today are more likely to mention traits in their beloved when asked why they fell in love with them.

SELF-FULFILLING PROPHECIES

When we perceive people as attractive—because of their appearances or personalities—we expect them to behave in ways that characterize attractive people. These expectations, in turn, encourage behaviors that make our expectations come true. A lovely example of this process was provided in a book written over sixty years ago by Edwin Ray Guthrie (1938).

The classmates of a shy and reserved young woman decided to conduct an experiment. (In another version of this story, the idea was suggested by their psychology instructor!) Their goal was to make their shy classmate feel attractive and desirable. The students made sure that one of them always sat next to her in class, in the cafeteria, or in any other social place on the campus; that one of them invited her to every social event and asked her to dance at parties. At first, the shy woman responded with shock and confusion. But with time, she started enjoying their advances, and developed a feminine self-confidence that was expressed in the way she dressed, did her hair, talked, and behaved.

The critical question was whether the positive change would transfer to other social situations. In order to find out, her classmates visited her other classes. They discovered that their shy and homely classmate continued to act like an attractive and self-confident woman who was sure of her desirability. But what was even more surprising, and exciting in its implications, was the fact that the men in those classes—unaware of the experiment underway and its progress—treated her as an attractive woman. They showed interest in her and pursued her.

The behavior of the men reinforced the shy woman's self-confidence and perception of herself as an attractive and desirable woman, which, in turn, caused her to behave accordingly. The more self-assured her behavior was, the more open she was with men; the more attention she gave to her appearance, the more responses she received from the men around her. With time, the experiment started affecting the men who took part in it. They no longer had to pretend to be attracted to their classmate. They came to see her as attractive and started competing earnestly for her attention. The students' attentions helped turn the ugly duckling into a beautiful swan.

THE STORY OF PYGMALION AND GALATEA

Greek mythology tells the story of a young and gifted sculptor named Pygmalion who lived on the isle of Cyprus. Pygmalion hated women and made up his mind never to marry. Nevertheless, or because of this, he invested all of his artistic genius in a sculpture of a woman. And the sculpture was beautiful; there was no living woman or sculpture that could compare to it in beauty. The sculpture transcended its static nature; it appeared to be a real woman standing motionless just for a moment.

So the legend goes, Pygmalion fell in love with his beautiful sculpture. His love was passionate and boundless. No man in love ever suffered so much pain. He kissed her seductive lips, but she didn't return his kisses. He held her in his arms, but she remained cold. His love drew the eye of Venus, goddess of love, and she decided to help him. She made the sculpture come alive. Pygmalion named his beloved Galatea and married her.

Guthrie's story is reminiscent of the love story of Pygmalion and Galatea (see Figure 7).

Our behavior influences the people around us. If a woman treats a man like the most caring and generous man on earth, she is going to help bring out more of his generosity. And if a man treats a woman like a strong able person, he is going to help bring out more of her competence. An elegant proof of the power of self-fulfilling prophecies is provided in a study by Mark Snyder (1993).

Young men and women were invited to take part in a study that, supposedly, examined the process of getting acquainted. The participants were asked to talk on the phone and try to get acquainted with an unknown person of the opposite sex. Before the telephone conversation, the experimenter entered each room in which a man sat, and took a photograph of him with a Polaroid camera. The experimenter explained that in order to help the conversation flow, the researchers had decided to give each subject a photograph of his or her telephone partner. Every man received a photograph of his supposed partner with whom he was going to converse. In truth, it was a photograph of a woman randomly selected from a group who had been pre-judged as either very attractive or very unattractive. The

women who took part in the study did not receive photographs and knew
nothing about the photographs that were given to the men. Every couple
spoke on the phone for about ten minutes on any subject they chose. Their
voices were recorded on separate tapes. Judges were then asked to listen to
the tape recordings of the women's voices only, and rate them on such characteristics as liveliness, warmth, intimacy, sexiness, and sociability.

Results of the study showed that the women who spoke to men who
thought they were talking to a beautiful woman, were friendlier, more open,
more flirtatious than women who spoke to men who thought they were
talking to an unattractive woman. In other words, the fact that the men
thought that the women were beautiful made the women act in ways that
fulfilled the men's expectations.

The conclusion is obvious—beauty and character are at least to some extent the result of an interaction between two people. The way we perceive a

person's appearance and personality influences that person's
self-perception and perception
of us. This perception, in-turn,
influences the person's behavior
which reinforces our perceptions. A man who treats a
woman as sexy and attractive
causes her to behave in a sexier
manner, at least in his presence.
This is the power of self-fulfilling prophecies. We can choose
to use this power or not.

Self-fulfilling prophecies
and positive illusions have positive effects on romantic relationships. Satisfying romantic
relationships reflect, at least in
part, the ability of people to see
their imperfect partners through
adoring eyes. A recent study
demonstrated this.

Three times during the
course of a year, one hundred
couples filled out questionnaires

FIGURE 7. *Pygmalion and Galatea* by Etiene
Falconet, 18th century.

that examined their levels of "partner idealization" and satisfaction from their relationships. Analysis of the data revealed that partner idealization worked as a self-fulfilling prophecy. The more the partners idealized each other the higher was the probability that they would stay together—even in cases where the couple had conflicts and reservations. Those couples in which the partners tended to idealize each other more at the beginning of the relationship reported a larger increase in satisfaction and a lower level of conflict during the year. And, among the couples in which the partners adored each other, each partner tended with time to accept the other's perceptions of him or herself—seeing the self more positively as a result of a partner's positive view. Contrary to the popular belief that love is blind, partners who adore each other are prophets. With time they shape the relationship according to their own visions (Murray et al., 1996).

Freud (1914) explained the idealization of the beloved as the "projection" of an "ideal self." The individual projects onto the beloved traits and values that the individual views as supreme, perceiving them as being in the beloved. Freud believed that in the progression from the immature stage of falling-in-love to the mature stage of love, the idealization of the beloved needs to be abandoned and replaced by a mature view of the beloved as he or she really is. The findings of the positive effect of partner idealization suggest that this isn't necessarily so. Positive illusions continue to have the power of a self-fulfilling prophecy even after falling-in-love has turned to love.

THE LOVER'S PERSONALITY

So far the discussion has centered on the personality of the beloved. What about the lover's personality? What personality dimensions make us more open to love, more comfortable in intimate relationships? The famous developmental psychologist Eric Erikson (1959) believed that we need to develop a strong sense of ourselves and know who we are before we can develop truly intimate relationships. A study in which the levels of people's self-identity were compared to the levels of intimacy in their relationships shows that Erikson was right (Kacerguis & Adams, 1980).

People without well-developed senses of identity are afraid of intimacy because they are terrified of being engulfed and losing themselves in relationships. It was shown that when people with a low sense of identity fall in love, their feelings are unusually intense, overwhelm them, and cause obsessive, tumultuous loves (Sperling, 1987).

Self-confidence influences our ability to give and receive love. People who have a high frequency of love experiences tend to have high self-confidence and low levels of defensiveness. (Dion & Dion, 1975). In order to be able to love, we first have to love ourselves and feel secure in out own lovability.

Another personality dimension that is related to the ability to love is self-actualization. Self-actualization refers to a person's constant effort to grow, to develop his or her inherent talents and capabilities. Abraham Maslow (1970) described the need for self-actualization as the highest in the human hierarchy of needs. He believed that being self-actualized is the foundation of the ability to give and receive love.

An early study that supported Maslow's theory showed that people who had been in romantic relationships within three years preceding the study were more self-actualized than people who had not been in intimate relationships during that time (Dietch, 1978). Later studies showed a more complex relationship between self-actualization and the ability to fall in love. On the one hand, being self-actualized was related to a richer and more satisfying love experience; on the other, a high level of self-actualization correlated with a lower need for romantic relationships (Dion & Dion, 1985). This suggests that self-actualized people enjoy love relationships more but need them less than people who are not actualized.

Greek philosophers distinguished among six styles of love: *best friends* love, *unselfish* and *sacrificing* love, *possessive* love, *playful* and *game-playing* love, and *romantic* love.[3] Studies show that insecure people who don't have a coherent sense of self and who are not self-actualized, tend toward a game-playing love; they have relationships with low levels of intimacy and high levels of conflict. People who are self-confident, self-actualized, and have a coherent sense of self, tend toward unselfish and romantic styles of love; their relationships are characterized by high levels of intimacy (Levy & Davis, 1988).

SUGGESTIONS FOR PEOPLE SEEKING LOVE

Suggestions Regarding Beauty

Look for a partner who is as physically appealing as you are. Despite the importance of physical attractiveness in the selection of super models and movie stars, when you are selecting a lover, the rule of thumb is not to choose the most attractive person possible. Rather, select the most attractive person among those similar to yourself in attractiveness. People who follow this general guideline are likely to have more harmonious and satisfying romantic relationships.

While beauty can be subjective and skin deep, it still plays an important role as one of the first screens in romantic relationships. This implies what most people know very well: that you should do everything you can to look your best when meeting someone you are interested in. If you are rejected because of an appearance that could have been enhanced with some effort, your potential mate will never have a chance to discover the wonderful treasures buried deep inside your unkempt appearance.

Suggestions Regarding Character

It ought to be encouraging that you need not have exceptional skills or abilities to find love. Neither should you look for a mate who has unusual skills or abilities. The emotional state that should guide the search for love is a feeling of pleasure, joy, and comfort. According to this criterion, despite its obvious subjectivity, people who are warm, sensitive, and considerate, who, preferably, have a good sense of humor—and who also like us—are the best candidates.

Suggestions Regarding Finding Love

Use the power of self-fulfilling prophecies. Treat your potential partners as if they were exactly what you want them to be—sexy, exciting, attractive. Your behavior will help bring out those traits in them. Work toward improving your self-confidence and toward actualizing yourself. Make a conscious effort to make yourself as attractive as possible by improving the attractive parts of your appearance and personality. Clearly, these suggestions require an enormous effort, can take a very long time, and may require professional help. Yet, as Ovid, the first century poet, wrote in *The Art of Love,* "To be loved, be lovable."

4

BIRDS OF A FEATHER
OR OPPOSITES ATTRACT?

Birds of a feather flock together.
    —A proverb

The starling went to the raven, because
it is of its kind.
    —Baba Kama, *The Mishna*

*N*arcissus was a beautiful youth. So great was his beauty that all the young women, as well as the nymphs, were in love with him, but he did not desire any of them. Rejected and despairing, many an admirer took her own life. But Narcissus was proud, stubborn, and heartless. Then, one day, a rejected admirer called out to the gods for vengeance, and Nemesis, the goddess of righteous anger, punished Narcissus. As he bent over a pristine pool of water to get a drink, Narcissus saw his own reflection and fell in love with himself. Now it was he who suffered the terrible pain of unrequited love, the despair of knowing that he would never consummate his love or possess his beloved. His gaze fixed on his reflection in the water, Narcissus died of grief and longing. When the nymphs went to bury his body, they couldn't find it. In the place where it had lain there grew a beautiful new flower that was given his name.

Like Narcissus, many people are attracted to their reflections, that is, other people who share the same characteristics.

"We had a lot in common. We both come from these highly intellectual neurotic couples, have an interest in the environment, not too much in a hurry to get into graduate school."

"When I discovered that we have a shared interest in biology I thought 'That's great! We have this in common!' Having things in common really helps."

"We have the same goals and interests. He loves to water-ski and that's my favorite thing. He's like my missing link. That's what he is. . . . We're both real open and communicators and we're both independent. We are both ourselves."

"We were both in an orchestra . . . I felt that we were similar. . . . We tended to think alike in many ways."

"We have a lot in common. We're both really affectionate, we both like to travel, and she plays tennis and I play. Everything we do together is fun."

"We're both musicians. . . . We are both loving people. We're best friends."

"What attracted me first was her looks . . . later that she's very much like me. We're very much alike. We don't want to get stuck with one person, we want to see other people."

"She was overweight, just like me. . . . She was nice, very nice. I felt comfortable with her."

"I'm attracted to people who are sensitive and quiet, because that's the way I am."

"She looks like me, same color tone."

"We're in the same religion and that's very attractive to me."

Analysis of the romantic attraction interviews suggests that, in one-third of the cases, similarity played a role in the initial attraction.[1] As can be seen from the above excerpts, the similarity appeared in many different areas: family background, personality traits, appearance, ways of thinking, goals and interests, and leisure activities. In all of these cases, interviewees saw the similarity as a positive factor that enhanced the original attraction and helped facilitate the development of the relationship.

Studies on who falls in love with whom show a huge range of variables in which intimate partners are similar. These variables include: age, appearance, height, weight, eye color, behavior patterns, professional success, attitudes, opinions, intelligence, cognitive complexity, verbal ability, education, social and economic class, family background, number and sex of siblings, feelings toward the family of origin, the quality of the parents' marriage,

race and ethnic background, religious background, social and political affil-
iations, acceptance of sex-role stereotypes, physical and emotional health,
emotional maturity, physical characteristics including physical defects, level
of neuroticism, moodiness, depressive tendencies, a tendency to be a "lone
wolf" or a "social animal," as well as drinking and smoking habits.[2]

The earliest statistical study that documented similarity between couples
is the study done by the British, Victorian psychologist Sir Francis Galton
(1884) toward the end of the nineteenth century. Galton, who developed
the method of statistical correlation, found a significant correlation between
husbands and wives not only in such obvious variables as age, race, religion,
education, and social status, but also in physical and psychological traits
such as height, eye color, and intelligence.

Over 100 years after Galton, studies have reached similar conclusions.
One study, involving 1,499 American couples, showed that the couples
were similar in a wide range of cognitive and personality traits (Phillips et
al., 1988). Another study, using British couples, showed that the couples
were similar in such diverse traits as intelligence, introversion, extroversion,
and inconsistency (Taylor & Vandenberg, 1988).[3] The authors concluded
that the similarity resulted from both physical proximity and personal preference. Which is to say that, among those who live in their neighborhoods,
study in their schools, or work in their offices, people choose those who are
similar to them in levels of intelligence and personality. Introverts choose
introverts and extroverts prefer extroverts.

People are more likely to choose, as a lover, someone who has similar
traits than someone who has different traits. Furthermore, the more similar
couples are in terms of personality, the more comfortable they are with each
other. This is manifested in greater compatibility and greater satisfaction
(Mehrabian, 1989).

Why does similarity enhance attraction and satisfaction in intimate relationships? One explanation suggests itself: similarities are generally rewarding whereas dissimilarities can be unpleasant. Consequently, couples who
are similar in attitudes, temperament, and behavior are more likely to stay
together over time (Hartfield & Rapson, 1992). Even those who build and
organize their thoughts and perceptions in similar ways are more attracted
to each other and find more enjoyment in each other's company (Burleson
et al., 1997; Neimeyer, 1984).

In addition, studies document similarity between couples in such physical features as height, size, and weight. Short men, it turns out, tend to
marry short women and tall women tend to marry tall men. Fat men tend

to marry fat women, and skinny women prefer skinny men. When the weights of 330 married couples were examined during four stages of their life cycle, it was discovered that even among young couples there was a similarity in the partners' weights. This correlation probably reflects people's original attraction to potential partners who are similar to themselves in physical appearance. It is less surprising that similarity was found in the couples' weights at the age of retirement—the probable result of similar eating habits and similar life styles (Schafer & Keith, 1990).

Another fascinating topic is the similarity found in a couple's mental health or illness. One of the studies that addressed this topic showed that husbands of schizophrenic women also tended to show symptoms of mental disturbance (Parnas, 1988). A study of people who suffer from depression revealed that in 41 percent of the cases, both parents suffered from a mental problem (Merikangas et al., 1988). Some evidence exists that moody people with depressive tendencies tend to be attracted to people who are similar to them in unhappiness. There is much stronger evidence that happy people are attracted to happy people. In all of these cases, it is clear that similarity in emotional makeup increases a couple's attraction to each other (Lock & Horowitz, 1990).

When we consider the long and impressive list of variables in which a couple can express similarity, a question suggests itself. Are some similarities more important than others? Evolutionary psychologist David Buss (1985) looked at this question and says the answer is yes. Age, education, race, religion, and ethnic background account for the highest correlations between partners; they also have the greatest effect on a relationship. Next in order of size and importance are similarities in attitudes, opinions, mental ability, social and economic status, height, weight, eye color, behavior, personality, number of brothers and sisters, and a large number of physical characteristics.

These correlations suggest that when we are looking for marriage partners, we eliminate first those whom we perceive to be inappropriate in the most important ways. They are too old or too young—"I never thought about him in a romantic way, because he seemed too old for me." They have too much or too little education—"I can't talk about issues that come up in my work with a man who didn't finish high-school and never reads." Their skin color, ethnic background, and religious background are too different from our own—"I could never get seriously involved with a non-Jew."

After passing the initial screening, people look at the other dimensions of potential mates. Here too, the greater the similarity, the greater the chance that the person will pass the test successfully. In the second screening, we assess basic values, similar social and economic status, personality, and behaviors. It would be very difficult, for example, for a liberal democrat to continue dating a racist fascist even if attractive and otherwise appropriate.

It is possible that underneath all these similarities exists a more basic, more fundamental similarity in genetic makeup. Indeed, a number of studies done in the last decade show that people are able to identify, and prefer as romantic partners, people who are similar to them genetically (e.g., Rushton, 1988).

Clearly, people tend to fall in love with, and choose as marriage partners, individuals who are similar to them. Fairy tales about great loves between Cinderella and the prince or between the beautiful call girl and the millionaire are very rare. This is probably why we enjoy hearing about them and seeing them in movies. In the original version of the movie *Pretty Woman*, the couple parted in the end. But at an early screening, viewers objected. They saw the story as a fairy tale and demanded an appropriate ending, which they got. When such miracle romances do occur, they usually don't lead to marriage. On the very rare occasions that they do, the marriages are characterized by a high number of conflicts.

The greater the similarity between a couple, the greater their satisfaction from the relationship. People who come from similar cultural and social backgrounds have similar expectations and assumptions. This makes communication between them easier and prevents conflicts. They don't need to discuss who does what and how, these things are mutually understood and accepted. Similarities in attitudes, interests, and personality also make communication easier; consequently, married couples who share these characteristics report greater happiness and satisfaction from their marriages (Caspi & Harbener, 1990).

From the long list of variables shared by couples, I have chosen five to discuss in detail. These variables play a special role in romantic attraction: similarity in appearance, attitudes, personality, psychological maturity, and genetic makeup.

SIMILARITY IN PHYSICAL APPEARANCE

A study done at a matchmaking agency demonstrated how similar levels of attractiveness affect the formation of romantic relationships. The agency gave its customers background information and a five-minute video of each potential partner answering a series of standard questions. If the customer expressed an interest in meeting one of the potential partners, the agency approached the person and asked for permission to release his or her name and phone number. The agency used a grading system to evaluate how a romantic relationship was developing. When one party was interested but the other party refused to release the name, the relationship received the lowest grade. After a couple had had two or more dates, the relationship received the highest grade. In addition, the agency graded each party's attractiveness in the video clip. The study examined the relationship between the attractiveness rating and the development of a romantic relationship. Results showed that the greater the similarity in attractiveness between a customer and a potential partner, the more likely it was that a romantic relationship would develop between them (Folkes, 1982).

Another study examined the progress of courtship by following couples for nine months. The more similar the partners were to each other in attractiveness, the greater interest they showed in continuing the relationship, the less likely they were to break up, and, with time, the more likely they were to express love toward each other (White, 1980). Other studies show that the similarity in attractiveness between a dating couple is smaller than that of a couple living together, and their similarity is smaller than that of couples planning to marry or already married (e.g., Brehm, 1992; Feingold, 1988). On those rare occasions when a significant difference exists between the attractiveness of romantic partners, it is explained by the exceptional qualities possessed by the less attractive member, as in the story of Beauty and the Beast.

With time, the role of physical attractiveness may diminish in importance. Nevertheless, when a partner's attractiveness changes drastically, it can have a major effect on the relationship, even after many years of marriage. A study of couples with sexual problems demonstrated this. The husbands who reported the highest number of sexual difficulties believed that they had remained as attractive as they were at the beginning of the relationship, while their wives had become less attractive than they used to be (Margolin & White, 1987).

WHY ARE COUPLES SIMILAR IN THEIR PHYSICAL ATTRACTIVENESS?

Equity theory offers one explanation. According to this theory, when choosing a partner, it is very important to us that we feel we are getting someone we deserve. The more similar the attractiveness of the partners, the more the relationship is perceived by the couple and by onlookers as equitable. The more attractive men and women are, the more attractive are the dates they choose. The more unattractive they are, the more unattractive the dates they have to accept (Berscheid & Hartfield–Walster, 1978).

The second explanation addresses the positive effect of repeated exposure. From the time we are born, most of us are surrounded by family members, especially parents and siblings, who tend to look like us. This repeated exposure causes people to develop a strong preference and attraction for physical features similar to their own. Indeed, there is far greater similarity between the photographs of married or engaged couples than there is between photographs of randomly selected couples (Hinsz, 1989).

A third explanation, is that, with time, couples tend to grow increasingly similar to each other. They eat the same foods, share the same leisure activities, and pay more or less attention to their appearances. When students were given yearbook pictures of couples who had graduated from high-school 25 years earlier, they couldn't guess who was married to whom. When they were given current pictures of the same couples, they were able to identify very easily who was married to whom (Zajonc et al., 1987). In other words, after 25 years of living together the couples came to look more alike.

Which explanation is correct? Probably all three. People tend to pursue and accept potential partners who resemble them, and, with time, people grow to look like their partners.

ATTITUDE SIMILARITY

After people have noticed and assessed the physical appearance of a potential partner, they go on to examine the person's attitudes toward issues they care about. It is on this topic of attitude similarity that most of the studies were done on the effect of similarity on attraction. The conclusion, over and over again, is the same—the greater the attitude similarity, the greater the attraction, and the greater the satisfaction in the relationship.

In thirty-five years of attraction research, Don Byrne (1997) showed that people are more attracted to others whom they perceive as sharing similar attitudes. In an early study, he began by identifying the attitudes of the students who were subjects in the study, and asking student judges to rate the physical appearance of each subject. Byrne then separated the subjects into couples who were either similar or dissimilar in their attitudes, and sent them on a date. After their dates, the couples who had similar attitudes were more attracted to each other than were the couples who had dissimilar attitudes. The attraction was greatest when the date was physically attractive *and* had similar attitudes. In a repeat check at the end of the semester, those students who had gone out with an attractive person with similar attitudes were most likely to remember the date's name and express a desire for another date (Byrne et al., 1970).

Don Byrne has repeatedly validated his findings on the effect of attitude similarity on attraction (1971; 1997). His studies took the following procedure. Subjects received a questionnaire in which they were asked about their attitudes on various topics—for example, "Do you believe in God?", "What are your political views?", and so on. Later, while participating in what they supposed was a separate study, the subjects were asked their impressions of another person and given a copy of that person's completed questionnaire. In fact, the questionnaire had been completed by the experimenter referring to the opinions expressed earlier by the subject. In some cases this questionnaire portrayed the other person as possessing very similar attitudes; in the remaining cases, the other person possessed very different attitudes.

Byrne discovered that the *ratio* of similar to different attitudes determined the level of attraction. The higher the ratio of similar to different attitudes, the greater the attraction. Neither the number of similar attitudes nor the kind of different attitudes had an effect. This finding was replicated with the very young and very old, and with both men and women who came from different backgrounds and lived in very different situations.

The effect of attitude similarity on attraction has been known for a long time. When Charles Darwin listed the causes for people's attraction to each other, similarity in attitudes and interests was at the top of his list. Darwin also mentioned expertise or excellence in some area, returned affection, and traits that are pleasant or admirable, such as loyalty, honesty, and goodness (1910). We will get back to some of these causes of attraction later.

Dale Carnegie (1982), who gave millions of his readers prescriptions on "how to win friends and influence people" recommended using the positive effect of similarity in attitudes and interests. "The royal road to a person's heart is to talk about the things he or she treasures most" (94). If a real similarity in attitudes doesn't exist, Carnegie recommended pretending that it does.

Why are we attracted to people who agree with us? Several explanations have been offered.

- A person who agrees with us validates our opinions. In other words, such a person gives us the pleasant feeling that we are right (Aronson, 1998). We are taught from a very young age that we can be punished for having the wrong opinions and attitudes. Consequently, when we find that someone else holds the same opinion or attitude as we do, our conviction that our own attitude is correct is supported. Since it is pleasant to feel that our view of the world is reasonable and correct, such social validation is rewarding and, hence, an element in attraction (Berscheid & Hartfield–Walster, 1978).

- When we know a person's attitudes, we can usually guess how that person is likely to behave. If a person perceives the world as we do, we feel fairly confident that it would be rewarding to spend time with that person (Berscheid & Hartfield–Walster, 1978). On the other hand, if he or she expresses attitudes different from our own, it may suggest a type of person whom we have found to be unpleasant, immoral, dangerous, or just plain stupid (Aronson, 1998).
- If we love ourselves, it only makes sense that we will love people who are similar to us (Berscheid & Hartfield–Walster, 1978).
- When we learn that others are similar to us, we assume they will like us; thus, we like them in return. When we perceive people as different, we tend to avoid them and thus reduce the chance that they will pass through our other attraction screens (Berscheid & Hartfield–Walster, 1978).
- People who are similar to us—in attitudes, personality, physical appearance, and background—seem familiar. And as we know, the familiar is more comfortable and pleasant to us than the unfamiliar.
- We are more likely to meet and get to know others who are similar to us in familiar surroundings. People from similar backgrounds are more likely to live in our neighborhoods, belong to the same clubs, and attend the same schools.

Despite this logical reasoning, it should be noted that attraction is not always the result of a true similarity in attitudes. When we like a person, we assume that he or she shares our attitudes. If I like you, I just naturally assume that you hold attitudes similar to mine and that our tastes and preferences are similar. The attraction develops an illusion of similarity, and the assumed similarity enhances the attraction (Marks & Miller, 1982).

The effect of assumed similarity on attraction can be explained by *Balance Theory*. According to this theory, people strive to organize their likes and dislikes in a symmetrical arrangement that results in balance. When two people like each other and agree about something, they create a state of balance. When they like each other and disagree, there is imbalance, an unpleasant state that motivates them to do something to restore balance (Orive, 1988).

One would assume that once we get to know people well, we would discover whether they indeed share our attitudes. Yet, several studies have found that husbands and wives tend to assume that they are far more similar to each other than they actually are.[4] In one of these studies, spouses were asked their opinions on various political issues, and, then, asked to imagine how each thought his or her spouse would repond. Results showed that the discrepancy between the real opinions of the husbands and wives was far greater than the discrepancy between their assumed opinions. It was also found that the more couples assumed that they shared attitudes and opinions, the more satisfaction they drew from the marriage (Levinger & Breedlove, 1966). This suggests that a couple's attitudes don't really have to be similar as long as the couple assumes that they are similar. It is possible, too, that in the interest of harmony, husbands and wives tend to emphasize their similarities and conceal or avoid areas of disagreement.

One variable that plays a particularly important role as a predictor of marital satisfaction is similarity in sex-role ideology (Grush & Yehl, 1979). Sex-role ideology can be traditional in assigning different and complementary roles to husband and wife, and it can be egalitarian in assigning equal roles and shared tasks. When both husband and wife share the same sex-role ideology, be it traditional or egalitarian, they are happier in their marriage than couples who do not. The reason is obvious. When a couple agrees on the roles of men and women in a marriage, they significantly reduce the probability of conflicts.

Similarity in sexual attitudes also bears directly on romantic attraction and marital satisfaction (Smith et al., 1993). Discrepancy in a couple's sexual attitudes predicts sexual dissatisfaction in both partners. Interestingly, the woman's sexual attitudes are a better predictor of sexual satisfaction in both the wife and the husband.

Similarities in a couple's social and communication skills are also important predictors of attraction and marital satisfaction. These similarities promote attraction by fostering enjoyable interactions. Indeed, married couples were found to be more similar in their levels of social and communication skills than were random, computer-generated couples (Burleson & Denton, 1992).

In summary, we like and are attracted to people who possess attitudes, interests, and social skills similar to our own, and we perceive ourselves to be more similar to people we like and are attracted to.

SIMILARITY IN PERSONALITY

The proverb "birds of a feather flock together" generally refers to an attraction between people of similar personalities. A number of the interviews at the beginning of the chapter refer to this attraction—"We're both real open" or "We're both really affectionate"—and a number of studies document it (e.g., Richard, et al., 1990; Marioles et al., 1996). However, the evidence for an attraction between people with similar personalities is far weaker than the evidence for an attraction between those with similar attitudes.

It seems that while similarity in attitudes serves as an important screening variable in the early stages of a love relationship, similarity in personality becomes important as the relationship develops. Indeed, a number of studies indicate that spouses who have similar personalities report higher levels of happiness and satisfaction from their marriages than do spouses who have different personalities (e.g., Caspi & Harbener, 1990; Richard, et al., 1990).

Why are we likely to be attracted to a personality similar to our own? For the same reasons that operated with similar appearance and attitudes: similarity in personality validates and reinforces our self-perceptions. In addition, a relationship with someone of similar personality helps us maintain the stability of our own personality. We surround ourselves with people similar to ourselves in an effort to keep our personalities stable in the face of the many situations, changes, and transitions that characterize our lives. In a longitudinal study at the University of California at Berkeley, an analysis of the criteria for mate selection showed that "homogeneity," which is to say, similarity, is a basic norm in marriage (Caspi & Herbener, 1990). In other words, we choose to love and marry people who are similar to us because the choice helps us maintain a stable personality. And, according to what has been called a *Theory of Narcissism,* as with Narcissus, we love in other people what we see and love in ourselves (Reader & English, 1947).

In one of the studies that tested the theory of narcissism, a personality test was given to female students at the beginning of their first year of school. Six months later they were asked to name the three classmates they liked most and the three classmates they liked least. Results of the study showed that the personality of the subject was similar to the personalities of her friends, but dissimilar from the personalities of the classmates she disliked (Izard, 1960). It is possible that the attraction to another with a similar personality is based on a similarity we sense intuitively but are not completely conscious of, that is, a similarity in emotional maturity.

SIMILARITY IN EMOTIONAL MATURITY AND MENTAL HEALTH

Family therapist Murray Bowen (1978) believed that a person's ability to separate from their birth families and develop as an independent individual defined his or her level of emotional maturity and mental health. He ranked people according to their levels of "differentiation" from their families of origin. At the bottom were people who were totally "undifferentiated"— unable to separate from their families of origin and still totally enmeshed in them. At the top were people who were totally "differentiated"—individuals who succeeded in separating from their families and had mature, independent, healthy self-identities. Bowen's important contribution to the subject of attraction to the similar is his notion that people choose as intimate partners others who are at the same level of differentiation, emotional maturity, and mental health.

Even when one of the partners, usually the husband, seemed significantly more differentiated, Bowen assumed that both partners actually function at a similar level of differentiation. My clinical experience supports Bowen's notion. When a crisis occurs in such a couple, the partner who has appeared to be less differentiated, very often funtions at a much higher level as the functioning of the supposed healthier partner deteriorates.

Harville Hendrix, a marriage therapist and pastoral counselor, popularized Bowen's ideas in his best-selling books. According to Hendrix (1992), all of us suffer from psychological injuries that happen during different stages of our development. We remain stuck in the stage in which the injury was the most serious. We are attracted to and choose as marriage partners people who are stuck in a similar developmental stage and suffered a similar psychological injury.

Individuals who have similar psychological wounds occasionally respond to their injuries in the same way; for example, they avoid intimate relationships and the risk of getting hurt. But married couples, despite sharing a level of psychological functioning, often exhibit opposite modes of coping; for example, as one partner approaches, the other withdraws. We will elaborate on the reason for this later in the book during the discussion of the unconscious forces influencing romantic choices.

GENETIC SIMILARITY

In recent years, the scientific literature on similarity and attraction has revealed evidence that genetic similarity plays a role in romantic attraction. Evolutionary psychologists believe that the natural selection process led humans to develop a biological mechanism that directs mate selection. This innate biological mechanism exerts a powerful influence on the sexual attraction a person feels toward a potential mate with optimal genetic similarity.

Evolutionary psychologist Philip Rushton (1988) documented the attraction to partners who are genetically similar by examining the results of approximately 1,000 paternity claims brought by women against men with whom they allegedly had borne a child. Since such a claim is resolved by a genetic test, Rushton was able to look at ten different genetic markers in both partners. He discovered that partners who were involved in a legal battle around a paternity claim—which is to say they had had sexual intercourse at least once and had some kind of an emotional connection—were closer genetically than were couples, from the same population, who were randomly matched by a computer. Furthermore, in all cases in which the paternity of the man was proven, there was a greater genetic similarity between him and the mother than there was in the cases in which the paternity was disproved. Clearly, genetic similarity is somehow detected and is romantically attractive.

The evolutionary psychologist Ada Lumpert (1997) quotes a series of studies that testify not only to the existence but the advantages of attraction between genetically similar couples. The greater the genetic similarity between romantic partners, the greater their fertility rates, the smaller their rates of natural abortions, and the healthier the children born to them. In addition, the more genetically similar a couple is, the greater their marital harmony, stability, mutual support, help, and satisfaction from their lives together.

If the greater the similarity, the greater the attraction, why aren't we attracted to members of our family who are most similar to us genetically? The reason is the operation of another genetically imprinted mechanism—the incest taboo. At the opposite end of the scale, neither are we attracted to those who are very different from us genetically, such as people of a different race.

OPPOSITES ATTRACT

I wanted you
that day on the beach
because you were different
and because you smiled
and because I knew your world
was different.
—R. McKuen,
Stanyan Street and Other Sorrows

While research and folk wisdom tell us that "birds of a feather flock together," folk wisdom also provides us with an opposing rule of human behavior, namely, that "opposites attract." While reading this chapter, the
question of attraction to the opposite probably crossed many a reader's
mind. After all, we all know that just as the opposite ends of a magnet attract each other, opposite personalities do as well. Let's examine the relevant
evidence.

> *"We look like total opposites. He's tall and dignified and I'm short and
> hysterical. We are opposites in terms of the way we look and the way we
> act, but because we get along so well we balance each other out. Or maybe
> we get along so well because we are opposites."*
>
> *"When people first see us they think that we kind of look weird, because
> I'm 5 foot 3, and he's 6 foot 5. 'You guys don't look like the perfect couple'
> she laughingly mimics. Then, after they get to know us and see how I know
> what he's thinking and how he does the same thing with me, they say 'You
> guys kind of click.' It just works really well between the two of us, and a lot
> of people have been commenting on it."*
>
> *"It's interesting. We come from totally different backgrounds."*
>
> *"He's very laid back. He could sit through my temper tantrums and not
> blink an eye."*
>
> *"We tend to argue about politics, and we tend to have different out-
> looks. He's in a different world—not in science. I learned a lot about
> banking and economics. It's fun."*

In all these quotes, the interviewee was attracted to an aspect that was
different in his or her romantic partner. In some cases, the difference is in
personality, in others, the difference lies in areas of interest, and in still oth-

ers, the difference is in physical appearance. In all cases, however, the difference is seen as a positive aspect that enhances the relationship.

There is a great deal of clinical as well as anecdotal evidence that opposites attract. Highly cerebral men are known to be attracted to highly emotional women, submissive people to dominant partners, strong women are attracted to weak men, soft and gentle men are attracted to aggressive women. There is also some research evidence that people in complementary relationships, specifically, submissive people with dominant partners, report more satisfaction than do people with similar partners (Dryer & Horowitz, 1997).

Differences can be more exciting than similarities. One of the early studies on this topic showed that while it is very nice to discover that we are liked by a person who holds views similar to our own, it is much more exciting to discover that we are liked by a person whose views are very different (Jones et al., 1971). The reason? When we are liked by a person who holds opinions different from ours, we assume that the person likes us because of who we are and not because of our opinions.

There are other rewards that differences can provide. When we interact with someone who holds different attitudes we are more likely to learn something new and valuable (Kruglanski & Mayseless, 1987). We are also more likely to find out that we are special and unique instead of being just like everyone else (Snyder & Fromkin, 1980).

ATTRACTION TO THE SIMILAR AND ATTRACTION TO THE OPPOSITE: A COMPARISON

Are we more attracted to people to whom we are similar or to people from whom we are different? Despite the evidence for the rewards obtained from people to whom we are different, the lion's share of the research on attraction indicates that similarity has far greater influence. Here are some examples. Similarity has been found to exert the major influence on the definition of the ideal mate (Rytting et al., 1992). Attitudinal similarity accounts for 81 percent of the determinants of interpersonal attraction (Shaikh & Suresh, 1994). Similar partners were found to be pleasurable and arousing, dissimilar partners repulsive (Krueger & Caspi, 1993).

Some couple therapists not only point to insufficient research support for the attraction of opposites, but view people's belief in this attraction as a very dangerous myth. It is one of those unrealistic beliefs, which also include a "match made in heaven," and the "perfect relationship," that creates unrealistic expectations that are bound to be disappointed. It has even been suggested that such unrealistic myths should be addressed in premarital counseling (Larson, 1992).

If there is such limited support for the notion that opposites attract, why do people continue to believe in it and view it as relevant to their own personal experience of love? A clue to the answer can be found in the words of the woman who said: "We are complete opposites . . . but we complement each other." In other words, it is not the differences per se, but their complementary nature that enhances the attraction (Nowicki & Menheim, 1991).

Indeed it seems that people are attracted to partners to whom, in general ways, they are similar—in background, values, interests, and intelligence—but whom they complement in a particular, significant, and opposing, personality dimension (Wilson, 1989).

Family therapist Murray Bowen (1978) believed that the general similarity that attracts potential partners to each other is one of psychological maturity, while the significant and complementary personality dimension operates as an opposing "defense mechanism". For example, a man who copes with stress by suppressing his feelings will be attracted to women who tend to dramatize their emotions.

The crucial factor that divides those people who are more attracted to partners similar to themselves from those who are more attracted to partners different from themselves, may be self-acceptance. Zehava Solomon (1986) analyzed the effects of similarity and compatibility on the romantic choices of couples. She discovered that people with high levels of self-acceptance chose partners whom they perceived as similar to themselves, whereas people with low levels of self-acceptance chose partners whom they viewed as different from themselves. A person's level of self-acceptance also influenced the degree to which he or she viewed the partner as different from the "ideal mate," and was willing to live with the compromise.

Returning to the question of what affects romantic attraction more, similarities or differences, the answer is, it depends on the similarities and differences in question, and on such things as the level of self-acceptance and style of coping. But the general rule is still the attraction of the similar. Furthermore, people who enjoy their interactions with their partners perceive their partners as similar to themselves. In other words, perceived similarity can act as an indicator of satisfaction in a relationship that, at times, can be satisfactory because it is complementary (Dryer & Horowitz, 1997).

SUGGESTIONS FOR THOSE SEEKING LOVE

Don't look for Prince Charming to come riding on a white horse from a far away land, or for an exotic and mysterious princess to arrive from a distant kingdom. The person who is similar to you in appearance, intelligence, attitudes, interests, emotional maturity, as well as background, is the person with whom you are most likely to live happily ever after. Furthermore, you are likely to find this most appropriate romantic and marriage partner in your nearest and most familiar surroundings. It is the, perhaps metaphorical, boy or girl next door with whom you are most likely to live in harmony and marital bliss. Once you have found someone who is similar to you in the important dimensions, look for someone whose personality complements yours in a way you find exciting and rewarding.

5

SATISFYING NEEDS AND RECIPROCATING LOVE

Love at best is giving what you need to get.
—R. McKuen,
Stanyan Street and Other Sorrows

There are many people who would never
have been in love if they had never heard
love spoken of.
—La Rochefoucauld, *Maximes,* 1665

Love begets love.
—Theodore Roethke, *The Motion*

As we follow the process of falling in love, we move from the conditions that make love likely, that is proximity and arousal, through features of the beloved, beauty and character, to relationship variables such as similarity. In this chapter, we focus on two more variables, namely, what the beloved does for us, and the amorous effect of knowing that the beloved is attracted to us.

Why these two variables? And why are they combined in one chapter? Because studies that investigated who falls in love with whom have identified the important roles played by satisfying needs and reciprocating love. In one such study, men and women were asked to describe in detail a time when they felt especially loving or as if they were falling in love. Analysis of their stories showed that the two most frequent causes for feeling loving or falling in love were: (a) the fact that the beloved provided something that the person wanted, needed, or loved; and (b) the fact that the beloved expressed love, need, or appreciation of the person (Shaver et al., 1978).

WHEN YOU THINK ABOUT A TIME WHEN YOU WERE IN LOVE, DID YOU FEEL THAT YOUR BELOVED PROVIDED YOU WITH SOMETHING YOU WANTED OR VALUED? DID YOU FEEL LOVED?

THE BELOVED SATISFIES IMPORTANT NEEDS

"He is caring and considerate. He's always saying 'make sure that you're doing what you want to do before thinking about me.' When he's with me, I know it's the most important thing."

"We are very good for each other. . . . She needed me, she needed someone who would respect her, and I needed her too."

"He's a very good listener. He really understood me. He got everything I said right off the bat. That was new. I'm a bit complicated but he would get things. When I asked him, 'How did you understand this?' he said, 'I just listen.' His comments were always right on the ball and he was supportive, friendly, understanding. And he was always interested in me and in being with me. He's always interested in what's best for me."

"She was so easy to talk to. I could talk to her about anything. She was very understanding."

"It's like he's always there for me. He's very supportive."

All of these speakers describe the beloved as someone who satisfies an important need. In slightly over half of the romantic attraction interviews, the interviewee attributed his or her attraction to the fact that the beloved provided something of value.[1]

Psychoanalyst Theodore Reik (1964) believed that people fall in love with each other for selfish reasons. They sense something lacking in themselves and seek the missing quality in a romantic partner. Thus, each partner provides a portion of the components required for a complete personality. For example, a rational man who is disconnected from his feelings and has difficulty expressing them, is attracted to an emotional woman who has difficulty controlling her emotions. The emotional woman who is uncomfortable expressing her intellect is attracted to the rational man.

The selfishness in this kind of romantic selection is not consciously articulated. The rational man who is attracted to the emotional woman is not saying to himself, "Here is someone who will complete me." What he is thinking, as indeed I was told by such a man, is, "She was cute and lively and seemed like a warm and sensitive person. She approached me and introduced herself. I tend to be rather closed and uptight with new people, but with her it was very easy. I felt very comfortable in her company." Likewise, the woman is not saying, "Here is a rational man who will complement my emotionalism." Rather, as the man's wife told me, she is thinking, "He looked very different from other men. He looked like a very smart man, a thinking man, a true intellectual. I was very attracted to him."

A similar idea about the utility of our romantic attractions was proposed by Bernard Murstein (1976) who explains who marries whom from the perspective of *Social Exchange Theory*. According to this economic model of human behavior, people's romantic choices, just like their market behavior, are motivated by a desire to maximize their earnings and minimize their losses. The more rewards—such as love, support, or sex—that a relationship provides, and the lower the cost of doing what one doesn't want to do, the more satisfying the relationship is and the longer it will last.

Murstein believes that attraction depends on the "fairest exchange value" of personal assets and liabilities that each partner brings to the relationship. He views people as rational beings who choose to marry a person who provides them with the best all-around package. According to Murstein, love is the feeling of mutual satisfaction that two partners derive from knowing that they got the best "exchange value" possible. In other words, they made the best possible deal.

This rather unromantic view of romantic choices is shared by other psychologists and sociologists who are convinced that we are attracted to people who provide us with the most rewards for the lowest price.[2] If people behave like rational, calculating, business people in other social relationships with colleagues, neighbors, and friends, wouldn't they be much more likely to do so when choosing a mate? Accordingly, it has been argued that the ideology of the marketplace has invaded and altered love and sex by transforming intimacies into commodities (Lee, 1998); people pursue the important goal of making a good deal by evaluating, rationally, the alternatives in the market. Here, for example, is the way renowned sociologist Erving Goffman describes such a romantic relationship: "A marriage proposal in our society tends to be a way in which a man sums up his social attributes and suggests to a woman that hers are not so much better as to preclude a merger or a partnership" (1952). Indeed, young urban professionals were said to consider each other's assets, including country house, income potential, schooling, and family, before deciding on suitable partners.

Does this steely-eyed materialism give a true picture of falling in love? At the beginning of this chapter, I quoted from an interview with a man who felt that both he and his future wife had made a good deal in getting together; he described the exchange between them in far more romantic terms. "We are very good for each" he said. "She needed me, she needed someone who would respect her, and I needed her too. . . . I feel sorry for people who don't have this kind of relationship. She makes me feel complete. What hurts most about being away from her are the simple things—going to the store, making lunch. The best thing is the actual living. We love each other and we love our relationship."

This man describes love as the main asset that he and his future wife brought to their lives together. Of course, love is only one of the assets couples bring to relationships. According to *Resource Theory*, people use six categories of resources when interacting with each other: *love,* warmth, affection, care, and comfort; *status,* which can either increase one's sense of self-worth or decrease it; *information,* advice or knowledge; *property,* money; *goods,* things; and *services* such as cooking or car repair (Foa & Foa, 1980).

In most interactions, people tend to exchange resources of the same kind, they return love when they receive love, and offer help or service when they receive help or service. When people were given descriptions of something they received from a friend—a hug, a compliment, or lecture notes—and were asked how and to what extent they were likely to reciprocate, the data showed clearly that they tended to reciprocate in kind—love for love and service for service (Brinberg & Castel, 1982).

A notable exception to the reciprocity rule of giving what we have received and receiving what we have given, is gender differences in romantic attraction. Analysis of personal advertisements indicates that women and men tend to offer different things and ask for different things when they are looking for romantic partners (Davis, 1990). We will get back to these differences later.

Dale Carnegie, in his best-selling book *How To Win Friends And Influence People* (1982), turns the link between attraction and satisfying needs into a recommendation. If you want someone to love you, writes Carnegie, express genuine interest in that person, be pleasant, smile, remember that a person's name is to him or her the sweetest and most important sound. Furthermore, be a good listener, encourage the person to talk about him- or herself, talk in terms of interests, make him or her feel important, and give honest and sincere appreciation. A number of studies support Carnegie's recommendations; we tend to like people who appreciate us and compliment us.[3]

HOW DO WE KNOW THAT THE APPRECIATION WE RECEIVE IS HONEST AND SINCERE?

Well aware that compliments are not always genuine, it is important to us that appreciation not disguise an ingratiation that is aimed at getting us to do or give something. In a number of studies, Edward Jones (1964), who studied ingratiation extensively, showed that interviewees liked most an evaluator who gave them a positive evaluation, as compared to a neutral or negative evaluation. But the liking dropped sharply when people suspected the evaluator's motives. This finding helps us understand why highly attractive people don't take seriously the compliments they receive for their performances. They assume, for good reason, that their physical attractiveness has influenced compliments that, in fact, are not genuine.

While we may like people who are positive and pleasant, who compliment us and express appreciation for our views, we respect more the people who are critical. We tend to view such people as more intelligent, even if unpleasant. In a study that demonstrated this, students received two reviews that had appeared in the *New York Times Review of Books*. The reviews were similar in style and quality, but one was very positive and the other was very negative. Results of the study showed that the students saw the negative reviewer as more intelligent, competent, and expert, and saw the positive reviewer as a nicer and more pleasant person (Amabille, 1983).

Criticism is always difficult to hear, hence Dale Carnegie's rule #1: Don't criticize, condemn, or complain. It is especially difficult when criticism comes from someone we respect. And it is doubly hard for people with low self-esteem, for whom approval and acceptance provide significant rewards, and criticism and rejection provide powerful punishments. In a classic study, people with low self-esteem were found to be more attracted to the people in a group who gave them positive evaluations, and more repelled by the people who gave them negative evaluations (Dittes, 1959).

It is important for people with low self-esteem to ask themselves if they prefer romantic partners who are pleasant, kind, and sensitive, who will compliment them, who will be good company and express genuine interest in them and the things that are important to them. Or do they prefer someone of superior intelligence, knowledge, and education from whom they can learn? Judgment and criticism can be part of the package when a person with low self-esteem chooses a brilliant and superior person as a romantic partner.

Of course, everyone wants a partner who is pleasant, kind, and sensitive, as well as intelligent and knowledgeable. And obviously a pleasant personality and an intelligent mind are not mutually exclusive. The point here has to do with the effect of one's own self-esteem on one's romantic choices. When a person with low self-esteem chooses a person to admire, the result is an asymmetry in the relationship in which one partner is an admirer and the other the admired. This kind of asymmetry is bound to create problems in the relationship later on. But when both partners in the relationship admire each other, the result is a positive loop of appreciation that can last indefinitely.

People prefer partners who most appropriately gratify important psychological needs, including emotional, intellectual, sexual, spiritual, and social needs. People looking for love need to assess the full picture of their psychological, as well as physical, needs and determine which needs are most important. These are the needs to look for in a romantic partner. The best candidate for gratifying those needs is someone whose needs are complementary.

COMPLEMENTARY NEEDS

Plato, the 5th century BC philosopher, had an interesting theory about the origin of love. In *The Symposium* he tells "the myth of Aristophanes."

> The myth describes a time primeval when humans were round with four hands and four feet, back and sides forming a circle. They had one head with two faces looking in opposite directions. These humans were also insolent, and the gods would not suffer such arrogance. So Zeus punished them by cutting them in two, thereby condemning each half to look for the other. When one half finds the other, "the pair are lost in an amazement of love and friendship and intimacy. . . . This meeting and melting in one another's arms, this becoming one instead of two is the very expression of 'the ancient need.' . . . The reason is that human nature was originally one and we were whole, and the desire and pursuit of that whole is called love."

Primeval humanity was divided into three kinds of people: men, women, and androgynous who were a union of the two. Men had a pair of masculine sex organs, women had a pair of feminine sex organs, and the androgynous had both a masculine and a feminine sex organ. After humans were cut in two, the man's separate halves that longed to be reunited became homosexuals; the woman's separate halves became lesbians. The separate halves of the androgynous became heterosexuals who are attracted to members of the opposite sex.

According to this Greek myth, people long to find in romantic love that which is missing in themselves. Here we come back to complementarity as a cause of attraction, not in the simplistic formulation of "opposites attract," but in the deeper meaning of mutually satisfying important needs.

Most people, like the split androgynous, fall in love with a person of the opposite sex, a person who has different and compatible sex organs. These biological sex differences are often associated with different gender roles. In traditional marriages, men and women are expected to exhibit different assets and skills and perform different tasks. Bread-winning has been "men's core role" and motherhood "women's core role" (Barnett, 1993).

Even in the growing numbers of egalitarian couples (Rabin, 1995), the attraction of complementary labor remains. A woman who hates cooking will find very appealing a man whose hobby is gourmet cooking; and a man who lacks any mechanical sense is likely to find a woman mechanic especially fascinating.

Robert Winch (1958) believes that love is the experience of two people jointly deriving maximum gratification for important psychological needs. In his theory of complementary needs, he argues that we are attracted to and marry people whose psychological needs complement our own. Psychological needs can be complementary in content, as in rational twined with emotional, or in degree, as in an alliance between strong and weak control needs. In a well-known study done over forty years ago, Winch conducted in-depth interviews with twenty-five married couples about their childhoods and current lives. The couples also responded to a series of personality tests. On the basis of the interviews and personality tests, the psychological needs of the couples were rated by five psychoanalysts. Their famous conclusion was that people tend to choose marriage partners whose psychological needs complement their own needs—more than they choose partners whose needs are similar to their own.

Romantic partners can also complement each other's sexual needs, intellectual needs, or spiritual needs. While some needs are better gratified when complementary, such as the match between a person who likes teaching and a person who likes to be taught, other needs are better satisfied when both partners share them. Couples who share spiritual journeys, political activism, or leisure time activities, find the actual sharing very rewarding.

RECIPROCATING LOVE

As the next quotes show, for some people, the most attractive thing about a romantic partner is the fact that he or she first found them attractive.

"What attracted me first? Flattery, the fact that she chased me. She did a lot more of the initiating than I did. It was flattering."

"He went through three different people to get my phone number."

"She's an attractive person, and she was interested in me, which is obviously attractive."

"What attracted me to her at first was the fact that she liked me (laughs). She was really attractive."

"What attracted me most was her choosing me. It was kind of strange. Really interesting but kind of strange."

Analysis of the romantic attraction interviews shows that in almost half the cases, an indication of attraction and romantic interest by the beloved played an important role in the initial attraction to him or her.[4] Feeling desired is clearly very attractive.

Elliot Aronson best summarized the influence of reciprocal attraction: "The single most powerful determinant of whether one person will like another is whether the other likes that person. What's more, merely believing someone likes you can initiate a spiraling series of events that promote increasingly positive feelings between you and the other person" (1998). For example, a man and woman are introduced at a party by a mutual friend and engage in a brief conversation. A few days later, the woman runs into the friend on the street, and the friend tells her that after the party the man had some very complimentary things to say about her, including the fact that he was very attracted to her. How is this woman likely to act next time she and the man meet? Chances are, the woman's knowledge that the man finds her attractive will lead her to like him; and she will behave in a way that lets the man know that she likes him, too. She will probably smile more, disclose more about herself, and generally behave in a more likable manner than if she hadn't learned that the man liked her. Faced with her warm and likable manner, the man's attraction and fondness for her will undoubtedly grow. The man, in turn, will convey his attraction in ways that make him even more attractive to the woman . . . and so on.

The rule of reciprocity in attraction works even when people assume erroneously that another person finds them attractive and likable. This was demonstrated in a study in which people were led to believe that another person either liked or disliked them. In subsequent interaction with the other person, those people who thought they were liked behaved in more likable ways. They were warmer, more pleasant, disclosed more about themselves, and agreed more with the other person than did the people who thought they were disliked. What is more significant for our discussion is that the people who erroneously believed that they were liked, were, in fact, liked more after the interaction. In other words, the behavior of the people who thought they were liked led others to reciprocate in kind (Curtis & Miller, 1986).

This finding demonstrates, once again, the power of romantic attraction as a self-fulfilling prophecy, a power used masterfully by Don Juan, who seduced endless numbers of women by giving each one the feeling that she was the most desirable woman in the world. People who treat potential partners as if they are exciting, sexy, and attractive, encourage them to respond that way. As we know, pretense influences not only the person on the receiving end, but the actor as well. This was even noted by the Roman poet, Ovid, in his counsel to lovers seeking romantic success: "Often the pretender begins to love truly and ends by becoming what he feigned to be" (*Ars Amatoria*).

Positive feelings generate positive feelings. A children's song describes the power of reciprocity of love with charming simplicity:

> Love is something if you give it away,
> you end up having more.
> It's just like a magic penny
> hold it tight you wouldn't have any.
> Lend it, spend it, you'll have so many
> they'll role all over the floor.

A word of caution. It should be obvious that in an ongoing romantic relationship, being loved more than one loves is not a positive experience—definitely not as positive as it was to discover that someone was attracted to you. It can evoke guilt, which can lead to anger, which can lead to some very negative feelings about the person who loves us too much, or more than we want to feel loved.

People who tend to find themselves in relationships in which they love too much, know well that it is impossible to force someone to love them. It is also inadvisable to cheat, bribe, seduce, demand, or threaten in order to get love. Forcing love on someone who is clearly uninterested will not make that someone's negative feelings turn into love. The only thing we can influence, to some extent, is our feelings. If we want to live a life of love, we have to be open to love, and we have to choose a romantic partner who is open to loving us.

SATISFYING NEEDS VS. RECIPROCATING LOVE.
WHICH PLAYS A GREATER ROLE IN LOVE?

In romantic attraction, how does the role of feeling loved compare to the other variables we have discussed, such as gratifying needs? An extensive survey of the stories people told about the partners they chose for love and marriage revealed eleven factors that influence this choice (Aron et al., 1989). Some of these variables have already been discussed and some will arise in later chapters:

1. Similarity, in attitudes, background, personality traits
2. Geographic proximity, propinquity
3. Desirable characteristics of personality and appearance
4. Reciprocal affection, or the fact that the other likes us
5. Satisfying needs
6. Physical and emotional arousal, experience with the unusual
7. Social influences, social norms and the approval of people in our social circle
8. Specific cues in the beloved's voice, eyes, posture, way of moving
9. Readiness for a relationship
10. Opportunities to be alone together, isolation
11. Mystery, in the situation or the person

WHEN YOU CONSIDER YOUR MOST MEMORABLE EXPERIENCE OF FALLING IN LOVE, WHICH OF THESE ELEVEN VARIABLES PLAYED THE GREATEST ROLE? WHICH OF THE VARIABLES DID NOT PLAY A ROLE AT ALL?

In order to examine the relative influence of these eleven variables, Aron and his colleagues (1989) examined three types of falling-in-love accounts. The first type was a lengthy and detailed account obtained from students who had fallen in love during the previous eight months. The students were asked to think for a few minutes about the experience of falling in love and then write about it in as much detail as possible. Content analysis of the variables in the stories, which averaged three pages, revealed that reciprocal liking was mentioned in practically all the stories. Desirable characteristics were mentioned in most of the stories, and satisfying needs appeared in less than a quarter of the stories.

The second type of falling-in-love accounts was obtained from participants in weekend seminars on Love and Consciousness. Participants, whose average age was 31, were asked to take part in a ten-minute exercise describing an experience of "developing a strong attraction to someone," of "falling in love," or of "falling in friendship." They were given 11 x 14 cm index cards on which they were told to "Just tell the story"—briefly describing how it happened, what they felt, and what resulted. One hundred of the accounts of falling in love were then compared to one hundred accounts of falling in friendship.

Content analysis revealed that two-thirds of these stories mentioned reciprocal liking and desirable traits of beauty and character in the beloved. Similarity and propinquity appeared in one-quarter to one-third of the stories. Satisfying needs was mentioned in only one-tenth of the stories!

Based on the results of both the long and the short love stories, a questionnaire was built, responses to which constituted the third kind of falling-in-love account. The respondents were asked to recall their most recent experiences of falling in love, especially the moment when they first felt a strong attraction, and then to rank their feelings on different scales. In the example relevant to this chapter, they were asked to what extent the person you fell in love with "filled your needs." In the analysis of their responses, once again, reciprocal affection and desirable characteristics appeared most frequently as the reasons for falling in love. Filling needs was mentioned in only about one-third of the cases.

It is interesting to note that the falling-in-friendship accounts gave relatively more emphasis to similarity and propinquity and somewhat less emphasis to reciprocal liking, desirable characteristics, and filling needs (Aron et al., 1989).

Why was filling needs mentioned so infrequently in all three types of the accounts of falling in love? One explanation is that satisfying needs is something people are uncomfortable admitting. We all prefer to believe that falling in love is pure of selfish motives. Aron and his colleagues asked people directly whether their beloved filled an important need for them. It is possible that respondents reported the socially desirable answer rather than the full extent to which filling needs affected their experiences.

In the romantic attraction study, young men and women described the development of their most significant romantic relationships. From these descriptions it is possible to infer how often filling significant needs played a role in the romantic attraction. When a young woman says, "He is very loving and makes every effort so I will enjoy myself. Like he knows that I

like champagne, so he always buys champagne when I arrive," it is quite obvious that what the man does for her plays a role in her attraction toward
him. And when a man says, "What attracted me at first was that she used to
buy things for me," it is clear that his attraction to her is associated with her
actions. Indeed, as was noted earlier, over half the romantic attraction interviews, as compared to less than a third of the cases in Aron's studies, reported that the partner's providing something of value, or satisfying an
important need, was part of the initial attraction. And when needs are complementary, the satisfaction is mutual.

The best way to end this chapter is with the finding I quote most often
to couples I work with. Over time, the love and rewards that people give are
related to the love and rewards that they receive from romantic relationships
(Robinson and Price, 1980).

SUGGESTIONS FOR PEOPLE SEEKING LOVE.

Use both the power of the reciprocity of love as well as the power of need
satisfaction. Starting with need satisfaction, it is important to address both
your needs and the needs of your potential partner. In other words, what do
you want and what are you willing to give? If you want to have your needs
met in a romantic relationship, you should first figure out what your most
important needs are. Is your need to be listened to and validated? To be
challenged and stimulated? To be cared for and supported? Once you figure
out what it is that you are looking for in a romantic partner, you can look at
a potential partner's willingness or ability to provide it. If the clear answer is
no, it is better to look elsewhere. Since you now know that people are attracted to partners who have either similar or opposite needs, your search
can be more focused, preferably leading you to someone whose needs complement your own.

The best strategy with a promising candidate is to be attentive, open,
warm, and pleasant. Show interest and be a good listener; give honest and
sincere appreciation only. But most importantly, be sensitive to your partner's needs and respect his or her right to feel, think, and do things differently—even if you are convinced that your way of expressing care is the
right way. Insensitive and excessive giving is as destructive to romantic relationships as withholding and distancing your love.

The information about the reciprocity of love leads to a more general
recommendation. Do not hold back love waiting for the perfect partner.
Giving love freely and generously to the less than perfect people who hap-

pen to cross your path can assure you of receiving many coins of love from the people around you. Among them you just might find your beloved. If we want to live a life of love we need to start the cycle of love. And then, very often, the love we give will come back to us in wonderful ways.

Sounds simple, doesn't it? Why it is then that so many people don't do this and sentence themselves to loveless lives? Why are some people attracted to those who torment them, cause them pain, and reject them? Why are so many attracted to those who don't reciprocate their love? These kinds of questions are addressed in the second part of the book.

6

FALLING IN LOVE AS A PROCESS

This bud of love, by summer's ripening breath,
May prove a beauteous flower when next we meet.
—Shakespeare, *Romeo and Juliet*

"*I* met him when I was a freshmen and he was a senior. We lived in the same dorm and he was always a nice guy, but you know, I really wasn't interested in him because he was so much older. I mean, three years can seem like a lot [laughs]. Here I was taking Freshman English and he was finishing his major. I mean, he was big-time. He was friendly and asked me out a couple of times, but nothing more than that at first. My heart didn't beat real fast. It wasn't love at first sight. We were just buddies. I never even thought about it for a year and a half. After that period we started getting closer. We were talking on the phone a lot. . . . We started doing things together. We liked a lot of the same things. . . . There was some tension at first because I still thought of him as a friend, but he didn't necessarily think of me that way. I felt great actually.*"

"*I thought she was gorgeous. From the first time I saw her I was really attracted to her. And then I got to know her. We were in a couple of classes together and we would do homework together and just joke around. And so sooner or later we just started going out. . . . She was a really neat person, fun to talk to . . . fun to get to know, and fun to hang out with, fun to goof around with or be intimate with.*"

"*I didn't feel physically attracted to him until we went out a couple of times. So it was a kind of gradual thing. It took a year before we were really close. . . . We knew each other because we went to the same school. He was a kind of all-around nice guy, friendly, warm. He had a friendly presence, a warm presence. And he was a kind of lively, good-humored sort. And I thought he was cute, nothing stunning, down to earth.*"

"*It was a classroom relationship. We sat next to each other and we sort of became good friends for a period of time, several months. I can't remem-*

*ber who wanted to become intimate, her or me, but it progressed. . . .
She's very pretty [laughs]. Others noticed it too."*

*"I didn't like him at first. I didn't like him at all. He didn't like me ei-
ther. We would kind of butt heads when we first met. We had the same
job, even though we were in different branches. . . . We were in class together and there was only one seat available and I sat next to him. I didn't
like him. I don't know. . . . He started talking to me, so we ended up being friends. And he was there for me after the divorce. . . . He was there
for me and I guess it just went on from there. It was different from any
other sort of attraction. It was the way he treated me, his ideas, his attitudes, his overall values and views about life."*

Content analysis of the romantic attraction interviews shows that in
one-third of the cases, falling in love was described as a gradual process.
Only in about one-tenth of the cases was love at first sight.[1]

When people fall in love, different variables play roles in different stages.
The backdrop of the entire process is cultural. From birth we are inculcated
with certain expectations about falling in love. In Western society, the romantic ideal calls for a man and a woman, rather than a same sex couple, to
meet, fall in love, marry, and live happily ever after. When a man and a
woman meet, they share these expectations of the way things ought to
progress between them.

In the getting-aquainted stage—more likely when a couples lives or
works at the same geographic location, and, preferably, when in a state of
emotional arousal—physical appearance is very important, especially to
men. But in order for a romance to spark, the partners need to feel a mutual
attraction to each other's personality. In order for the romantic spark to
ignite, the partners need to perceive that they share a similarity in such
things as background, personal assets, attitudes, and emotional health. And
for a romance to evolve into a committed relationship, the partners need to
feel that their love is reciprocated and gratifies their needs. This chapter
describes the process that combines these different variables, namely, falling
in love.

A romantic relationship starts in different ways. It may be love at first
sight—"From the first time I met him there was something that attracted
me to him," or it may develop after years of friendship—"We knew each
other five years, no, four years, as friends. I called him when I moved up
here and then it started getting more serious." A romantic relationship may

start at a significant encounter—"It was a set up. We talked the whole night," or evolve into a deep connection over time—"At first, I wasn't attracted to her, [but] we talked a lot and became closer and closer. . . . Then I became more attracted to her."

In all cases a state of acquaintance, such as friendship or mere physical attraction, develops into a state of passionate, romantic love—a development that has been documented in many studies (Berscheid & Reis, 1998). In secular Western society, at the end of the twentieth century, romantic love is considered a very important element in the choice of a mate. And even in the arranged marriages of some traditional societies, romantic love is an important background criterion (de Munck, 1998).

Despite the different starting points and different rates of development among romantic relationships, there is usually a certain point at which both partners say "This is love!" This turning point starts a series of physiological changes (Fisher, 1998) and is often preceded and marked by a very special mutual gaze. Victor Hugo described the power of this gaze in *Les Misérables* (1862):

> Few people dare now to say that two beings have fallen in love because they have looked at each other. Yet it is in this way that love begins, and in this way only. The rest is only the rest, and comes afterwards. Nothing is more real than these great shocks which two souls give each other in exchanging this spark.

THE STAGES OF FALLING IN LOVE

How do people fall in love? Several theories rest on an assumption that romantic relationships go through certain steps that occur in a certain order; thus, the falling-in-love process is described as a series of stages. In some theories falling in love happens in two stages, and in others, it happens in three or even four stages. But all stage theories assume that there is a qualitative difference among the different stages.

According to the *two-stage theory* of love proposed by Judith Rodin (1987), falling in love involves a two-step screening process. People screen first for those they consider unsuitable. They don't notice these people when they meet, and they forget them right away. A typical example is screening for age. Many young people don't even notice older people because they don't perceive them as potential romantic partners. When someone doesn't fit our selection criteria we simply don't notice them. Thus the unsuitable becomes invisible. In the second stage, people select the most appropriate partners among those who are judged suitable.

The initial automatic screening of unsuitables is influenced by social norms that dictate for us the category of people that contains suitable marriage partners. Robert Winch coined the term "candidates field of eligible spouse" to describe the range of people with whom we are permitted to fall in love and marry (1958). In other words, the society or specific sub-culture in which we live determines the first stage of screening that happens even before we start operating our own love filters. The Berkeley sub-culture, for example, tolerates inter-racial marriages more than most other sub-cultures in the United States.

Most societies use similarities in background and social assets as their main selection criteria. Societal norms tend to prefer that marriage partners be from the same race, social and economic class, religion, and age group. A person who doesn't conform to these social dictates, such as an old man who marries a very young woman, is often criticized and ridiculed, and can become the object of jokes and gossip. Reactions of this sort teach both the person to whom they are directed, as well as the people watching from the sidelines, who is appropriate and who is inappropriate as a marriage partner.

Societies influence the screening process of romantic partners in two major ways. Most prominently, social norms reward people who follow the norm and punish those who deviate, as, for example, when friends and relatives shun or express outright criticism of an unsuitable, potential partner. Secondly, societies arrange meetings between people who are judged to be suitable romantic partners, meetings such as parties in schools, workplaces and clubs, or social events arranged for single people of a certain age group and a certain social or economic status (Kerckoff, 1974). Societal agents such as parents, teachers, friends, and the media teach the social norms. They reward and encourage suitable romantic connections and discourage unsuitable ones.

Only after people pass through this social screening and choose a suitable partner from the field of eligibles can falling-in-love take place. And, according to another stage theory of love, it, too, happens in two stages. In the first stage, shared values are most important; in the second stage, compatibility of needs is most important. A study that inspired this theory looked at predictors for the continuance of relationships. Agreement about values served as the best predictor for couples who had been together less than a year and a half, whereas the best predictor for couples who had been together more than a year and a half was complementarity (Kerckoff, 1974).

It seems that in the first stage of a developing romantic relationship, a similarity in values and interests is especially important. Disagreement about values that even one of the partners considers central to his or her life significantly limits the possibility of a romantic relationship. Consider, for example, a devoutly religious woman who finds herself attracted to a man who is a committed atheist. If she cannot see herself building a life with this man, she will no doubt try to quench her attraction to him. Or, as in the plot of a recent movie, consider a cowboy who loves open spaces and makes his living raising cattle; he is attracted to a urban woman who loves theatre, concerts, the opera, and works in the publishing industry. Since it is unlikely that two such people will be able to make a living and be happy and contented in the same place, it is unlikely that a relationship between them will succeed in going beyond the stage of attraction or romance.

It is important to recall, however, that when people are strongly attracted to each other, they are very capable of ignoring such glaring differences; they assume that they can overcome incredible odds with the sheer power of their love.

Only growing intimacy can provide couples with the foundation of trust that enables them to reveal their deeper psychological needs to each other. Most people have to feel a certain degree of security in the relationship before they can remove their defenses and admit their more infantile, immature, and, some say, neurotic needs. This is why complementary emotional needs become central in the later stage of the relationship.

The most famous *three-stage theory* of love was proposed some twenty years ago by Bernard Murstein (1976). According to this theory, in the first stage of a love relationship, the *stimulus* stage, external features such as physical appearance have the greatest impact. In the second stage, the *value* stage, the attraction is based primarily on finding similarity in values and interests. In the third and last stage, the *role* stage, the couple examines whether they function well in the various roles related to their identity as a couple, the friend, lover, roommate, husband or wife components.

In the stimulus stage, people know only what they can learn from minimal interaction. Attraction is a function of the other's physical, mental, and social attributes. Potential partners assess and arrive at an overall evaluation of the other, which each compares to his or her own overall attractiveness. Only if both partners perceive each other's attractiveness as roughly equal to their own can the relationship progress to the value stage. When a man and a woman begin dating, they talk about their attitudes toward different things. If they discover that their attitudes are similar, their attraction grows and they can move to the role stage in which they become concerned about their ability to function as a unit. How is each member of the couple expected to act in certain situations or roles? How are holidays and birthdays celebrated? When one is depressed is the other expected to help, or leave him or her alone? Should a wife develop an independent career? And so on. When both partners discover that the other behaves in a way that fits their expectations, and that their needs and roles are complementary, the relationship can become highly satisfying.

Even though all three components—stimulus, value, and role—influence the development of a romantic relationship, each component becomes central only during one developmental stage. For example, in the second stage the attraction is based primarily on similarity in values and less on physical appearance or satisfying role requirements.

Other stage theories talk about four stages of falling in love. One of these theories focuses on rewards and roles rather than compatibility in deep psychological needs. In this theory, the development of a romantic relationship happens in the following four stages:

1. the exploration stage, in which rewards and cost of the relationship are weighed;
2. the negotiation stage, in which the relationship is defined and the behaviors that bring the most rewards to both partners are learned;
3. the commitment stage, in which mutual dependence develops between the partners as a result of their deepening involvement with each other;
4. the final formalizing stage, in which both the couple and the people around the couple view the relationship as sanctioned by society (Backman, 1981). Not a word about love!

According to yet another multiple-stage theory of love, all romantic relationships start with the attraction based on similarity, which causes feelings of comfort and closeness—"You also love staying in bed and reading on stormy nights?! That's incredible!!" When couples feel close and comfortable with each other, they start opening up and self-disclosing. Only after they feel and express empathic understanding for each other in the stage of self-disclosure, can the relationship move on to the next stages. The final stages of a love relationship demand compatibility in the interpersonal roles that have to do with being a couple, meaning the way in which each makes a commitment to the relationship and contributes to the identity as a couple (Lewis, 1973).

One of the most complex and comprehensive stage theories of love was proposed by Avner Ziv (1993). The theory is based on interviews with men and women, young and old, married and single, who were asked to describe an experience in which they fell in love. Analysis of the interviews suggested that falling in love involves emotional, behavioral, mental, and social components. Ziv combined all these components into a four-stage model of falling in love.

1. Attraction. This stage results from past experiences and physical attributes, physical beauty being the most prominent among them.
2. Examination. The partners examine the extent of their social compatibility in terms of social and economic background, their intellectual compatibility derived from education and areas of interest, and their emotional compatibility or feeling of comfort with each other. Since both partners know at this stage that they are on trial, they try to present as positive a picture of themselves as possible.
3. Self-revealing. This is the stage in which intimacy is created, the stage in which deeper thoughts and feelings, including negative ones, are revealed to the partner.
4. Mutual expectations and satisfying needs. In this stage, each partner learns about the expectations of the other, and makes a conscious effort to respond to these expectations in all economic, emotional, social, and sexual areas.

When a couple first meets, if there is an attraction between them, the romantic relationship will start. If there is no attraction, it will not. As the relationship progresses, and they examine each other, if there is no social, intellectual, or emotional compatibility, the relationship will end. If compatability exists, the relationship will continue evolving. With intimacy growing between them, the couple starts revealing vulnerabilities and negative sides to each other. If either partner doesn't understand or fears what is revealed, the relationship ends. If they understand and are empathic to each other's vulnerabilities, the relationship continues to the stage of mutual expectations. If partners don't satisfy each other's needs and expectations, the relationship is terminated. If the needs and expectations of both partners are filled, the result is love—mutual dependence respectful of each partner's independence.

Which one of these stage theories of love is the correct one? Or, better still, is any of the theories correct? One critical question in the evaluation of any stage theory is the question of the order of the stages. In Murstein's theory, for example, does the value stage always precede the role stage? Or are couples able to deal with role issues—"Will she be able to be a professor's wife?" "Can I invite him to the office?"—before they have examined their similarity in values? A number of studies have shown weak evidence for the existence of fixed stages in the development of intimate relationships. One of these studies referred specifically to Murstein's stage theory (Stephen, 1987). Another study asked newly-wed couples to describe how their relationship had evolved. Analysis of their stories revealed different patterns of development—from the first meeting until the marriage (Surra & Hyston, 1987). The romantic attraction interviews that served as the basis for this book also show that, in the development of their relationships, couples go through different stages at different times and at different paces.

Even if we accept the assumption that romantic relationships change and evolve with time, it does not mean that we have to accept the existence of definite stages in which different variables play key roles. Indeed, there are several theories that describe in great detail the evolution of an intimate relationship without needing to describe distinct stages. Here is the evolution of a romantic relationship according to one such theory. The couple starts meeting more frequently and for longer periods of time. They feel comfortable when together and make efforts to meet again and again. They become more open with each other, are less reserved, and are ready to express negative feelings. They develop a unique style of communication. They develop an ability to predict each other's expectations, feelings, and views. They adjust to each other's behaviors and goals. Their investment in the relationship and its importance for them grow. They consider each other in their goals. They feel growing affection, trust, and love. They view the relationship as unique and irreplaceable. They see each other as partners (Burgess & Huston, 1979).

In another example, the development of a romantic relationship is described in terms of the growing influence and interdependence of the partnership. As the partners' influence on each other grows, and as their mutual dependence grows, the relationship becomes closer and more intimate. Since this is a gradual development that takes time, only long-term relationships can achieve true closeness, intimacy, and love (Kelley et al., 1983).

In yet another example, couples first choose each other according to physical traits, but only stay together or marry if they are also similar psychologically. The proof? While married couples and dating couples have a similar number of shared physical traits, married couples have significantly more (11 to 1) shared psychological traits (Keller & Young, 1996).

Finally, I would like to propose that falling in love is the result of a *funnel-shaped screening process*. There are no distinct stages in this process, but "love screens" at different points of the funnel (Pines, 1996). The first five chapters of this book described these various love screens. Now we can see how they operate in the funnel-shaped process of falling in love.

In order to enter the funnel, people need to grow up in a society that acknowledges and values romantic love; they need to be socialized to expect falling in love (the subject of the introduction). When potential partners meet and get to know each other, such determinants as geographic proximity (the subject of the first chapter) define the pool of potential romantic partners. A state of emotional arousal (the subject of the second chapter) increases the probability that a pleasant encounter will be defined as romantic love. Only after they meet and are ready to fall in love, are potential partners likely to notice each other's exciting appearance and pleasant personality (the subjects of the third chapter). Having noticed each other and concluded that they deserve each other's romantic attention, they start discovering through heart-to-heart talks whether they have similar backgrounds, values, and interests (the subject of the fourth chapter). The greater the similarity in social, intellectual, spiritual, emotional, and psychological traits, the greater the feelings of comfort and validation, and the greater the desire for closeness. The greater the discrepancies between the partners, the more misunderstandings and conflicts that can break up the relationship. A notable exception, however, to the rule of attraction to the similar, lies in the existence of areas, many of them unconscious, in which the attraction is to the opposite or the complementary. With the growing intimacy, a couple's deeper, more infantile, psychological needs are revealed, and, with them, each other's mutual ability to satisfy those needs, which increases the reciprocal attraction (the subject of the fifth chapter).

Even this summary doesn't do justice to the complexity of the process of falling in love. Perhaps it is better this way, because the result is the subjective feeling of every couple that their experience of falling in love was unique only to them and could have happened to no one else in the whole world. Han Suin says it most poignantly in the preface to *A Many Splendoured Thing* (1952).

> "Do you really think, then, that other people get as much pleasure and happiness out of their bodies as we do?"
>
> "Dear Love, even the paunchy, ugly people of this world believe they love as much as we do and forever. It is the illusion of all lovers to think themselves unique and their words immortal."

I cannot end the discussion of stage theories of love without mentioning my favorite theory proposed by one of Italy's great sociologists, Francesco Alberoni (1983). According to Alberoni, the significant stages of a romantic relationship are simply "falling in love" and "love." If falling in love is like taking off or flying, then love is like landing. Falling in love is being high above the clouds. Love is standing firmly on the ground. If falling in love is like a flower, then love is like a fruit. The fruit comes from the flower, but they are two different things. "And there is really no point in asking if the flower is better than the fruit or vice versa. By the same token, there is no point in asking whether the nascent state is better than the institution. One does not exist without the other. Life is made of both."

Falling in love is a positive, energizing process that causes both physiological and psychological changes. Arthur Aron demonstrated the positive influence of love on people's self-concept. Over a ten-week period, he followed students who were in love and students who were not in love. Results of the comparison revealed that the students who were in love expressed greater self-confidence and higher self-concepts. In addition, they expanded the scope and range of their self-definitions, probably as a result of their partners admiring certain aspects in their personalities that they had ignored or under-appreciated (Aron et al., 1995). In other words, falling in love helps develop self-confidence and more expansive personalities. Clearly, falling in love is a very positive and highly recommended experience.

GENDER DIFFERENCES IN THE PROCESS OF FALLING IN LOVE

In the romantic attraction study, a very small gender difference divided the frequency with which young men and women described falling in love as a process.[2] However, a significant difference divided the genders in their perceptions of the direction of the process. Men were more often initially attracted to the physical appearances of the woman, followed by a discovery of their personalities. Women, on the other hand, frequently felt no initial physical attraction. The attraction followed the development of friendship and emotional intimacy. To put it more bluntly, for many men, the physical attraction caused the relationship; for many women, the relationship caused the physical attraction.

Here are examples of the way women described the development of their relationships.

> "The relationship started as a friendship. I was actually going out with his roommate so I spent a lot of time in their house and we became close friends. We got to know each other really well. We got to be close friends before we became involved. As soon as the other relationship was over, he and I became very romantically involved. I felt very attracted to him because I loved him so much. He had been attracted to me ever since we met. He initially told me that he loved me. I wasn't interested in him. Then I started falling in love with him."

> "I wasn't attracted to him at the beginning, but he was there during the difficult time. He's not a macho type. I didn't have to put on an act. He was always nice to me, really understanding when I was upset. Now we have a friendship behind the relationship. It's like he's my best friend. It's pretty serious right now. We're talking about moving in together."

> "I didn't find him particularly sexy. We were just buddies. Then we started getting closer. On our first date I didn't really know what to expect, I wasn't really thinking about him in a romantic way. I guess he had a different idea than I had. So there was some tension at first because I still thought of him as a friend."

And here are examples of how men described the development of their romantic relationships.

> "I liked her. She would tell you it was for the wrong reasons because I was always looking at her. She's slightly top heavy and my eyes were always wandering. And she knew it too. . . . Before we really got into the relationship we talked about a lot of things."

> "I thought she was gorgeous. From the first time I saw her, I was really attracted to her. And then I got to know her. She was a really neat person."

> "It started initially as a sexual thing. I met her in the students' office.

She was a secretary in the office. We started talking. There were interesting things about her physically. . . . Also her personality. She's one of the nicest people I've met."

These quotes suggest that for many men the initial sexual attraction is dominant. It makes them listen to the woman they are attracted to, be attentive and supportive. For many women, the attention, the listening, and the support are the most attractive, and are what make them fall in love. Men should remember this when they want to conquer a woman's heart!

What is the reason for this gender difference? One explanation has to do with gender stereotypes and gender roles that define the correct courtship behavior for men and women (Basow, 1992). During the getting-acquainted stage, men are supposed to take the initiative. Women can hint their interest by flirting, but not initiate directly. One study discovered fifty-two nonverbal courtship patterns of women flirting with men to attract their attention (Moore, 1985). Despite the sexual revolution and the openness and tolerance that characterize romantic relationships today, women who take the initiative with men are often still perceived negatively (Green & Sandos, 1983).

According to young singles' scripts for a first date, men are expected to be more influenced by the physical appearance of their dates and women are expected to be more influenced by the emotional closeness and intimacy. For both men and women, sexual attraction is expected to be important. All these expectations are part of a well-defined social script. The script is so familiar that when young men and women are asked to describe the order of events on a first date, the similarity in their descriptions is amazing (Rose & Frieze, 1989).

The feminine script of courtship behavior emphasizes attractive physical appearance, ability to carry on a conversation, and control of sex, usually by refusal. The masculine script covers planning the date, be it a dinner, a concert, or a movie, paying for it, and taking the initiative in sex. For example, women who break the script by taking the initiative sexually, are perceived as aggressive and masculine. Men who break the script by demanding that the woman pay her share of the meal, are perceived as cheap and ungentlemanly. These scripts structure and exacerbate the differences between men and women. The penalties for breaking their scripts force men and women to comply with them.

Gender differences exist in courtship and in the move from courtship to committed relationship. While women tend to be more cautious during the courtship stage, men tend to fall in love faster and stronger (Rubin et al., 1981). In the move from courtship to committed relationship, women tend to move faster, while men tend to be more cautious.

Women's cautiousness, especially about sex, can function not just as part of a script, but also as part of a social norm. In a survey conducted among American female students, for example, it was discovered that 30 percent of these young and educated women sometimes said no to sex when they actually meant to say yes. Women's token resistance to sex is culturally prescribed and is part of the mating game (Muehlenhard & Hollabaugh, 1988). It is comforting to note that after the initial stages of courtship in which both sexes behave according to the socially prescribed scripts, men and women tend to fall in love at a similar pace and level of intensity.

Another explanation for the gender differences in the process of falling in love arises out of the difference in men's and women's innate programming for mate selection. This difference is a major topic of evolutionary theory, which we will discuss extensively in the next chapter. As we will see, according to this theory, different evolutionary developments have dictated different courting strategies for men and women (Buss, 1994).

Before concluding the discussion of gender differences in the process of falling in love, I want to address an assumption in the evolutionary theories. According to this assumption, these gender differences, because they result from evolutionary dictates, are universal. This assumption has received a great deal of criticism arguing against a universal, biological, explanation and in favor of a cultural explanation. The findings of an anthropological study that examined the courtship patterns in several North American countries support this criticism (Perper, 1989). These findings show that courtship is a well-defined process of specific meaning and prescribed verbal and nonverbal content. The subjective experience of this process is the development of strong mutual feelings of attraction and sexual arousal. None of this is very new, of course. But the findings are augmented by comparing the parts of the falling-in-love process that were shared by different cultures to the parts that were not shared. Since the latter were found to be unique to each culture, it was possible to conclude that the gender differences in courtship are not universal. This suggests that the evolutionary theories that present themselves as universal, may be nothing more than ethnographic theories that describe how men and women in certain cultures view the process of mate selection, a description that includes some very narrow assumptions about the roles of men and women. In other words, even if there are certain differences between men and women in their approach to falling in love and choosing a mate, there are also some powerful social and cultural influences that can account for these differences.

Furthermore, as most people know from personal experience, there is a very personal and private aspect to falling in love. This is the aspect that lies behind the choice of a particular man or woman from all the eligible, appropriate, and attractive, potential partners that people meet. It is this choice of one particular person from all the appropriate people in the world, that gives love its magical quality. In the words of the 15th century poem, *The Nut-Brown Maid*:

> For in my mind, of all mankind
> I love but you alone.

SUGGESTIONS FOR PEOPLE SEEKING LOVE

Be aware of your love screens. Think about the two people with whom you were most in love. What do, or did, they have in common? Was it something about their looks, their personalities, their intelligence, their social standing, their sex appeal, the way they treated you, or the fact that they loved you? The quality, or qualities, they have in common says more about you than about them. The commonalities point to the screens you use for choosing a romantic partner.

Once you have identified your love screens, try to evaluate to what extent these screens are truly yours. Are they part of a social script you adopted that doesn't really suit you—or doesn't suit you any longer? The more honest you are with yourself, and with potential partners, about your true love screens, the more likely you will be to find a partner who will pass through them successfully.

It is also important to recognize the mating script in your own social group. But be ready to abandon, as fast as possible, the gender related part of the script in order to assure yourself of a genuine and authentic love relationship.

7

ON GENDER AND LOVE, STATUS AND BEAUTY

Solomon

Behold, thou art fair, my love; behold, thou art fair; thou
hast dove's eyes behind thy veil; thy hair is like a flock of
goats, that cascade down from mount Gil'ad. . . .
Thy lips are like a thread of scarlet, and thy mouth is
comely; thy cheek is like a piece of pomegranate within
thy locks. . . .
Thy two breasts are like two fawns, twins of a gazelle,
which feed among the lilies. . . .
Thou are all fair, my love; there is no blemish in thee. . . .

The Daughters of Jerusalem

What is thy beloved more than another beloved, O thou
fairest among women? What is thy beloved more than
another beloved, that thou dost so charge us?

The Bride

My beloved is white and ruddy, distinguished among
ten thousand.
His head is as the most fine gold, his locks are wavy, as
black as a raven . . .
—*The Song of Songs,* Old Testament

WOMEN TALK ABOUT THE REASONS THAT MADE THEM FALL IN LOVE WITH THEIR PARTNERS

"*I was attracted to his personality. I also thought he was very sexy. He carried himself well and dressed nicely. He was a very real and honest person. He comes off as being very confident, almost cocky. That's what
attracted me to him. . . . He is a very loving person. There's nothing he
wouldn't do.*"

"*We were both in an orchestra, so at first it was just as friends. When I saw him for the first time it was totally dark, and he started talking about the stars. He knew all about astronomy and astrology and seemed very knowledgeable. But he was also very funny and had an odd sense of humor. . . . I felt comfortable talking to him. I felt we were compatible in many ways.*"

"*We met at a party. I ignored him. I was with someone else. He asked around, discovered where I worked, and came after me. It was very passionate. I thought he was handsome. . . . He was very reserved and that attracted me. He keeps things close. Feels like he's special. He's busy all the time. He has three businesses and works all the time.*"

"*He noticed me before I noticed him. . . . He looked too old for me but he was always there to listen. He is very reliable. If he says he'll do something, I know he'll do it. He takes care of me and he's loving. He spoils me.*"

MEN TALK ABOUT THE REASONS THAT MADE THEM FALL IN LOVE WITH THEIR PARTNERS

"*She's very pretty. I was attracted to her. I talked to her and we have a lot in common. She was very responsive and fun, intelligent.*"

"*I thought she was really striking. I was really attracted to her. I don't like picking up women but I was so attracted to her that I came over and started small talk.*"

"*She was good-looking. I immediately noticed that. Then I saw she was friendly and we had things in common. She was pretty and nice. I got along with her.*"

"*I remember thinking that she was pretty. What attracted me most was her looks, at first. Later, that she's great. She's nice. . . . There was something about her, she would put my mind at ease.*"

"*She's a very pretty woman. What attracted me first was her looks. Later, she's very much like me. She's giving towards me. She cares a lot.*"

"*She's very attractive, very pretty. Good looks rank higher for me than it does to the average person. She knows she's attractive . . . has presence . . . is very aware, a serious person.*"

GENDER DIFFERENCES IN ROMANTIC ATTRACTION

Do these quotes suggest a gender difference in the romantic choices of men and women? Most of the attraction variables presented in the first chapters of the book did not. Men and women seem to be equally influenced by physical proximity, arousal, pleasant personality traits, similarity, satisfying needs, and reciprocity in love.[1] Only the importance of physical appearance revealed a significant difference between men and women. Most of the men, as compared to less than half of the women, mentioned physical appearance as triggering the initial attraction to their partners. Furthermore, men described physical appearance as playing a far more significant role in their romantic attractions.[2]

Other studies, as well, have documented a gender difference in the effect of physical appearance on romantic attraction. Particularly persuasive evidence was provided by Alan Feingold (1992) who reviewed studies based on questionnaires; studies based on personal ads; studies that examined the impact of physical beauty on popularity with the opposite sex; and studies that manipulated the attractiveness of members of the opposite sex.[3] All four types of studies showed a gender difference in the predicted direction: physical appeal, even if important to women, is far more important for men.

It is noteworthy that the gender difference found in men's and women's responses to questionnaires was larger than the difference found in their actual behavior. In other words, men are less influenced by women's appearance than they say, and women are more influenced by men's appearance than they say. What they say may reflect social expectations more than personal preferences.

While men emphasize physical attractiveness, women more often look for social and economic status, ambition, strong character, and intelligence in a potential mate. The greatest gender difference was found in the attraction to status and ambition, which are related to a man's earning ability. Indications that men are more romantically attracted to beauty, and women to status, were found to be valid in studies totaling hundreds of subjects in different age groups and in different cultures. No gender difference was found in the attraction to such traits as a pleasant personality and a good sense of humor: both men and women like and value these qualities equally.

The following is a list of attributes that some people consider in their decisions to marry. Please rate on a 7-point scale (where 1 = not at all, and 7 = very much) to what extent you would be interested in marrying someone who

_____ is younger by five years or more.
_____ was married in the past.
_____ has children.

_____ is not likely to hold a steady job.

_____ belongs to a different religion.

_____ is of a different race.

_____ will earn far less money than you will.

_____ will earn far more money than you will.

_____ is not physically attractive.

_____ has more education than you have.

_____ has less education than you have.

_____ is older by five years or more.

This very list was presented to an unusually large and representative sample that included over 13,000 single men and women, age 19 to 35, from different social classes. The results of the study showed, once again, that beauty as well as youth are more important to men than to women, while earning ability is more important to women than to men.

Women were more willing than men to marry someone unattractive, or someone older by five years or more, if that someone earned more and had more education than they did. Men, on the other hand, were more willing than women to marry someone younger by five years or more, someone who was not likely to hold a steady job, who was likely to earn far less, and be less educated than they were (Sprecher et al., 1994).

Is it personal economic shortages that lead women to put such an emphasis on financial resources? Not necessarily. In a recent study, young men, young women, middle-aged men, and middle-aged women were asked about their criteria for choosing a mate. The four groups were asked to (a) estimate their own earning potential; and (b) rate the importance of various characteristics in a potential mate. Results of the study showed that men gave a higher rating to "a nice looking appearance" while women gave a higher rating to "good economic potential." Nothing new so far. However, there was a correlation between the income young women, themselves, expected to earn and the income they wanted a potential partner to earn. The higher the personal income, the more importance women gave to the income of their partners. In other words, the emphasis was not the result of a personal lack of economic resources. The fact that this correlation did not exist among older women suggests that the variables that influence romantic attraction can change during different stages of life and different periods of history (Weiderman & Allgeier, 1992).

Another study used photographs of models and models in bathing suits to demonstrate gender differences in (a) the ability to determine romantic attraction by means of visual scan; and (b) what types of information men and women need in addition to a visual scan. Results showed, once again, that for men a visual scan of a potential partner's "physical attributes" was enough to establish a "pool of coitally acceptable partners." For women, information about a partner's "nonphysical attributes," such as ambition, status, and dominance, was needed to establish a pool of partners who were potentially acceptable for sexual liaisons and "higher investment relationships," which is to say, marriage (Townsend & Wasserman, 1998).

WHAT ARE WOMEN AND MEN ASKING FOR, AND WHAT ARE THEY OFFERING?

A content analysis of 1000, classified, "lonely hearts" ads shows that men seek "cues to reproductive value"—physical appearance and youth—while women seek "cues revealing an ability to acquire resources"—maturity and actual or potential financial security. Women also seek to ascertain a man's willingness to provide resources in the form of time, emotion, money, and status. Both men and women offered those traits sought by the opposite sex. Men, favoring casual relationships, were more promiscuously inclined

WRITER SEEKS 65+ educated, moral, articulate, poised, person empathetic to feminist. Liberal democrat. Send background in own handwriting between fifty to hundred words.

HONEST, CARING, CHRISTIAN, SWF, Full figured, humorous and fun to be with. Enjoys most sports, talking and cuddling. ISO SDWM 27-42 No drugs, or drinkers. Serious replies only.

NATURE LOVER 53 y.o. blue eyed professional female, lives in the mountains, is looking for fun loving professional male 50-65 to share canoeing, hiking and romantic dinners by the fire.

WANTED WHITE MALE Intellectual snob, must be 5'4" tall or taller. Sense of humor is a plus. I'm in my 40's and I'm a very attractive white female, brunette/brown eyes, 5'2" 125lbs.

SUN AND BEACHES SWF, 51, enjoys the beach, boating, dining out, movies, travel, dancing. ISO gentleman with similar interests, affectionate, financially/emotionally secure.

SWF, 21 ISO SWM, 19-26. Love is the answer, but while you are waiting for the answer, romance raises some pretty good questions.

ACTIVE, HAPPY SWPF available for LTR. 41, 5'3, "weighty", brown hair, hazel eyes, ISO intelligent, open-minded, kind-hearted, tolerant, spiritual, mellow fellow of wit and character. Mail Box 700

LIFE MATE WANTED: DWM seeks slender to medium N/S, WF under 64, sensuous, passionate, affectionate, loving, classy dresser to jeans, who loves holding hands, country and popular music, slow dancing, movies, video's, cooking, dining out, some sports, cards, good conversations, quiet times, gardening, home life, for a life time of happiness. Mail Box 705

SEEKING SPECIAL LADY: SWM, 35, 5'10", DDF, muscular build, handsome, respectful, loyal, compassionate, protective, charming, personable. ISO SF, must enjoy cuddling, romance, dining, walks on beach. If interested call Voice box #8634.

SWPF, 34, N/S stunning brunette. ISO tall, strong, dynamic, blue-eyed Irishman (S/DPM 32-40) for committed relationship. Passion for golf, baseball, fun, romance, laughter, communication, kids.

ATTRACTIVE 39, DPCBF, ISO DPCBM 41-50, intelligent, honest and loving, easy going gentleman that appreciates friendship first. ND/NS, financially secure and caring that enjoys sports, movies, dining out, music etc. DDF, photo appreciated.

GIRL EINSTEIN with artistic touch ISO witty male 30-36 with similar fondness for dark humor and propensity for creativity

LOOKING FOR THAT CERTAIN SOMEONE: are you looking for me? Intelligent, articulate, creative, caring, silly, wise, thoughtful, quiet, communicative SWF50, ISO S/DWPM with brains n' spark 45+.

5'2" BUNDLE OF ENERGY Slim, NSSWF likes dancing, swing music, movies, travel, biking, walking, gardening. ISO fun loving energetic, NSSWM 55/65. To share in life's good times.

ARE YOU MY RHETT BUTLER? S/DNSPM 45-55 needed to tame this Scarlet. Must be dashing, daring and an incurable romantic. Love of golf and/or dancing a bonus.

FIGURE 8. *The Personals.* What are women and men asking for and what are they offering?

than women, who favor long-term, monogamous relationships (Greenlees & McGrew, 1994). (See examples of "lonely hearts" ads in Figure 8.)

Other studies show that, more frequently than women, men engage in sexual fantasies about someone other than a partner, and may pursue someone else while in a dating relationship (Yarab et al., 1998). When male and female students were asked about the physical appearance and professional level of an acceptable partner at various degrees of intimacy and commitment, women were more likely to prefer, or insist, that sexual relationships occur in the context of intimate emotional involvement with the possibility of marriage (Townsend & Levy, 1990). Not surprisingly, sex appeal as a specific element in physical attraction was also found to be far more important in the romantic interest of men than in women's romantic interest (Cunningham, 1986). While physical attractiveness is more important to men, quality of communication is more important to women (Sprecher & Duck, 1994).

Age is another variable that affects the different romantic choices of men and women. An examination of personal ads in the United States, the Philippines, Europe, and India shows that young men prefer women their own age, but as they grow older, their preferences change to younger women. The age preference of women doesn't change as they age but remains steady for men older than themselves (Kenrick & Keefe, 1992). An examination of marriage licenses granted during the fifty-year period between 1928–1978 also shows that in 75 percent of the cases, the husband was older than the wife (Patterson & Pettijohn, 1982).

As we have seen, men and women also differ in their preferences for height in a mate. While the majority of women prefer a man who is taller than they are (Pierce, 1996), most men prefer women who are shorter than they are. As a matter of fact, shortness is more of a liability for a man than tallness is an asset (Jackson & Ervin, 1992). Women not only prefer to look up to their husbands, they also tend to marry up, while men tend to marry down, leaving unmarried women at the top of the worlds of politics, science, and business, and unmarried men in prison at the bottom.

Men and women are attracted to different personality traits. One such personality trait is dominance. Four different studies showed that expressions of dominance in men increased their sexual appeal for women. Dominant behavior does nothing to enhance women's attractiveness to men. Interestingly, while dominant behavior increased the sexual appeal of men, it did not increase the degree to which they are liked (Sadalla et al., 1987).

Does this mean that women are sexually attracted to all dominant men?

Not necessarily, because in order to appeal to women, dominant men have to demonstrate other traits as well, such as a willingness to help, empathic ability, and a willingness to cooperate. Presumably, such men are more likely to invest in their offspring (Ellis, 1992).

The attraction of women to dominant yet helpful men was demonstrated in three studies in which young women watched a video showing a man being dominant, or not; and helpful and cooperative, or not. Findings showed that women found the men who were cooperative and helpful much more attractive physically and sexually, and more socially desirable as potential mates. Dominant men were found to be more appealing than submissive men, but only when they were helpful and cooperative. Men who were dominant and egotistical did not appeal to women (Jensen-Campbell et al., 1995).

WHAT CAUSES THE GENDER DIFFERENCES IN ROMANTIC ATTRACTION?

In their separate answers to this question, two theories—one, evolutionary, the other, psychoanalytic—rest on an assumption that gender differences in romantic attraction are real. Conversely, the separate answers of two social theories rest on an assumption that these gender differences are *not* real. One social theory explains the differences as the operation of sex-role stereotypes; the other argues that individual differences in romantic attraction are more significant than gender differences. If you are not interested in any of these explanations, you can skip right to the recommendations for people seeking love. For those who are interested, I will discuss each theory in some detail.

GENDER DIFFERENCES IN ROMANTIC ATTRACTION: EVOLUTIONARY THEORY

According to evolutionary theory, gender differences in romantic attraction are the result of biological differences between mammalian males and females. Because only females give birth, their investment in their offspring through gestation, birth, and nursing is far greater than the male's. In addition, women can produce far fewer offspring over a limited duration, while men can produce offspring from puberty until they die. As a result, men and women are attracted to different qualities in their potential mates. A woman looks for a man who is willing to commit to her and her offspring, and who is able to provide for them; a man looks for a woman who can bear children. In other words, different requirements for genetic survival dictate different criteria for mate selection in the two sexes. In men, evolution dictates preferences for qualities that indicate a woman's ability to procreate, namely, youth and beauty. In women, evolution dictates preferences for qualities that indicate a man's ability to obtain resources, namely, earning potential and status.

She Loves His Success, He Loves Her Youth And Beauty

If romantic attraction is the result of genetic imprints that are different in men and women, these imprints cause each gender to be attracted to different qualities in potential mates. The evolution of these, and other, sex differences is one of the central themes in Darwin's theory. Charles Darwin (1871) believed that evolution occurs in a continuing process of change through which different traits are selected because of their greater adaptability to environmental demands. This process of "natural selection" favors those individuals who adapt better to their environments. The evidence for "good adaptation" is simple—more offspring in the next generations. A trait appears by chance, is found to serve the ability to produce offspring who can survive, and reappears through natural selection.

To these basic Darwinian concepts, modern sociobiologists added the term "parental investment," meaning the energy invested by parents in giving birth and raising an offspring.[4] Sociobiologists argue that the larger the difference between the sexes in their parental investment, the larger the differences between their criteria for romantic attraction. In humans, the differences between the sexes start with the difference between the sperm and the egg. The slow-moving egg is 50,000 times larger than the fast-moving sperm. Women release one egg per month, as compared to hundreds of millions of sperm produced by men every day. This is why, says evolutionary psychologist Ada Lumpert (1998), a woman is very cautious about her egg, while a man spreads his sperm around. Sperm is cheap and the man has nothing to lose. The further and faster he wanders, the greater his chances of success. A woman carries the baby in her womb for nine months; she nurses and takes care of the baby after the birth. A man invests something like ten pleasant minutes in passing his sperm into the womb of his partner; even if we add the time involved taking her to the maternity ward, the difference in time invested is still very large. Because her parental investment is so much greater than his, the optimal way for the female to ensure having as many healthy offspring as possible is characterized by caution; his way, by speed. Since she is going to invest so much time and energy in her offspring, she has to be very sure before she starts that they will survive.

The difference between her caution and his speed puts them in the stereotypical situation in which he pushes her to agree to sexual activity, and she resists, saying, "Wait." So he waits and she assesses his loyalty. Will he stay with her after they make love? Will he help her raise their offspring? He promises he will. So they make love, and she is exposed to the danger that despite his promise he will get up and leave. Dishonesty is a common strategy and everyone can promise eternal love. The greatest danger a woman must guard against is a man's abandonment of her and her offspring. So the female guards with extra caution, her instincts tuned to detecting liars. She searches for a man who is loyal, who doesn't abandon, but stays and lends a hand.

An examination of the romantic attraction interviews indicates that loyalty is indeed an attractive male trait for women. "He is very reliable. If he says he'll do something, I know he'll do it." "He is honest, he is moral, he is smart, he is responsible, he is everything you can want." "He goes out of his way to help people, and you can rely on him. He doesn't play the kind of games that some men play with women." "I can trust him. He's responsible." "With him I know that if he says he'll be somewhere, he's really going to be there."

Sociobiologist David Buss (1994) emphasizes the role of evolutionary processes in creating different mating strategies for men and women. Since women can have a smaller number of children than men can, women look for men of means who can provide for them and their offspring. This is why women measure men according to their earning potentials, as seen in their status, money, ambition, and diligence, and why they are attracted to expressions of love, such as expensive restaurants and gifts, that demonstrate men's economic resources. Alternatively, from adolescence through old age, men can produce children; so men measure women according to their youth, health, and beauty, and are attracted to shows of affection that symbolize a woman's fertility.

Buss organized a huge cross-cultural study that involved over fifty researchers and close to ten thousand people in thirty-three countries, six continents, and five islands. Once again a consistent gender difference was found in the importance of earning potential versus physical attractiveness. Women gave the greatest weight to signs of men's earning potential—ambition and hard work—while men gave the greatest weight to signs of women's fertility—youth and beauty (Buss et al., 1990).

Many other studies have examined a particular culture or a certain aspect of mate selection. A study of mate preferences among the Kipsigis women in Kenya, for example, found that the women prefer men who offer "high quality breeding" as evidenced by their numbers of inhabitable acres of land. Furthermore, Kipsigis women prefer single men, followed by monogamous men, and, finally, polygamous men. When several women are married to one man, even a rich man, it reduces the "quality of breeding" they can provide for their offspring. Kipsigis women try to minimize this risk as much as they can when choosing a mate (Mulder, 1990).

A study done in India showed that while physical appearance is important to *both* men and women, caste and economic security exercise different gender appeal. Indian men will ignore the economic security of a potential partner if she is from a similar caste, while women will ignore the caste of the man if he is sure to provide economic security (Suman, 1992).

Men And Women, Love And Sex

Evolutionary psychologists argue that while birds as well as humans exhibit the connection between mate selection and parental investment, romantic attraction intervenes in humans as the "active ingredient" in mate seeking, courtship, and flirting (Trost & Alberts, 1998). While romantic love was co-opted by evolutionary forces to maintain the pair bond, humans, or more specifically, human males, have evolved both short-term and long-term "reproductive strategies" (Kirkpatrick, 1998). In short-term mating, men have faced the "adaptive problem" of finding sexually accessible women. As a result, men express a preference for sexual availability in short-term partners. Such short-term partners require different attraction tactics than long-term romantic partners. Indeed, when the effectiveness of different mate-attraction tactics was evaluated, a show of resource potential was judged most effective for men seeking a long-term mate, whereas furnishing immediate resources (giving money or buying a drink), was judged most effective for men seeking short-term partners (Schmitt & Buss, 1996).

Similar findings emerged when men and women, age 17 to 43, were asked about the tactics they use to attract potential marriage partners. Women who expected an investing partner said that they tried to attract him by behaving modestly and emphasizing their sexual fidelity. Women who expected a non-investing partner flaunted their sexuality in order to get pre-parental investment from as large a number of men as possible. Men who believed that one should invest in children were more likely than other men to emphasize this willingness and ability to invest as a way to attract women. They were also likely to emphasize their sexual fidelity. Men who did not believe in the importance of investing in children demonstrated their sexuality and their attraction to women as a way to attract them (Cashdan, 1993).

Emphasizing those traits in yourself that are likely to attract the opposite sex may seem a legitimate and acceptable tactic, but it can also be considered deception. Not surprisingly, there are gender differences in "patterns of deception" in "mating strategies." When men talk to other men, they tend to exaggerate their success in general, and their sexual conquests in particular. On the other hand, when they talk to women, men exaggerate their commitment, their honesty, and their ability to generate resources. Women try to enhance their physical appearances in the company of men as part of a strategy for attracting a mate (Tooke & Camire, 1991).

One of the biggest differences between men and women has to do with their approaches to sex without love.[5] A famous study on this subject was done by Douglas Kenrick and his colleagues (1993). Young men and women specified their minimum criteria for twenty-four different traits when evaluating (a) a date, (b) a sexual partner, (c) an exclusive dating partner, (d) a marriage partner, and (e) a one-night sexual liaison. Findings showed that gender differences were greatest for casual sexual liaisons, with men's criteria consistently lower than women's. Men's criteria were as high as women's criteria for marriage partners.

Similar findings are reported in a recent study that compared men's and women's minimum standards for short-term and long-term relationships. Once again it was found that both men and women expressed higher minimum standards for long-term relationships, and that women were far more selective than men when considering potential short-term mates (Regan, 1998).

An amusing study was conducted on a university campus. An attractive young man and an attractive young woman approached students of the opposite sex and offered to go to bed with them. Seventy-five percent of the male students approached by the young woman and *zero* percent of the female students approached by the young man accepted the offer (Clark & Hatfield, 1989).

What about women who are as sexually active as men? Interviews with highly sexually active men and women showed that in women, but not in men, the large number of sexual partners was related to emotional vulnerability and anxiety about the partner's willingness to invest in the relationship. This may reflect women's difficulty in dissociating sexual pleasure from the partner's emotional involvement (Townsend, 1995).

In recent years the evolutionary theory has been gaining force and followers. All of the studies mentioned in this section support the claim that physical appearance is more important to men, while status and economic success are more important to women. She loves his success and he loves her beauty, as we see in the famous example in Figure 9.

Evaluation of Evolutionary Theory

With the growing popularity of evolutionary theory grew the number of its critics. One of those critics, a biologist, noted the great leap that evolutionary theorists make "from the seemingly innocent asymmetries between eggs and sperm" to such "major consequences" as female fidelity, male promiscuity, women's disproportional contribution to the care of children, and the unequal distribution of labor by gender (Hubbard, 1990). Another critic, this time a primatologist, argues very convincingly that evolutionary theorists' notion of "the coy female" persists "despite the accumulation of abundant openly available evidence contradicting it." Why, then, does such a notion persist? The reason is a cultural congruence. Since the evolutionary explanations for the competitiveness and promiscuity of men, and the choosiness, sexual inhibition, and flirtatiousness of women fit many elements in popular culture, "coyness" became one of the most commonly mentioned attributes of women in the evolutionary literature (Hrdy, 1988).

With regard to gender differences in romantic attraction, evolutionary theory attempts to use the same concepts to explain contradictory behaviors—not only why women are coy, but why they flaunt their sexuality; not only why men are promiscuous, but why they emphasize their sexual fidelity. Despite this theoretical

FIGURE 9. *Prince Charles and Princess Diana. The apotheosis of the successful man and the beautiful woman.*

flexibility, there are numerous findings that do not fit evolutionary theory. In addition, there are other convincing explanations for the gender differences in romantic attraction and mate selection strategies.

Most of the theories that oppose evolutionary theory offer a social explanation for the gender differences in romantic attraction. While evolutionary theory views romantic love as a cultural means to a biological end (de Munck, 1998), the social theories emphasize the role played by social forces such as social norms and sex-role stereotypes.

GENDER DIFFERENCES IN ROMANTIC ATTRACTION: SOCIAL THEORIES

The evolutionary explanation of the gender differences in romantic attraction, as well as the psychoanalytic explanation that will be discussed later, are based on the assumption that gender differences in romantic attraction are real. They are both challenged by social explanations that are based on the assumption that these gender differences are *not* real. According to one explanation, gender differences in romantic attraction result from the operation of social forces such as gender-role stereotypes, social roles, social norms, and differences in social power. Socialization toward different gender roles and scripts and different norms for men and women dictate different preferences in a potential mate.

According to another social explanation, based on social construction theory, reality is socially constructed. The similarity between men and women in most things, including romantic attraction, is far greater than the differences. Therefore, individual differences and social differences in romantic attraction should be noted and emphasized more than gender differences.

Here is an example of a study that achieved results similar to those of evolutionary theorists, but was explained by a social theory. In terms of determining the choice of a romantic partner for both short-term, sexual, and long-term, meaningful, relationships, men and women rated the importance of physical features, demographic variables, and personal qualities. Findings showed, again, that men placed greater emphasis on the physical appearance of their prospective romantic partners, while women placed greater emphasis on the personal qualities. In the context of a meaningful, long-term relationship, however, both men and women weighed various personal qualities more heavily than physical characteristics. Contrary to the evolutionary explanation of the effect of innate genetic programming, these findings were explained by the effect of sex-role stereotypes and traditional sex roles on the romantic preferences of men and women. Since all of us are influenced by the masculine and feminine stereotypes dominant in our culture, we tend to choose partners who fit those stereotypes (Nevid, 1984).

A review of a large number of studies on the topic led the six researchers who conducted the review to conclude that gender differences in romantic attraction and affiliation resulted from "a common, perhaps representative, stereotype" (Benton et al., 1983).

Gender-Role Stereotypes And Their Influence On Romantic Attraction

Gender-role stereotypes are those rigidly held, oversimplified beliefs that males and females possess distinct psychological traits and characteristics—solely by virtue of their sex. Such overgeneralizations tend to be widely shared in a given culture (Basow, 1992). While the division by sex is one of the most basic classifications of every known human society, the division of labor and the behaviors and traits of males and females differ in different societies. Consequently, the associations people have for the words "masculine" and "feminine" are characteristic of the society and specific sub-culture in which they live.

What function, if any, do stereotypes serve? And what were they created for? Simply to help us process social information faster. Since we cannot possibly process the endless amount of information we absorb through our senses, we organize that information into different cognitive schemas. A *schema* is a cognitive framework, acquired through experience, which directs the way we process new incoming information. After a schema is created it influences the way new information is absorbed, explained, processed, and remembered. We categorize people according to social schemas. To some of those schemas we belong, to others we do not belong. There are many social groups to which we can belong, groups that are defined by such things as race, religion, nationality, profession, political views, and, of course, gender. A gender schema is a cognitive framework that reflects social beliefs about men and women. Sexual schemas influence people's responses to sexual-romantic cues, sexual desire, and romantic attachment (Cyranowski & Andersen, 1998).

To all apparent purposes, there is nothing wrong with stereotypes. After all, they are nothing more than cognitive schemas that help us make sense of the ocean of information threatening to drown us every moment. The problem is that while organizing and processing all this information, we make mistakes. And these mistakes tend to be consistent. One notable example is that we tend to see groups to which we don't belong as more homogeneous than groups to which we do belong. Thus women tend to assume that men are closer to the masculine stereotype than men really are, and men tend to assume that women are closer to the feminine stereotype than women really are. In a study that demonstrated this, men and women examined sentences that described masculine and feminine stereotypes, such as, "Losing a competition is depressing" or, "Taking care of a baby is a way of showing love." Findings showed that both men and women assumed that a higher percentage of members of the opposite sex agreed with these stereotypical sentences than the members of the opposite sex actually did (Park & Rothbart, 1982).

By their nature, stereotypes perpetuate themselves and acquire the power of self-fulfilling prophecies. In a study that demonstrated this power, men and women arrived at the laboratory presumably to participate in a study that explored the influence of communication on decision-making in organizations. Out of sight of each other, they were asked to use a signaling board to negotiate with a co-worker about the division of labor on different tasks. Some of the tasks were stereotypically masculine, for example, repairing an electrical outlet; some were stereotypically feminine, such as decorating a birthday cake; and some were neutral, such as painting a chair. One- third of the men were told that they were negotiating with a man, one-third were told they were negotiating with a woman, and one-third were told nothing.

Findings showed that women who were thought by their partners in the negotiation to be men, chose more masculine tasks, whereas the women who were thought by their partners to be women, chose more feminine tasks. The reason? The women behaved according to the men's expectations. When the men thought they were negotiating with a woman, they chose masculine tasks for themselves and tended to compromise less when a conflict arose. These behaviors caused the women to behave in ways that confirmed the men's expectations. In other words, the men's expectations, based on gender-role stereotypes, produced behaviors that confirmed these stereotypes (Skrypneck & Snyder, 1982). The different behaviors of the women thought to be men, and the women thought to be women, suggests that these are not innate sex differences that evolved during thousands of years of evolution. Rather, these are differences that result from gender-role stereotypes and self-fulfilling prophecies.

Gender-role stereotypes are a social product and they define normative behavior. Stereotyped women are perceived as feminine and stereotyped men are viewed as masculine. Since it is important to people to be accepted and popular, they feel pressure to behave according to gender-role stereotypes. At the getting-acquainted stage of a romantic relationship, it is important to make a good impression. This forces both men and women to behave according to gender-role stereotypes more than they might otherwise behave.

Most people behave according to the appropriate stereotypes, especially when they are expecting to meet an attractive potential mate. This was demonstrated in a classic study that involved four groups of women. One group was told that they were going to meet a very attractive, and brilliant, Ivy League student who held conservative views. The second group was told that they were going to meet a very attractive and brilliant, Ivy League student who held liberal views. The third group was told they were going to meet an unattractive and mediocre student who held conservative views at a mediocre university. The fourth group was told they were going to meet an unattractive, and liberal, mediocre student at a mediocre university. The women were asked to describe themselves and were told that their descriptions would be given to the man. These same women had also participated in a previous, unconnected, study in which they had given detailed descriptions of themselves.

Results showed that the women who thought they were going to meet an attractive, conservative man described themselves as more feminine and less intelligent. The women who thought they were going to meet an attractive, liberal man described themselves as less feminine and more intelligent. The women who thought they were going to meet an unattractive man didn't alter their descriptions of themselves. The changes in self-presentation of the first two groups of women were not related to the women's real views, either conservative or liberal (Zana & Pack, 1975).

In a thirty-year-old study that is still relevant today, eight hundred women were given three questionnaires covering "self perception," "the ideal woman," and "the ideal woman as seen by men." Comparison of the responses that the women gave to the three questionnaires revealed a small discrepancy between their perceptions of themselves and their perceptions of the ideal woman. However, there were very large differences between their own views of the ideal woman and their assumptions about the male view of the ideal woman. When men described the ideal woman, their responses were very similar to the women's descriptions of the ideal woman. But there were big differences between the men's descriptions of the ideal woman and the women's descriptions of the male's ideal woman. Men's descriptions of the ideal woman were less conservative than the women thought she would be (Steinman & Fox, 1970).

Similar findings emerged when men were asked to describe themselves, the ideal man, and the ideal man as seen by women. In similar fashion, there was a big discrepancy between men's perception of women's ideal man, and women's true ideal. Men thought that women preferred family men. In fact, there was a great similarity in the descriptions of the ideal man by both men and women.

Do Stereotypes Have a Basis in Reality?

Carol Martin believes that the answer is a definite no. Martin (1987) showed that when students are asked about the traits that characterize men and women, they describe the familiar stereotypes. When they are asked to describe themselves, the stereotypes disappear almost altogether. An exercise I do in my classes on the psychology of gender shows the same thing. I ask my students to write the traits they associate with masculinity and those they associate with femininity. The traits they invariably mention describe sex-role stereotypes. When I ask them how many of the traits describe themselves, it turns out, to their great surprise, that almost none do.

Other studies also show little basis for stereotypes. When men and women were asked what attitudes and qualities they, personally, and members of their sex value, there was a big similarity in the values of men and women. Both sexes value such traits as honesty, responsibility, and open-mindedness. These are characteristics that are not included in studies of sex-role stereotypes. Nevertheless, when they were asked about the values of the other sex, the stereotypes appeared; women exaggerated the importance that men attribute to achievement, and men exaggerated the importance that women attribute to nurturing. The conclusion, gender differences are far smaller in reality than they appear to be in stereotypes (Unger, 1975).

Here is the paradox. Both men and women play their prescribed sex roles and then complain about the results. Couples are first attracted to each other because each fits the stereotype. She is attracted to him because he is strong, silent, masculine, assertive, and skilled. He is attracted to her because she is warm, sensitive, open, and verbal. Later she will complain that he doesn't talk and he will complain that she's a nag (Tavris, 1992).

Why are people attracted to potential mates who are stereotypically masculine or feminine in light of the evidence that relationships of men and women in traditional gender roles are far from optimal and are generally worse than those in androgynous roles? One answer that was offered is that the attraction to stereotypes reflects a conflict between what old genetic imprints and past values dispose people to do and what the present culture prescribes, such as more androgynous relationships (Ickees, 1993).

A recent study in which instrumentality, a masculine trait, and expressiveness, a feminine trait, of potential partners were manipulated, shows that, indeed, both men and women prefer androgynous partners who combine both these traits over sex-typed partners (Green & Kenrick, 1994).

Another study has shown that women were most attracted to "masculinity with a feminine touch" (Cramer et al., 1993). In this study, young educated women either listened to prerecorded responses or read verbatim transcripts of two men answering questions on topics such as car repairs, career opportunities, and romantic interests. One set of answers was constructed to reflect stereotypically masculine activities and interests; the second set reflected stereotypically masculine *and* feminine activities and interests. Findings showed that women rated the androgynous man as more likeable, intelligent, moral, mentally healthy, appropriate, and honest than they rated the masculine man.

Attraction to a stereotypical macho man can be dangerous, because traditional gender roles have been associated with sexual aggression. Hyperfeminine women who adhere to a traditional gender role were found to be attracted to macho men, preferred them as husbands and sex partners, and thought they resembled past and current boyfriends. These women also reported more attraction to, and interest in, nonconsensual sexual dates, as well as less anger, and more sexual arousal. These findings point to the risk associated with the attraction to macho, aggressive, and coercive men, namely, sexual aggression (Maybach & Gold, 1994).

Gender stereotypes convey a clear message about how men and women are supposed to behave toward each other, who they are supposed to be attracted to, and how they are supposed to express this attraction. Men are supposed to be attracted to "feminine" women, and women are supposed to be attracted to "masculine" men (Basow, 1992). Similarly, handsome men are seen as masculine and beautiful women are seen as feminine (Gillen, 1981).

Nevertheless, when the traits *most desired* in a mate are examined, no gender differences are found (Goodwin, 1990; Smith et al., 1990). Furthermore, when the types of men most attractive to women are examined, it turns out that women prefer feminine to masculine men as both friends and romantic partners. Income contributes to a man's romantic attraction only when the man has desirable personality traits, suggesting that women consider income only after personality criteria are met. In fact, a man's personality factors relate more consistently to his romantic appeal to women than do his success factors—and a man's belief in gender equality has the greatest influence on his attractiveness to women (Desrochers, 1995).

Gender-role stereotypes have more influence during the early stages of young people's romantic relationships than they do on more established, long-term relationships involving older people. A Dutch/German study demonstrated that while young, single people follow the stereotypical male preference for good looks and female preference for financial prospects, older people value a steady relationship and exhibit a stronger desire for home and children, chastity and ambition (de-Raad & Boddema, 1992).

Young men and women whose personalities are shaped by gender-role stereotypes in their late teens, continue to be influenced by, and shape their romantic relationships according to these stereotypes in their young adulthood. In an ongoing study of personality and gender differences in romantic attraction, I found that the closer to one of the gender-role stereotypes young people's personalities were at age 18, the more this predicted their intimate relationships at age 23 (Pines, 1998b).

Even studies that were presented as theoretically supporting the evolutionary perspective can be explained by gender-role stereotypes. In the study of personal ads, for example, it can be said that women emphasize traits such as economic status because it fits the masculine gender stereotype. Men, on the other hand, emphasize an attractive appearance because it fits the desirable feminine stereotype (Davis, 1990).

The Influence of Social Norms

Social theorists are convinced that gender differences in casual sex provide no proof for evolutionary theory. They explain these differences as social forces, such as social norms, that dictate the appropriate behavior for men and women when offered casual sex (Hyde, 1993). Furthermore, the famous study that demonstrated a gender difference in its approach to casual sex, also showed that men are as choosy as women are when it comes to selecting a marriage partner (Kenrick et al., 1993).

Clear, yet different, norms influence the "average" man and woman's sexual expectations of a dating relationship. Men generally expect sexual intercourse after approximately nine to eleven dates, fewer than women's expectation of approximately fifteen to eighteen dates (Cohen & Shotland, 1996). When asked about possible responses to hypothetical encounters between a man and a woman, men are likely to choose more responses leading to sexual activity and to express greater sexual desire (Leigh & Aramburu, 1996).

There are different sexual scripts for men and women (Chafetz, 1975). According to the masculine sexual script, a man who has casual sexual relationships is a playboy or a Don Juan. According to the feminine sexual script, a woman who has casual sex is a slut. Since the label "a playboy" is rather positive while the label "a slut" is very negative, the labels, or more accurately the norms behind them, dictate very different behaviors for men and women.

Even if there is a significant gender difference in their *approach* to casual sex, it does not mean that there is a difference between men and women in either level of sexuality or romantic attraction. The stereotype that women have little interest in their sexual functioning, or are unable to function sexually at a level similar to that of men, is just that, a stereotype with little base in reality (Small, 1992).

Other scientists who discovered gender differences in romantic attraction also chose to explain them by referring to the functions of various social forces. They argued that women were not genetically programmed to be pragmatic about love, social reality forced them to be (Dion & Dion, 1973). Social norms, and not genetic programming, dictate what is attractive in a potential mate (Aron & Aron, 1986).

Another social variable—power—has been used to explain gender differences in romantic attraction (Low, 1990). Women choose men who are older, taller, wiser, and more educated because they make it "natural" for them to be weaker. Similarly, men choose women who are younger, shorter, less intelligent, and less educated because they can more easily maintain their social power. Neither the men nor the women are necessarily aware of the fact that their romantic choices are influenced by power considerations. Their sex-role socialization and the acceptable social norms make it easy for them to be.

Even when the findings reported by David Buss, the leading proponent and spokesman of the evolutionary perspective, are examined carefully, the main finding is not of gender differences in romantic attraction and mate selection, but rather of gender similarity. In one of his studies it was discovered, for example, that the most important traits in a potential mate, for both men and women, are kindness and consideration (Buss & Barnes, 1986).

Self-evaluation also influences romantic attraction. A study showed that men with a low self-concept are more attracted to traditional women, whereas men with high self-concept are more attracted to modern, liberal women. Why? Liberal women are perceived as more assertive, self-confident, and independent than traditional women, and may present a threat to the sense of independence and control of men with a low self-concept. In an attempt to enhance their egos when they feel threatened, these men need to reject non-traditional women. A man who is sure of himself is not threatened by women and therefore does not have a need to criticize assertive and independent women (Grube et al., 1982).

In summary, some studies contradict evolutionary theory predictions, and even the results of evolutionary studies can be explained by social norm theory. Occasionally, rather than demonstrating a difference, even evolutionary studies actually illustrate a greater similarity in romantic attraction between men and women.

GENDER DIFFERENCES IN ROMANTIC ATTRACTION: PSYCHOANALYTIC THEORY

We turn now to the third fascinating theory that attempts to explain gender differences in romantic attraction. Several well-known feminist psychoanalysts agree with evolutionary theorists about the existence of significant gender differences in romantic attraction, but they explain them very differently.[6] These theorists believe that gender differences in romantic attraction and romantic love are not the result of a biological imperative but rather the result of different childhood experiences and different developmental tasks that boys and girls face growing up in a patriarchal society such as ours.

Their explanation for gender differences in love starts with a fact so obvious that most of us don't even acknowledge it. As poet Adrian Rich states it, we are all "of woman born" (1976). All of us, men and women alike, are born to a woman. This simple biological fact carries an enormous psychological significance. Since a woman gives birth and nurses, the woman in most human societies, even if she is not the biological mother, is almost always the baby's primary care giver. "No fact of our early life has greater consequences for how girls and boys develop into women and men, [and] therefore for how we relate to each other in our adult years" writes Lillian Rubin (1983).

Because a woman, most often the mother, takes care of them in the first months of their life, a woman is the first "love object" for both baby boys and baby girls. It is she with whom they form their first attachment and first

symbiotic bond, the bond they will later try to recreate in their adult romantic love relationships. During these first stages of development, their love for
her is both emotional and erotic. When they develop the ability to differentiate self from other, mother is for both baby boys and baby girls the first object of identification. In order to develop a mature personality both boys and
girls have to accomplish two tasks: develop a sense of self that is separate and
autonomous and develop the ability to relate to others (Blatt & Blass, 1996).

The accomplishment of these two tasks is related to the development of
gender identity which begins at about age one and a half. This developmental process is different for boys and for girls. Boys, in order to develop a
masculine gender identity need to suppress their emotional attachment to
Mother and shift their identification to Father. Since his penis defines him
in this stage ("I have a penis like my father, that's why I'm a man like him"),
it becomes the center of the man's masculine identity. The infantile identification with Mother is repressed, and defenses are erected against the needs
and emotional experiences of infancy. When men fall in love, they find
again the emotional bond with a woman. The boyhood conflict between
longing for the symbiosis with mother and anxiety about losing himself in
this symbiosis is repeated in intimate relationships. Men long for closeness
and intimacy with a woman but are also terrified by it (Rubin, 1983).

As a result of the early separation from mother, the basic masculine self is
separate and autonomous. Being different from women is central to masculine identity. Boys have an easier time establishing ego boundaries that make
them feel separate and independent, and a harder time developing a masculine gender identity. Later on, it is easy for most men to be independent and
maintain firm ego boundaries, but they have a hard time being intimate. In
other words, men accomplish easily the developmental task of self-definition
but have a harder time accomplishing the task of relatedness.

Girls don't need to separate from mother in order to develop a feminine
gender identity. As a result, for most women it is easy to develop a gender
identity, to be like Mother, and easy to be intimate, but difficult to develop
an independent self and establish firm ego boundaries. In other words,
women easily accomplish the developmental task of relatedness, but have a
harder time accomplishing the task of self-definition.

As a result of these different developmental processes, the basic masculine self, one of independence and separation, derives satisfaction in competition and achievements (Pleck, 1977), whereas the basic feminine self, one
of relatedness, derives satisfaction from being in an intimate relationship
(Miller, 1976).

For boys, while the emotional attachment to Mother is suppressed, the bodily bonding of infancy, which is to say the erotic or sexual aspect of the attachment to her, is left undisturbed and is later transferred to other women. For girls the erotic attachment to Mother must be denied, shifted to Father, and, later in life, transferred to another man, while the emotional involvement and identification with Mother remains intact.

Since women had to repress their sexual attraction to Mother, but not the emotional connection, the emotional connection is dominant in their love experiences. For them, there is no satisfying sexual relationship without an emotional connection. On the other hand, since men had to repress their emotional connection to Mother but not the sexual attraction, the sexual connection is dominant in their romantic relationships. This is why "for men, the erotic aspect of any relationship remains forever the most compelling, while for women the emotional component will always be the most salient" (Rubin, 1983).

Psychological development also affects the different roles of words and sex for men and women. Since the repression of the attachment to Mother happens at such an early age for boys, men do not connect feelings with words the way women do. For men, physical connection is at the center of intimacy. For women, words are at the center of intimacy (Rubin, 1983).

Because of these different childhood experiences, women, more so than men, look for commitment, intimacy, and security in their intimate relationships, whereas men look for physical appearance and sexual appeal in potential mates. Indeed, in the romantic attachment interviews, women described romantic relationships with higher levels of intimacy, commitment, and security than the relationships men described. And, as noted before, men described the physical appearances of their mates as playing a more important role in their romantic attractions.[7]

One result of these different processes is a dance of intimacy in which one partner, most often the woman, is the pursuer, and the other partner, most often the man, is the distancer. One extreme example of the distancer in the dance of intimacy is the commitment-phobic man. Often this is a man that a woman doesn't even notice. But he pursues her with such enthusiasm and determination that she can't ignore him. His most impressive trait is his ability to express love. Contrary to most men, this type of man can talk for hours about feelings, show vulnerability, bond, and appear truly intimate. The woman, who is dazzled by this outpouring of verbal sensitivity, starts to think that she has found her true love. But when the woman finally surrenders and reciprocates his love, he disappears. At first she is convinced that something terrible has happened to him. After all, he had never failed to arrive for a date or call when he promised he would. She starts searching for him, only to realize that she doesn't actually know where he lives. He always came to her house when they went on a date, something she viewed as yet another testimony of his love of her. She doesn't know where he works; he was kind of vague about it and seemed much more interested in what she was doing, which was also wonderfully flattering. She doesn't know his family or any of his friends because they always spent time with her friends. Gradually it dawns on her that Prince Charming is really gone. Men like him are capable of expressing their need for a symbiosis only as long as the woman is not interested in them. The minute she reciprocates their love, their anxiety about being engulfed surfaces and they run away. After the woman has overcome the trauma of his disappearance, and has given up on him, he can reappear in her life as enthusiastic as ever, with some feeble explanation for his disappearance. She learns very quickly that the only sure way to hold a man like this is by refusing him.

THERE ARE NO SIGNIFICANT GENDER DIFFERENCES IN ROMANTIC ATTRACTION: SOCIAL CONSTRUCTION THEORY

While both the evolutionary and psychoanalytic theories assume that gender differences in attraction are real, studies of sex-role stereotypes assume that they are not real, but rather an attempt on the part of both men and women to behave according to prescribed social norms. An even more extreme position is taken by social constructionists who argue that the similarities in romantic attraction between men and women are far greater and more significant than the differences between them. The individual differences among men and among women are more important than the gender differences between men and women.[8]

Social construction theory rests on the belief that reality is socially constructed (DeLamater & Hyde, 1998). There is no, one, particular "reality" that is simultaneously experienced by all people. Different cultures have their own unique understandings of the world. Yet people are not passive recipients of these societal scripts. They actively construct their perceptions of the world and use the culture as a guide. Social construction ideas have been applied to many areas, among them, intimate relationships (Gergen & Gergen, 1992) and romantic love (Beall & Sternberg, 1995).

According to social construction theory, romantic love is a social construction. Societies differ in their understanding of the nature of romantic love. And even within the same society, romantic love has been conceptualized differently in different times and periods in history. Within as complex a society as Northern America, there are different sub-cultures and ethnic groups that have different conceptions of romantic love (Jacobson & Christensen, 1996). The cultural influences far outweigh genetic and evolutionary influences.

Social constructionists quote studies showing that men and women look for similar things in a mate. Studies done at a university and a dating club show, for example, that both men and women put at the top of their lists of desirable traits in a partner, kindness, consideration, honesty, and a sense of humor (Goodwin, 1990).

An analysis of personal ads also showed that the most desirable traits of a potential mate are understanding and a sense of humor (Smith et al., 1990). After the relationship has been established, the partner's sensitivity and ability to be empathetic and intimate correlate with satisfaction from the relationship in both men and women.

Another study, which investigated men's and women's values in heterosexual relationships, found no evidence for women's allegedly greater concern with having a secure, committed, sexually exclusive relationship. Most of the men and women who participated in the study valued equally these features of intimacy (Cochran & Peplau, 1985).

A review of studies on differences in the genders' approaches to sex shows that women have a strong interest in their sexual functioning and are able to function sexually at a level similar to that of men. Furthermore, in many societies, especially Western societies, women have sex outside of marriage regularly with no concern for punishment or criticism. On the whole, women are expressing their sexuality far more freely than it was common to think (Small, 1992).

Sexuality as an aspect of courtship varies as the ages of the people in the courtship vary, not just because of life experience and comfort with oneself, but also because of when sexual libido peaks for women. Women tend to peak in sexual functioning in their 30s and 40s—a later age than men—and have the capacity to be multi-orgasmic.

Instead of a view of sexuality that emphasizes the differences between men and women, social constructionists emphasize the subjective experience of every individual. The ideal relationship between two sexual partners, either heterosexual or homosexual, is "intersubjective" —that is, two individuals who treat each other as subjects rather than objects and delight in each other's uniqueness (Goldner, 1998). An intersubjective relationship is the exact antithesis of a sex-role stereotyped relationship that rigidly defines the different roles of men and women. Jessica Benjamin (1998) describes an intersubjective sexual relationship using a joke she heard from a friend who grew up in Long Island.

> One full-moon night in midsummer, the horseshoe crabs all come out from the water onto the bay shore, where they mate amid clattering of shells. Then they all light up and say to each other, "It was good for me. How was it for you?"

Benjamin writes, "Obviously, the joke lies in the attribution of human intersubjectivity to crabs: concern with each other's pleasure, respect for the inevitable difference between my experience and yours."

If our individual differences are so large and the focus on them so beneficial to our intimate relationships, why then are so many people and so many researchers and theoreticians convinced that men and women are attracted to different things in a potential mate? Carol Tavris (1992) believes that "human beings love to divide the world and its inhabitants into pairs of opposites," we/them, good guys/bad guys, and, of course, men/women. "Western ways of thinking emphasize dualisms and opposites, and pose many questions of human life in fruitless either/or terms." Are we uniquely human or basically mammalian? Are we shaped by nature or by nurture? After we divide things, the same tendency makes us emphasize the differences between them. When parents who have two children are asked to describe them, they tend to describe them as opposites; if one is an "angel," almost always the other one is a "devil." The oversimplification hides the fact that the similarity is much greater than the difference.

GENDER DIFFERENCES IN ATTRACTION: SOCIAL CONSTRUCTION THEORY VS. EVOLUTIONARY THEORY

Social construction theory views gender differences in romantic attraction as minor and as the result of primarily cultural forces; evolution theory views them as large and as the result of innate, biologically based differences. The greatest differences are assumed to be in the male's attraction to physical appearance and the female's attraction to status. Which theory is correct?

In order to answer this question, I looked at the romantic attraction interviews, and compared the responses of the 93 young American men and women to the responses of the 89 young Israeli men and women (Pines, 1998a). Results of this gender by culture comparison provide partial support for both the evolutionary and social construction theories.[9]

As predicted by evolutionary theory, more men were attracted to the physical appearance of their partner than women; 80 percent of the men and 53 percent of the women mentioned the physical appearance of their partner when describing why they fell in love. There was no difference, however, in the frequency with which men and women mentioned status as a cause of attraction; 4 percent of the men and 4 percent of the women mentioned status.

On the other hand, culture did have an effect on the importance of status. While 8 percent of the Americans interviewed were attracted to the status of their partner, almost none of the Israelis, 0 percent, were. Americans were also more influenced by propinquity, 63 percent, as compared to 46 percent of the Israelis, and by similarity, 30 percent, as compared to 8 percent of the Israelis.

Interestingly, gender differences were found where evolutionary theory had not predicted that they should be found: women were found to be significantly more likely than men to attribute arousal to romantic attraction, namely, 30 percent of women versus 16 percent of men. And gender differences were not found where they were expected: men were as likely as women to be attracted to someone who satisfied their needs, namely, 56 percent of the men versus 58 percent of the women.

These findings, as well as other findings reported throughout the chapter, suggest a need for an integrated theory of romantic attraction that combines some aspects of evolutionary theory with the contributions of the social theories. While there have been several attempts to offer such an integrated approach, there also have been those who believe that such an integration is impossible. It has been argued, for example, that although research may show an integration of biological and social influences, such different approaches as evolutionary psychology and social construction theory cannot conjoin (DeLamater & Hyde, 1998).

I myself believe that an integration of evolutionary theory, psychoanalytic theory, social norm theory, and social construction theory is not only possible, but necessary. Each of these theories highlights an important aspect of the way men and women experience falling in love. Biological forces, the physical excitation of falling in love, which I will describe later in the book, affect falling in love. Different childhood experiences influence the different romantic choices of women and men. And social norms prescribe the mating game. Nevertheless, falling in love remains the most private and unique experience.

SUGGESTIONS FOR THOSE SEEKING LOVE

What should those seeking love conclude from all this? It is possible, of course, to simply conclude that it is important, especially for women, and especially on the first date, to try and gain maximum benefit from physical appearance. And it is important for men to appear successful and ready to commit. But it is also possible to conclude, as the social constructionists suggest, that what both men and women are looking for is a partner who is kind, considerate, and fun to be with. Luckily, these are traits that, with effort, can be adopted and developed. But social constructionists are saying something else, too. They are saying that each one of us is a unique individual, and that our uniqueness is more important than the similarities we share with our own sex or the differences that divide us from the opposite sex.

As I was writing this, a young man arrived for his therapy session. He is a very handsome and bright young man who is finishing his law degree and comes from a very wealthy family. Nevertheless, he has never been in an intimate relationship. Wanting very much to have such a relationship, and realizing that there must be a problem if he continuously fails to establish one, brought him to therapy. In this session he talked about his difficulty in bringing out his "true self," that part of him that is "sensitive and vulnerable and easily hurt" when he meets new women. "Women expect a man to be strong and sure of himself," he told me. By not being himself, and by behaving according to the masculine sex-role stereotype, he kept himself from the true intimacy he longed for.

This young man has two choices: (a) either play the dating game and present a mask of the masculine persona, or (b) take the risk and present his true self. He is familiar with the first option, and if he chooses to continue with it, he may only get to know the feminine persona that women will present in response. If he chooses the second, and scarier, option, the woman he likes may well reject him because she perceives him as, in his words, "weak and feminine." Since the hope is that once the bridge of first acquaintance has been crossed, the couple can go beyond stereotypes to a truly intimate relationship, the path chosen ought to be the one likely to lead to this end.

Part Two

UNCONSCIOUS CHOICES

How We Choose The Lovers We Choose

The heart has its reasons, which reason knows nothing of.
—Blaise Pascal

Lovers and men of intellect cannot mix . . .
Lovers who drink the dregs of the wine reel from
   bliss to bliss:
The dark-hearted men of reason
Burn inwardly with denial.
   —Talal al-Din Rumi, *Lovers and Men of Intellect*

*P*eople often express an amused surprise when they hear about the effects such situational variables as proximity and arousal have on falling in love. But they readily agree that such variables do indeed have an effect and often have examples of their own to prove it. People usually express less surprise, however, when they hear about the influence of similarity in background and attitudes, a pleasant personality, and physical beauty—qualities found in the beloved. These are the kinds of things "everybody and his grandmother" know about falling in love. Research data about reciprocal attraction, filling needs in romantic love, the process of falling in love, and gender differences in romantic attraction, help people organize information that they already had in one form or another.

But even after a detailed discussion of the situational and conscious determinants of falling in love, people can be left with a strong feeling that something is still missing. Somehow missing from the studies and theories, interesting and amusing as they may be, is the most important, significant, and mysterious element—the magic of love. The studies do not explain why it is that we fall in love with one person and not with another who is more similar in background and attitudes, whose personality is more pleasant, appearance more impressive, and whom we see more often. The theories do not explain why one person makes us "walk on air" as if we had found our "match made in heaven," as if we had known him or her our entire lives, even though it's been only two weeks. Why does another person, who is a far more appropriate mate according to all the relevant criteria, leave us cold? These are the kinds of questions the second part of this book addresses. Here, we will focus on the unconscious processes in falling in love. Because they are unconscious, these processes are difficult to observe directly and study empirically. As a result, unlike the first part of the book, the second part relies less on empirical research, and more on clinical evidence.

8

OPENNESS TO LOVE

Benedick. I could find in my heart that I had not a hard
  heart, for, truly, I love none.
Beatrice. I thank God, and my cold blood . . . for that I
  had rather hear my dog bark at a crow than a man
  swear he loves me."
  —Shakespeare, *Much Ado About Nothing*

"*I'm single and I don't have a boyfriend. I would say I have never had
a boyfriend. . . . Other people are more excited about just being
with someone than being with someone in particular. I had a few good
male friends, but as far as a romantic relationship goes, I just was not
ready emotionally. I was just not used to it. Most people were moving faster
than I was and I just wasn't very comfortable . . . I have no problem being friends with men, but it's sort of a struggle getting into a romantic
thing. Something about it just didn't feel right to me . . . the whole idea
just scared me.*"

"*I've been kind of shy. I haven't pursued relationships with girls my age.
I'd like to, but I hadn't bothered to. I'd like to get married, have kids, but
the bachelor life suits me. I'm in no rush. It'll happen eventually. Once in a
while I may think about it when I see a couple on the street. I'm kind of
reclusive. I don't like partners.*"

"*I have never been in a romantic relationship, not really. I got buddies
and stuff . . . I'm a tough guy to get along with. I have a bad problem
with the physical aspect of the relationship. When you find someone you
like, they don't always like you. I don't tell them what I feel. It's tough
'cause I can be guessing wrong . . . Like this woman in the place where I
work. We'd go out and hang out, but she didn't want to get involved. So I
never confronted her. I was asking her out but she would say I'm busy. I
never confronted her on it. We used to get into huge arguments. We were
very similar. That scared me. She was getting to the core of me. There were
things about me I didn't want her to know.*"

A tenth of the men and women interviewed about their significant intimate relationships said that at age 23 they still had never been in a romantic relationship.[1] Their romantic involvements with members of the opposite sex had not gone beyond one or two dates. Other interviewees talked about highly intimate and highly satisfying relationships of many years. Some people had had only one such significant relationship at this age; some had had two or even three significant relationships. A small number, 2 percent, of the people, all of them men, had had four or more significant, intimate relationships.

There are people who fall in love easily, very intensely and repeatedly, some even claiming that they cannot live without love. And there are others who have never been in love and are convinced that all the stories about the intensity of romantic love are either vast exaggerations or straight out lies (Tennov, 1979). One of these, a good-looking man and a highly respected journalist, told me recently that he is convinced that passionate love is an invention. He himself has lusted after many women and he knows what sexual passion is, but he has never fallen in love.

Why is it that some people can find love and a romantic relationship easy and satisfying, while others want desperately to have a truly intimate relationship but fail? Why do still others avoid relationships all together? The answer to this question is not simple. One major explanation has been provided by *Attachment Theory,* formulated first by British child psychoanalyst John Bowlby (1982).

Like Freud and most of the psychoanalytically oriented theoreticians and researchers that followed him, Bowlby believes that early childhood experiences, most of them unconscious, have the most profound impact on adult love relationships. For Bowlby, the key is "attachment," the first stable love relationship that the baby develops. The ability to attach is innate, but the form it takes depends on the relationship that the baby has with a "primary caregiver," most often the mother. Bowlby believes that an infant needs a reliable, ongoing attachment to the primary caregiver, and that the infant suffers grievously, even irreparably, if that attachment is interrupted or lost. He developed the concept of "internal working models" to describe how the infant's sense of self and sense of others unfold through interactions with that primary caregiver.

The major premises of attachment theory are that:

- intimate relationships of adults are guided by internal working models constructed from early childhood relationship experiences;

- these models shape an individual's beliefs about whether he or she is worthy of love and whether others can be trusted to provide love and support;
- these models also influence the kinds of interactions individuals have with others and their interpretations of these interactions.

Bowlby believes that the inborn human need for attachment is the result of an evolutionary development. Babies are born with a repertoire of behaviors that are aimed at obtaining and preserving closeness to a "strong and wise caregiver." The maintenance of the closeness is related not only to the baby's inborn repertoire, but also to the ability, willingness, sensitivity, and accessibility of the caregiver. The experiences the baby has with the caregiver are internalized into mental models of the self and the other. These internalized working models are generalized to other relationships. The internal model changes with development because, despite being genetically imprinted, it is sensitive to environmental influences. The internal model is responsible for all the patterns of attachment, including first and foremost, romantic attachment.

While John Bowlby is the theoretical father of attachment theory, Mary Slater Ainsworth is its empirical mother. She provided empirical evidence for a number of conclusions intuited from the theory. Mary Ainsworth, a student of Bowlby, conducted experimental observation of babies. She and her students observed 76 babies and their mothers in their homes. The observers paid attention to each mother's style of responding to her infant in such areas as feeding, crying, cuddling, eye contact, and smiling. Each mother-baby pair was observed for a total of seventy-two hours, spread over eighteen observation sessions, each lasting four hours. One-year-old babies were taken by their mothers to the laboratory and experienced a procedure termed "strange situation." Mother and baby were put in a toy-filled room where a friendly research assistant greeted them and invited the baby to play with the toys. The infant was observed as the mother left the room three times for three-minute intervals. During two intervals the research assistant was in the room, during another interval the baby was alone. Ainsworth identified three distinct patterns in the baby's reaction to the room full of toys, to the mother's departure, and to her return.

The *securely attached*, about two-thirds of the babies, were infants who were ready to explore the room on their own, but turned around once in a while to make sure Mother was there. They protested or cried on separation, but when the mother returned, they greeted her with pleasure, frequently stretching out their arms to be picked up, and molding to her body. They were relatively easy to console.

The *anxiously attached* or *ambivalent*, about 10 percent, seemed anxious and insecure. They tended to cling and were afraid to explore the room on their own. They became terribly anxious and agitated upon separation, often crying profusely. They sought contact with Mother when she returned, but simultaneously arched away from her angrily, resisting her efforts to soothe them.

The *avoidant*, about 20 to 25 percent, gave the impression of independence. They explored the new environment without using their mothers as a secure base, and they didn't turn around to be certain of the mother's presence. When the mother left, the avoidant infant didn't seem affected; but an examination of the infant's heartbeat showed a very strong response. And when she returned, the infant snubbed or avoided her.

Because Ainsworth and her team had observed the mother-baby pairs in their homes, she was able to make specific associations between the babies' attachment styles and the mothers' styles of parenting. Mothers of securely attached babies were found to be more responsive to the hunger signals and crying of their infants and to readily return the infants' smiles. Mothers of anxiously attached babies were inconsistent and unresponsive to the baby's needs. Mothers of avoidant babies rejected their infants either physically or emotionally (Ainsworth et al., 1978).

In other words, the three attachment patterns seen in the laboratory were directly related to the ways the babies were mothered. The insecure babies developed strategies that helped them cope with a mother's rejection or inconsistency.

The anxious baby tries desperately to make mother pay attention and love him or her. The baby senses that when the begging is loud enough or the scene dramatic enough, Mother responds because of guilt. This is why the anxious baby clings to Mother or tries to punish her when she doesn't respond. The baby is addicted to Mother and to the effort to change her.

The avoidant baby chooses the opposite strategy. This baby learns to suppress and ignore needs and emotions. The baby is angry at Mother and distances from her even while remaining as attached to her as the anxious baby. Since pleas for attention have been rejected in an insulting and hurtful way, the baby says in effect to the rejecting mother: "Who needs you anyway? I can manage on my own!" At times grandiose feelings about the self are added to this response—"I'm perfect and I don't need anyone"—

suggesting the early development of a narcissistic personality.

Often, the mother's inattention results from the emotional deprivation she herself had suffered in her childhood. Her baby's emotional needs remind her of her own infantile needs that she had succeeded in repressing at great effort. The reminder generates an internal anger, depression, and rejection, which she then expresses toward her child. In this way, the problem is transferred from one generation to the next in a multi-generational pattern.

In succeeding studies, researchers showed that the attachment patterns formed in infancy persist in adulthood. The patterns of intimate relationships that people exhibit as adults are powerfully influenced by the types of relationships they had with their primary caregivers, most often the mother. When the primary caregiver is consistent, stable, trustworthy, and responsive, the baby will develop a sense of security in love, and, as an adult, will feel comfortable and satisfied in love relationships. When the primary caregiver is not consistent, stable, and trustworthy, and if the baby is abandoned or rejected, then the baby will develop an adult pattern of anxiety and ambivalence about love, or else will attempt to avoid altogether the dangers involved in intimate relationships (e.g., Bartholomew & Horowitz, 1991; Shaver & Clark, 1994).

A famous series of studies conducted by Philip Shaver and Cindy Hazan used a measure of adult romantic attachment that was inspired by Mary Ainsworth's work (Hazan & Shaver, 1987; Shaver & Hazan, 1993). These studies, as well as numerous others, demonstrated the existence of three romantic attachment styles.

Secure. Adults with a secure attachment style are comfortable depending on others and having others depend on them. It is relatively easy for them to become emotionally close to people. They feel themselves valuable and worthy of love and respect. They can trust people; they believe that people have good intentions and can be counted on in an hour of need. They develop intimate relationships easily and don't worry about being alone or about someone getting too close to them. They are not overly concerned about abandonment or dependency; and they tend to score high in sensitivity to others, and low in compulsive giving.

Avoidant. Adults with an avoidant attachment style tend to be isolated. They are uncomfortable being close to others; they find it difficult to allow themselves to depend on others, or to trust others completely. They are nervous when anyone gets too close; and, often, their partners in a relationship want them to be more intimate than they are comfortable being. They have many separations but suffer less from relationship termination. They are loners, uncomfortable in relationships involving intimacy and closeness; they have more one-night stands and are more likely to be unfaithful and enjoy loveless sex.

Anxious-ambivalent. Adults with an anxious-ambivalent attachment style see others as reluctant to get as close as the adults would like. They often worry that their partner doesn't really love them, or won't want to stay with them. They are seeking such high levels of closeness and commitment that they scare away potential partners who often view them as clingy and suffocating. They are insecure and invest too much in relationships. They tend to think that people don't value them as much as they should and that, in general, people are untrustworthy. They often separate again and again from the same partner and tend to be jealous in relationships. They have low self-concepts and reveal too much about themselves. They worry about being abandoned and their love not being reciprocated, and they worry about being too close and dependent. They tend to get a high score in compulsive giving and a low score in sensitivity.

The three attachment styles influence not only the way people act in romantic relationships and caregiving styles, but also their sexual styles. *Secure* individuals are willing to experiment sexually, but do so in the context of a continuing relationship. They enjoy nearly all physical and sexual contact from cuddling to oral sex. They are unlikely to engage in one-night stands or to have sex outside the primary relationship. *Avoidant* individuals take less enjoyment from almost all physical, as opposed to sexual, contact, are more likely to engage in one-night stands, have extramarital sex, and are more likely to think that sex without love is pleasurable. *Anxious* individuals like the physical, nurturing, aspects of the relationship, but enjoy sex less.

A recent study of adult attachment styles in a large, nationally representative sample involving thousands of people shows that 59 percent are securely attached, 25 percent are avoidant, and 11 percent are anxious (Mickelson et al., 1997). I think it is fascinating to note that these percentages are very close to Ainsworth's original observations in infants some twenty years earlier.

Childhood adversities such as physical abuse and serious neglect have the most consistent association with insecure, adult attachment styles, and relate strongly to anxious and avoidant adult attachment. Psychopathology in a parent has a strong association with insecure attachment. A parent's substance abuse is related to avoidant attachment. Financial adversity during childhood is related to insecure adult attachment. The adult attachment styles are related to people's ability to function in romantic relationships (Brennan & Shaver, 1995).

Kim Bartholomew divided the avoidant category into two, thus changing the three adult attachment categories into four (1990). In the measure she developed, that is used in the context of an interview, people are categorized on the basis of the following four descriptions.

Secure. It is easy for me to become emotionally close to others. I am comfortable depending on others and having others depend on me. I don't worry about being alone or having others not accept me.

Fearful Avoidant. I am somewhat uncomfortable getting close to others. I want emotionally close relationships, but I find it difficult to depend on others or to trust them completely. I sometimes worry that I will be hurt if I allow myself to become emotionally too close to others.

Preoccupied. I want to be completely emotionally intimate with others, but I often find that others are reluctant to get as close as I would like. I am uncomfortable being without close relationships, but I sometimes worry that others don't value me as much as I value them

Dismissing Avoidant. I am uncomfortable with close emotional relationships. It is very important to me to feel independent and self-sufficient, and I prefer not to depend on others or have them depend on me.

Attachment styles can be measured as early as 12 months of age, and in the absence of major environmental change, persist into adulthood (Stein et al., 1998). The nature of the early relationship between a mother and her baby influences what that baby as an adult will think, feel, and believe about intimate relationships. Will the adult trust others or not? Will he or she expect love or rejection in intimate relationships? These are learned responses acquired very early in life in response to the degree of sensitivity and consistency received during infant care-taking.

Attachment styles also affect coping. An interesting study shows that attachment style influences the way couples respond to an anxiety-provoking situation. In the study, both husbands and wives filled out an adult attachment measure. The wives were told that they were going to take part in an activity "that produces anxiety in most people." The husbands were told that they would take part in a neutral activity. The couples were videotaped as they waited together. Analysis of the videotapes showed that it was possible to predict the couples' behavior in the waiting room from their attachment style measures. The secure women sought the closeness of their husbands, while the avoidant women kept their distance. The men showed a similar pattern of behavior. The secure men gave their wives support in words and physical contact when their wives' anxiety went up, while the avoidant husbands shunned their wives. The ambivalent men and women did not show a consistent pattern of behavior (Simpson et al., 1992).

CRITICISM OF ATTACHMENT THEORY AND RESEARCH

While attachment theory has inspired a large and steadily growing body of research, it has also raised a fair amount of criticism. Some criticized Ainsworth's "strange situation" for being an artificial base for data that could not generalize to real life situations. Some criticized the overemphasis on the influence of the relationship between the baby and Mother. Doesn't Father have an influence? And what about siblings, other relatives, teachers, and close friends? Others criticized the tendency to blame Mother for everyone's problems. Doesn't a romantic relationship that ended badly have more of an impact than Mother's handling in the first months of life? Still others criticized the overemphasis on childhood experiences. After all, we continue to evolve and learn from relationships throughout our life.

Ainsworth's response to these criticisms is to say that both she and Bowlby believe that our internal attachment model is sensitive to environmental influences and that people continue to influence us throughout our lives. She extends attachment theory beyond infancy and to "affectional bonds" throughout life, including kinship bonds, friendship bonds, and, of course, sexual pair-bonds (Ainsworth, 1989).

Sexual pair-bonds involve three systems: reproductive, attachment, and care-giving. Although sexual attraction may be the most important component at the falling-in-love stage of a romantic relationship, those relationships that depend entirely on the sexual or reproductive component are likely to be short-lived. As the relationship persists, the attachment and care-giving components become more important and sustain the pair-bond even when sexual interest has waned. Attachment and care-giving interact to make for a reciprocal give-and-take. Each partner, at some times and in some ways, looks to the other as stronger and wiser, and the other reciprocates by providing care, comfort, and reassurance that promote feelings of security.

SELF-CONFIDENCE AND OPENNESS TO LOVE

How do you feel and act when you are in love? Do you feel secure in yourself and in the love given to you? Do you avoid getting close and intimate? If so, is this why you are not in an intimate relationship, or are there really no appropriate candidates? Are you longing for a relationship but allow your anxiety and ambivalence to scare potential partners away? It seems rather obvious from all the predictions and studies generated by attachment theory that our self-concept and self-confidence influence our ability to give and receive love.

In an early study on self-esteem and romantic love, students were asked to fill out a questionnaire that examined their level of self-confidence along with their tendency to feel threatened and respond defensively. Then they were asked about their love experiences. Results showed that the students who reported the highest number of falling-in-love experiences had high self-confidence and low defensiveness (Dion & Dion, 1975). *In order to love others, we first must love and respect ourselves.* Attachment studies indeed show that secure individuals are more self-confident, less neurotic, more extroverted, more agreeable, and more open to new experiences than avoidant and anxious individuals (Mickelson et al., 1997, Shaver & Brennan, 1992).

The conclusion that in order to be able to love others we first must love ourselves is not big news in psychology. Eric Erikson argued some forty years ago that we have to develop a strong and positive sense of ourselves before we can develop and sustain intimate relationships (Erikson, 1959). A study that examined the relationship between self-identity and intimacy showed that Erikson was right. People with a highly developed sense of identity had relationships of greater intimacy than did people with undeveloped self-identity (Macerguis & Adams, 1980).

People whose sense of identity is not well-developed are afraid of intimacy because they are afraid to be engulfed. And their anxiety is well founded. When people with a low sense of self fall in love, their love is especially powerful, often taking complete control of them and becoming the main focus of their lives. The result is compulsive, destructive, desperate love (Sperling, 1987).

Does self-confidence always imply greater openness to love? Not necessarily. With greater self-confidence come higher expectations and standards for an appropriate romantic partner. In a study that illustrated this, an attractive, well-dressed, young man approached a succession of young women who were waiting to receive the results of a personality test they had taken. As each woman waited, the young man started talking to her, indicated that he liked her, and asked her for a date. At that moment, the experimenter walked in, and showed her to another room where she received the results of the personality test. Half of the women read very positive evaluations that were aimed at raising self-confidence. The other half read very negative evaluations that were aimed at reducing self-concept and self-confidence. The experimenter then asked each woman how much she liked various people, such as a teacher or a friend, and, since "there was space left on the page," how did she evaluate the young man who approached her in the waiting room? Results indicated that the women who received negative evaluations and felt less confident, expressed greater liking for the man who showed an interest in them (Walster, 1965). The greater the insecurity and doubts we have about ourselves, the greater our liking and appreciation for a person who likes us.

Similar findings were reported in a study on how self-esteem and physical attractiveness affected the search for a romantic partner. In the study, male students who took an intelligence test received false information about their performance; some were told that they had done very well, others that they had failed miserably. Afterwards, during a break, the experimenter joined the subject for coffee. A female student, part of the experiment, waited in the coffee shop. When the experimenter and subject entered the coffee shop, the experimenter *discovered* the female student, who sat alone, joined her, and introduced the subject. In half of the cases, the female student, with the help of makeup, hairstyle, and appropriate clothes, looked very attractive; in half of the cases, she was made to look very unattractive. The experimenter noted whether or not the subject expressed romantic interest in the young woman. Did he try to make her stay longer? Did he offer to pay for her coffee? Did he express a desire to meet her again? Did he ask for her phone number? Analysis of the observation data indicated that the students who felt more sure of themselves, because of their great success in the intelligence test, expressed more romantic interest in the young woman when she looked attractive. On the other hand, the students who felt less self-confident, because they had performed miserably, expressed more interest in the young woman when she looked less attractive (Kiesler & Baral, 1970).

The less sure of themselves people are, the more they need love and respect, and the more likely they are to be attracted to people who offer those rewards. The more sure of themselves people are, the less they need approval, acceptance, and love; they are likely to be more choosy and less likely to fall in love with just anyone who offers them love. Like a hungry person who will eat anything, an insecure person is likely to choose someone less attractive because that kind of person is less likely to reject him or her and more likely to offer love and appreciation.

In women, self-confidence is related to physical attractiveness. Women who had been rated for attractiveness by objective judges were asked to describe their romantic preferences. All women preferred to date a high-status man, such as a physician or a lawyer, over a low-status man, such as a janitor or a waiter. Nevertheless, unattractive women were willing to go out with men holding jobs in the middle of the scale, such as an electrician or a clerk; attractive women were not (Rubin, 1973).

This brings us back to the discussion of the relationship between self-confidence and various love styles.[2] You may recall that insecure people who don't have a coherent sense of self and are not self-actualized tend toward a game-playing style of love; they have relationships with low levels of intimacy and high levels of conflict. People who are self-confident, self-actualized, and have a coherent sense of self, tend toward unselfish and romantic styles of love, and their relationships are characterized by high levels of intimacy (Levy & Davis, 1988).

BARRIERS TO FALLING AND STAYING IN LOVE

The question of readiness for love is of great interest for clinicians who work with individuals who are incapable of sustaining intimate relationships. I am currently working with two such individuals, a young man and a young woman. Both are very attractive physically, intelligent, and charming. Both want desperately to be in an intimate relationship. Both have a very long list of relationships that lasted from one date to several weeks. But none evolved into the kind of truly intimate relationship they both want.

The man, who loves folk dancing and is a wonderful dancer, often falls in love with his female partners. He dazzles them with his openness, readiness to talk about feelings, his ability to express love. Each is delighted to receive the love poem he left at night in her mailbox and is ready to join him in this larger-than-life love story. Their amazement lasts a week, or two, or three, and then it turns to distress. He is simply "too much." Finding a love poem every time you open your mailbox, every time you put your hand in your coat pocket, every time you open a drawer, is not thrilling, it's suffocating. In therapy, when he asked me if I wanted to see his poems and I said yes, he brought 682 poems to the next session. The women try to distance themselves from this flood of love, and tell him that they need some space, but he insists on being true to his feelings and expressing his love. When they can't take it anymore, they break up with him.

The woman is a very attractive, professional woman who meets many men through her work. Men are dazzled by her beauty, intelligence, and feminine charm. They pursue her and she responds enthusiastically, falling madly in love, convinced every time that she has found her Prince Charming. The mutual enthusiasm lasts a week or two and then the men start distancing themselves as she overwhelms them with her phone calls, her generous gifts, and her physical presence—she likes to arrive unannounced and surprise them by cleaning or cooking for them. When they hint that they need some space, she insists that she is a genuine person who needs to express her feelings. So she continues flooding them with her love, and sooner or later, they walk away, assuring her each time that she's a wonderful person. It is they who don't deserve all the love she has to give.

One of the most famous psychoanalysts to address the psychological barriers to falling in love and maintaining an intimate relationship is Otto Kernberg. Kernberg believes that the ability to love reflects the developmental level of the individual (1974). Internal models of love that are based on childhood experiences with important people, most notably, Mother, influence adult relationships. In order to fall in love and maintain a love relationship, an individual has to reach a certain emotional depth and maturity. "A capacity for relating to one's own self in depth as well as to others seems to be a basic precognition for a deep and lasting relation between two people who love each other" (Kernberg, 1980).

Kernberg describes people's ability to love on the following five-point scale.

Total inability to love. This most extreme end of the scale represents an inability to establish relationships that involve sexual love. It characterizes the extreme examples of a narcissistic, schizophrenic personality structure. A narcissistic personality is characterized by unrealistic feelings of grandiosity and a ceaseless need for admiration. The total involvement with the self prevents the establishment of intimate relationships. Schizophrenia is a very serious mental illness that causes serious disturbances in perception, motivation, and emotion.

Sexual promiscuity. The second pattern expressed is usually, but not always, heterosexual. It characterizes a less extreme form of narcissistic personality disorder, and people who suffer from it are capable of establishing intimate relationships. But since they tend to treat others as tools for their own gratification, their intimate relationships tend to be immature, incomplete, and often sexually focused.

Primitive idealization of the beloved and childish dependence. The third pattern is clinging and characterizes borderline personality disorder. People with this disorder tend to have very unstable interpersonal relationships and swing between total idealization and total dismissal of the other. They also tend to be emotionally unstable, impulsive, and desperate to prevent a real or imagined abandonment.

Ability to create stable relationships, without the ability to enjoy full sexual satisfaction. The fourth pattern characterizes less serious personality disorders and neuroses. Neuroses, according to psychoanalytic theory, are disturbances that originate in an unconscious conflict that creates anxiety. The anxiety pushes the individual to use various defense mechanisms that distort reality.

A healthy combination of sexuality and sensitivity to the other, and deep intimate relations. This fifth pattern is at the other, positive end of the scale.

The different levels on the scale represent different levels of "personality organization." The stage in which a "developmental failure" occurred determines the level of the adult's personality organization.[3] In order to understand what a developmental failure is, we first need to understand what normal development is.

Our personality is the result of a developmental process that the noted psychoanalyst Margaret Mahler calls "psychological birth" (Mahler et al., 1975). Mahler believes that psychological birth is not the same as physical birth. She and her colleagues followed "normal children of average mothers" from birth to age three. Their observations led them to conclude that psychological birth requires a successful passage through a number of stages.

Autistic stage. The first stage in a baby's life, birth to 2 months, during which the baby responds only to internal needs and periods of sleep are longer than periods of being awake.

Symbiotic stage. When the baby's sensitivity and response to outside stimuli grow, at 2 to 5 months, the baby moves to this stage. Here, there is no differentiation between self and non-self, between baby and mother. This symbiosis, *this experience of oneness with Mother, is the building block for the ability to love and all future love relationships.* The successful passage of this stage depends on the mother's ability to mother and the baby's ability to accept mothering. The symbiotic stage explains why people who fall in love allow their ego boundaries to collapse and feel at one with the beloved; and why people who fall in love are emotionally closed to loving anyone else. Symbiosis, and thus falling in love, is by definition between two.

Separating from Mother. When a baby has, what famous child doctor and psychoanalyst Donald Winnicott (1976) calls, "good enough mothering," the baby can start separating from Mother and develop an independent self-identity. Winnicott did a great favor to concerned mothers by assuring them that in order to raise an emotionally healthy baby they don't need to be perfect mothers, only "good enough." The process of separation from Mother and the development of an independent self happens, according to Mahler, in four stages.

Differentiation, 6 to 9 months. At this stage, the baby starts differentiating from Mother. The baby explores the world with eyes, hands, feet, and mouth. The development of this differentiation can be seen in a baby who sucks his or her fist. The expression of wonder and endless fascination on the baby's face indicates a beginning understanding that both the sensation in the mouth and on the fist are one's own and the baby can make them happen. It has been said that the baby's first reality testing is reality tasting. Only when the baby is able to differentiate between self and what is not self, can the baby start internalizing objects, that is, people, relationships, and things. Mother is the baby's first love object, and therefore also the first object the baby internalizes. As the baby starts separating from Mother, elements of her are internalized. Those internalized elements become a part of the baby's own independent, inner world.

Practicing, 10 to 16 months. After the baby has internalized Mother, or elements of the mother, the baby can tolerate being separated from her. At this stage the child starts to practice separating from Mother. The baby has an affair with the world and is full of enthusiasm and growing independence. At the beginning of this stage the baby crawls, at the end of the stage the toddler walks. Children at this stage love to play the game of "getting away from Mom." The mother has to be able to tolerate the baby's distancing and encourage the development of an independent self by recognizing the child's individual needs and preferences. When the mother encourages her child's independence, but at the same time is there, her child learns that separation can be enjoyable and exciting and does not mean a loss of love.

Rapprochement, 17 to 24 months. This stage of refueling is characterized by growing independence followed by a retreat, separation and return for love. It is important for Mother to allow her child to get away from her, but be there with a loving hug and nurturing when the newly acquired independence gets too scary.

Consolidation of individuality, 24 to 36 months. An inner world of internalized love objects enables the child to form stable emotional relationships, postpone gratification, tolerate frustrations, and enjoy the functioning of an independent self.

When the child passes these four stages successfully, the result is a "psychological birth"—the first step in the development of an autonomous personality with a unique and coherent self-identity capable of facing challenges, forming attachments, accepting others, and withstanding separation and conflict. An individuated person is able to maintain long-term love relationships even after the first drive was satisfied, and despite frustration, disappointment, and attacks. Such a person can postpone gratification, suffer frustration, and enjoy the functioning of an independent ego. Such a person can also distinguish self from other, and truly enjoy the other person's separate identity.

Throughout the process of separation-individuation, the primal conflict between longing for the infantile symbiosis, or the yearning for the perfect bond, and the need for independence, or the fear of being engulfed and losing individuality, expresses itself. This conflict returns in full force in adult romantic relationships.

The dual needs for closeness and for independence exist in each and every one of us, and in all romantic love relationships. Neither one is preferred and neither one exists all the time. Rather, there is an ongoing interplay between the two. Couples in romantic love relationships need to consciously allow, and move back and forth between, close intimacy and independence.

WHAT HAPPENS WHEN SOMETHING GOES WRONG?

A traumatic experience in one of these developmental stages can cause a fear of separation or an impulse towards merging. Abandonment, even if temporary, causes mortal dread and is imprinted as such. When the child's drive toward independence is suffocated by the parent's anxiety, the child develops a fear of suffocation and a strong need for space, independence, and autonomy. When the child's need for closeness is frustrated by a parent who pushes for independence too early, or is not there to defend the child in need, the child develops a fear of abandonment and an unusually strong need for closeness and merging. These unconscious needs define the choice of a romantic partner and influence the couple's dynamic.[4]

Failure in the process of separation-individuation results in the absence of a separate, independent self.[5] At times, people with such a fragile sense of self develop a "borrowed identity." They adopt the values of their family of origin or other people. They can't separate from their family and all their emotional energy is invested in it.

When the self is fragile, the person needs constant assurances and cannot stand criticism or rejection. His or her goal in life is to be loved and accepted by others. Such a person will always try to be what the other wants. A mature self, on the other hand, has boundaries. The self-concept of a person with a mature self is far less influenced by the opinions and feelings of others.

It is important to note that this view of the separated and individuated person as a model of mental health has been criticized by feminist writers as being a masculine model. In other words, the ideal of mental health is in fact a masculine stereotype.[6] What is described as normal development is characteristic of a patriarchal society where Mother is the primary caregiver rather than a partner in shared parenting.[7]

This brings us back to Otto Kernberg (1974) who believes that the ability to love reflects a level of emotional depth and maturity, and that this development can be described on a scale. What determines the personality's level of organization is the stage in which a developmental failure occurred in the process of separation-individuation, and the seriousness of the trauma that caused it. The ability to love and to maintain love relationships represents success in the process of separation from the primal symbiosis with Mother, and the development of an independent and differentiated self. The ability to love can be described on a continuum. On one end is the ability to achieve a deep and stable relationship with complete sexual satisfaction, a testament to success in the process of separation-individuation. On the other end is a total inability to have an intimate relationship that involves love and sexuality, which testifies to a serious failure in the process of separation-individuation. The earlier the developmental failure happens, and the more difficult the trauma associated with it, the more likely it is to severely affect development and the ability to love.

SCHIZOID PERSONALITY DISORDER

I cannot end the discussion of the ability, or inability, to love without addressing the personality disorder that is most relevant to the subject, namely, schizoid personality disorder. People who suffer from it treat all people with suspicion and distance; they tend to avoid all close relationships including sexual love relationships. They see in intimate relationships the threat of being controlled or their inner world invaded. When they are married or in an intimate relationship, schizoids express little interest in their partners and do not share their thoughts or feelings. They lack, almost altogether, an interest in social involvement and basic social skills, such as carrying on a conversation. They show no interest in either praise or criticism from other people. Since their emotional expression is limited, they are often perceived as cold and distant.

The social world of schizoids is very limited. They have very few intimate relationships, few friends, if any, and tend to be extremely isolated. When emotional issues arise in social contacts, they feel tremendous discomfort, and tend to escape the discussion of emotions by introducing a theoretical or abstract discussion. In comparison to the poverty of their social lives, their inner worlds are rich in fantasies and daydreams. It is noteworthy that people with a schizoid personality disorder usually do not experience the lack of intimate relationships as a problem and do not want to change.[8]

Things are different for people who find themselves without intimate relationships. They experience great distress with their situation and want very badly to change it. While it is true that people can do very little about the love they did or did not receive as children, adults can choose to be conscious of their attachment styles, and how the style affects their intimate relationships.

SUGGESTIONS FOR PEOPLE SEEKING LOVE

Do you feel secure in your ability to love and be loved? Do you avoid getting close and intimate? Are you longing for a relationship, but, because of your anxiety and ambivalence, manage to scare potential partners away? Instead of finding faults in their partners, as witnessed by many years of fruitless searching leaving them still unable to find an appropriate partner, people who are searching for love can try to figure out why they respond the way they do to others in general, and to candidates for a romantic relationship in particular. Even if awareness does not necessarily imply change, it is an important first step in the right direction.

9

THE SON FALLS IN LOVE WITH "MOTHER," THE DAUGHTER WITH "FATHER"

The innumerable peculiarities in the erotic life of human beings, as well as the compulsive character of the process of falling in love itself, are quite unintelligible except by reference back to childhood and as being residual effects of childhood.
—Sigmund Freud,
Three Essays on the Theory of Sexuality

WOMEN TALK ABOUT THE MEN THEY LOVE

"*I think I attract men who are like my father, very carefree and open . . . For the most part I like men with his characteristics.*"

"*I try to make him fatherly toward me. I made him spoil me like my dad did. He's like my dad in being vulnerable and trusting people.*"

"*What's weird is that he's definitely a combination of my step-dad and my real dad. A lot of things that seem to make me attracted to someone come from my step-dad. He's extremely talented. He is good with his hands. I mean he can fix things. He's also kind of casual. His smile, things like that. But he can also be kind of opinionated, like my dad. He can be condescending like my dad. I think I used to play the role with him that I played with my dad.*"

"*He's like my dad in being very career oriented. He talks about work a lot. He brings his work mind home with him. My dad did that. And he'll make decisions for you if you let him. He can have a short fuse too. That's kind of like my dad.*"

"*My father is reserved. He thinks about things before he says them. He [the boyfriend] is sort of like that too. Neither of them is really concerned about immediate gratification type of things.*"

"He's kind of similar to my father in that he has a strong sense of determination. Whatever he does, he'll try to do to the best of his ability. They are both very caring about me."

MEN TALK ABOUT THE WOMEN THEY LOVE

"She is similar to my mother in terms of not having a mean bone in her body and in being real easy going. Then you feel guilty, which you don't when they're being selfish. My mom is like that."

"She is very warm and loving, like my mother. And she takes care of me and spoils me like my mother used to spoil me."

"She sort of has the same granola look like my mother, not a lot of makeup, dresses casually. And she is laid back like my mother."

"Sometimes my mother doesn't like to be bothered. They are similar like that."

"She is overly dependent on me, that's a similarity between my Mom and her. And she spoils me in a lot of ways, like she buys things for me."

"She takes care of me and worries about me like my mother."

"She's a genuinely nice person. In that she's like my mom."

Sigmund Freud, a man of the Victorian age and a brilliant thinker, provided the pioneering psychoanalytic theory about the unconscious roots and development of adult love relationships. Many theoreticians and researchers have expanded and refined Freud's early concepts in creating their own theories about the roots of romantic love. One of these is Bowlby's attachment theory, discussed in the previous chapter. These theories continue to be refined by modern day psychologists who study both early childhood development and later adult development.

In his less-than-one-hundred-page book, *Three Essays On The Theory Of Sexuality* (1905), Freud explained romantic love according to his psychoanalytic theory, and described the roots of romantic choices, both normal and perverse, in men and in women.

The over-simplified translation of the complex process Freud described is the formula familiar to all of us—a man falls in love with a woman who reminds him of his mother; a woman falls in love with a man who reminds her of her father. These reasons are "unconscious," which is to say the individual is unaware of them.

IS YOUR PARTNER SIMILAR TO YOUR MOTHER OR FATHER?

In response to this question a significantly higher percentage of men than women described their partners as similar to their mothers, and a significantly higher percentage of women than men described their partners as similar to their fathers.[1]

Freud believed that the attraction to people who remind us of our opposite sex parent is a universal, biologically based phenomenon, related to the developmental processes of early childhood. In his conceptions, romantic love is a socially accepted expression of the sexual drive that he termed *libido*. Libido is the energy that life instincts use to perform their tasks, be it individual survival or racial propagation. Different from attachment, libido is akin to the biological drive of hunger or thirst that pushes for gratification. People are born with different levels of libido.

It is interesting to note that the Greeks called the bonding instinct of the baby to Mother, *Eros*, a word that is associated with romantic love. In its origin the word had the wider connotation of life force. Freud also saw Eros as a life instinct opposed to *Tanatus*, the death instinct, the unconscious and destructive wish to die.

Freud was the first to emphasize the decisive role played by the early years of infancy in laying the foundations of an individual's adult personality. He believed that the personality was formed by the end of the fifth year, and that subsequent development consisted of elaborating on this basic structure. Other psychoanalysts expanded Freud's formulation both backward, to earlier stages, and forward, to later ones.

THE PSYCHOSEXUAL DEVELOPMENT OF THE CHILD

According to Freud's theory of infantile sexuality, in order to achieve mature sexual identity, a child needs to pass successfully through different stages of psychosexual development, which occur in response to innate biological drives. Every stage is defined (a) by an "erogenous zone" of the body, a specific area that provides the focus for sexuality, pleasurable sensuality, and instinctual drive; and (b) by an "object" that provides the sensual pleasure, that is the thing, condition, or behaviors that can satisfy the drive.

At the first stages of life, a baby's libido is directed toward oneself, loving oneself in narcissistic love and enjoying one's body in "autoerotic" enjoyment. Later, if the development is healthy and normal, the baby can start to direct the libido outside, and love people outside the self. These people then become the baby's "love objects."

The first stage in the psychosexual development of a child is the *oral* stage that takes place during the first year of life. The child's sexuality is centered on the mouth. The principal source of pleasure derived from the mouth is eating, or the "incorporation" of food; it involves suckling and sucking and, with the growth of teeth, biting. These two modes of oral activity, eating and biting, are the prototypes for many traits seen in adulthood. Pleasure derived from oral incorporation may be "displaced" to other modes of incorporation such as acquiring possessions or knowledge. Oral aggression may be displaced to other modes or metaphors of biting such as criticism and sarcasm.

The baby's "love object" in the oral stage is the feeding breast. This is why "a child sucking at his mother's breast has become the prototype of every relation of love. The finding of an object is in fact a refinding of it" (88). "When children fall asleep after being sated at the breast, they show an expression of blissful satisfaction which will be repeated later in life after the experience of sexual orgasm" (Freud, 1917, 388). Even after sexual activity becomes disconnected from feeding, an important part of this initial sexuality remains and helps prepare for the choice of a mature love object that can bring back the lost happiness of this early stage of life.

In this stage of development, Mother is "teaching the child to love" (Freud, 1905, 89). In other words, Mother's love is necessary for adult romantic love. However, both too much and too little love can be harmful. The lack or the loss of love causes anxiety in romantic relationships, so that with intimacy, the anxious person behaves like an abandoned child. On the other hand, too much love makes it difficult for a person to be without love for even a brief period of time, or alternatively, to manage the relationship with very small amounts of love.

Second is the *anal* stage that takes place during the second year of life. At this stage, the sexuality of the child is centered on the anus, and is expressed in the enjoyment of both holding back and releasing feces. Depending on the toilet training and the parents' feelings concerning defecation, the child will develop certain traits and values. If parents are very strict, the child may hold back feces and later in life may become stingy and obstinate. Or else, in response to the parents' pressure, the child may respond with rage by defecating at the most inappropriate times. This is the prototype for traits such as messy disorderliness, temper tantrums, cruelty, and wanton destructiveness. However, when the parents praise the child extravagantly after a bowel movement, the child feels that producing feces is extremely important and as an adult is likely to demonstrate creativity and productivity.

In the oral and anal stages, there is no difference between boys and girls.

Children in these early stages are autoerotic and the love object for both boy and girl is Mother. From the third stage, the phallic stage, the psychosexual development of boys and girls diverges.

The *phallic stage* takes place between ages three and five. During this stage, sexual feelings associated with the functioning of the genital organs come into focus. The phallus and external genitalia fascinate boys and girls. They masturbate and express interest in the sexual organs of others. Childhood sexuality is at its peak at this stage, and its influences shape adult sexuality. However, the sexual impulse is different for a boy and a girl. Because of the so-called natural attraction to members of the opposite sex, the son is attracted to his mother and the daughter is attracted to her father.

The pleasures of masturbation and the fantasies that accompany it set the stage for the appearance of the Oedipus complex. According to the Greek tragedy that became famous thanks to Freud, King Oedipus killed his father and married his mother (see a retelling of the story on pages 150–151). Freud believed that like Oedipus, every boy is in love with his mother and views his father as a hostile competitor, and every girl is in love with her father and views her mother as a competitor. The boy wants to possess his mother and remove his father, the girl wants to possess her father and displace her mother.

Because of the forbidden sexual attraction to Mother, the boy imagines that his powerful rival, Father, is going to harm him. His fears center on harm to his genitals because they are the source of his lustful feelings. He is afraid that, in a jealous rage, his jealous father will remove the offending organ. This *castration anxiety* induces an identification with Father which assures the boy that Father will not harm him, while also giving him some vicarious gratification of his sexual impulse toward Mother. "Anatomy is destiny" declared Freud. The anatomical differences between the sexes cause a different process during this stage in girls and a different resolution of the Oedipal conflict.

As the boy discovers his phallus, the girl discovers her clitoris and views it, because of the pleasure it provides, as a phallus equivalent. When she discovers the inferiority of her sex organ, a cavity as compared to the boy's glorious protruding sex organ, it is a traumatic experience with far reaching consequences. The girl holds her mother responsible for her castrated condition and resents her for it. She transfers her love to her father because he has the valued organ. Her love for Father, and for other men, is mixed with envy because they possess something she lacks. *Penis envy* is the female counterpart of castration anxiety in males. Penis envy expresses the desire of the girl to have a phallus. The girl envies those who have a phallus and like the boy interprets its absence as a punishment, that is, castration. She imagines that she has lost something valuable, while the boy fears he is going to lose it. Her penis envy and his castration anxiety are called collectively the *castration complex.*

The boy's Oedipal complex is resolved, under the pressure of castration anxiety, by identification with his father. The boy hopes that if he imitates Father, Father will not hurt him and he can have a wife like Mother when he grows up. The girl's Oedipal complex is resolved, under the pressure of penis envy, by identification with her mother. The girl hopes that if she imitates Mother, she can have a husband like Father when she grows up.

THE STORY OF OEDIPUS

When a baby was born to King Laius of Thebes and his wife Jocasta, the oracle of Delphi told the king that he would be killed by his son. In order to avert this terrible prophecy Laius bound the baby's feet and ordered him abandoned on a lonely mountain, certain that within a very short time, the baby would die.

But his servant took pity on the baby and gave him to Polybus, King of Corinth, who named him Oedipus, "wounded feet," and adopted him as a son. When Oedipus grew up he left his house in Corinth because of a terrible prophecy from the oracle in Delphi. Once, again, the oracle prophesied that Oedipus was doomed to kill his father, and, the oracle added, marry his mother. Oedipus thought he could escape his cruel fate by abandoning his home and going into exile.

During his wandering, Oedipus met his real father at a crossroad. Laius, who had four companions with him, tried to push Oedipus off the road and hit him with a staff. In his anger Oedipus attacked Laius and his companions and killed them. Only one man remained alive to carry the news to Thebes. The man, too embarrassed to tell the truth, told the people of Thebes that their king was killed by a band of robbers. The people did not try to verify the story because they were preoccupied with a disaster that had befallen their city. The Sphinx, a monster in the form of a winged lion with a woman's face and breasts, stood at the entrance to the city and asked passers-by a riddle. The person who answered the riddle correctly would be allowed to continue. The person who did not,

In his early writings, Freud termed the Oedipus conflict in girls the *Electra complex*. In Greek tragedy, Electra loved her father and convinced her brother to kill their mother who had betrayed their father and caused his death. It is important to note, however, that with the intellectual honesty characteristic of him, Freud admitted that he didn't understand the psychosexual development of women with the same clarity that he understood the psychosexual development of men.

Women psychoanalysts, such as Karen Horney (1922, 1967), indeed criticized the Freudian conception of female sexuality and argue that as women experiment with sexuality, they have a positive, rather than an inferior experience of loss. Horney also argues that women do not envy the

would die. No one had been able to answer the riddle and the monster had devoured them all. The city was under siege and famine was closing in.

Then Oedipus, the wise and the brave, arrived in Thebes and offered to solve Sphinx's riddle. "What creature walks on four in the morning, on two at noon, and on three at night?" asked the Sphinx. "A man does," answered Oedipus. "As a baby he crawls on four, as an adult he walks on two feet, and in his old age he leans on a cane." This was the correct answer, and on hearing it, the Sphinx killed itself; the people of Thebes were set free. Seeing Oedipus as their savior, they offered him the throne. Oedipus gladly accepted, married the widow of the slain King Laius, and became the king of Thebes.

Years later, when Oedipus and Jocasta's two children were grown, Thebes was hit by a devastating plague. Oedipus sent a messenger to Delphi with an urgent plea to Apollo to come to their rescue. The messenger came back with the announcement that the plague would be over only after King Laius' assassin was punished. Oedipus started searching far and wide for the king's murderer, only to discover to his great horror that he himself was the man, and that King Laius was his own father. When the horrible truth that he had killed his father and married his mother was revealed to Oedipus, he blinded himself and left Thebes for a life of exile. His mother/wife killed herself.

After many years of wandering in exile, Oedipus came to terms with his cruel fate, understanding that while he was not at fault, he was still responsible for his actions.

glorious penis, but rather, the societal power that having a penis in a patriarchal society represents. We will get back to this criticism in the last section of this chapter when we evaluate Freud's theory.

Resolution of the Oedipal conflict is necessary before the boy can develop a masculine gender identity by identifying with his father, and before the girl can develop her concommitant feminine gender identity. Resolving the Oedipal conflict is also necessary for both boy and girl to be able to detach themselves from their first love object and "displace" it as adults, in other words, to fall in love with other people.

Freud described two processes that interfere with this normal development, fixation and regression. *Fixation* occurs when development is halted temporarily or permanently. A child who becomes fixated at an early stage of development continues in adulthood to derive the gratification characterized by that early stage. Gratification from smoking or overeating as an adult, for example, may suggest an oral fixation. Fixation can result from too much or too little gratification of a need.

Regression means a retreat to an earlier stage of development. A young married woman who has difficulties with her husband, may return to the security of her parents' home. Regression is usually determined by earlier fixation, that is, a person tends to regress to the stage of previous fixation.

When boys and girls do not pass through the Oedipal stage successfully, they remain fixated at this stage and cannot detach themselves from their infantile love object. When they grow up, such men remain in love with their mothers and are incapable of loving fully other women. In my clinical practice I have seen quite a few men like this. Typically, he gets married and declares that he loves his wife who, invariably, is a "wonderful mother." But for some "inexplicable reason," he is not attracted to her sexually. He is, however, very attracted sexually to all other women. But he never loves any of them. His love is reserved for the mother who is the wife. This type of split has been termed the *whore/Madonna complex.*[2]

Other men with unresolved Oedipal complexes are attracted to many women and fall in love easily, each time convinced that, this time, they have found the perfect woman they have been looking for. But shortly afterwards, they discover that this one, too, is not the one, the one for whom they will continue to search but never quite find.

Women who fail to resolve their Oedipal conflicts remain in love with their fathers. There are amongst them those, like Anna Freud, who remain attached to their fathers all their lives and never marry[3] (see Figure 10). Others marry men whom they view as inferior to their father and thus deserving only of cold criticism. Women with an Oedipal fixation tend to be non-responsive sexually. The sexual problems these women have, as well as the sexual problems men with a whore/Madonna complex have, can be explained by the operation of the incest taboo. Since the husband or wife psychologically represents a parent, he or she is forbidden sexually.

Even when the Oedipal fixation is less severe, its influence is clearly evident. For example, a young man falls in love with older women who represent his mother, or a young woman falls in love with older men who represent fatherly love or authority.

The oral, anal, and phallic stages are collectively called the *pre-genital* stages. They are narcissistic and autoerotic, meaning, the child obtains gratification of the sexual drive from the stimulation and manipulation of his or her own body.

The fourth stage is a prolonged *latency* period. These are the quiet years between age five and adolescence, in which the sexual impulses are held in a state of repression. The child's love for the parent of the opposite sex is forgotten and the sexual drive is latent, thus this stage's name. The child starts school and the libido is directed to new interests and new people. A screen of forgetfulness covers the experiences of early childhood.

During adolescence and the fifth, *genital*, stage, the focus is again on the genitals, but now some of the narcissistic love of the pre-genital stages becomes channeled into other love choices. The adolescent begins to love others and is sexually attracted to people outside the family. Yet the love objects of the Oedipal stage influence the love choices of adolescence. The old family love objects get

FIGURE 10. Sigmund Freud and his daughter, Anna (1913). Anna Freud, a well-known psychoanalyst and the author of *The Ego and the Mechanisms of Defense,* continued the work of her admired father but never married.

renewed *libidinal cathexes*, or libidinal energy, invested with powerful emotional energies. But since they now arouse the incest taboo, they have to remain unconscious. From this age on, the adolescence's task is to differentiate from the parents and become a separate and autonomous individual.

For a boy this means displacing the libidinal cathexes to mother and substituting for her a woman outside the family. For a girl it means displacing the libidinal cathexes to father and substituting for him a man outside the family. Finding a love object is in fact *re-finding* it. The infantile desire for the parent is displaced by a desire for a sexual partner.

Even after reaching adulthood and sexual maturity, the love of a son for his mother and the love of a daughter for her father have the greatest influence on their choices of a person to love and marry. But it is not the only influence. Despite the importance of the parental love, it is not the only kind of love a child experiences. Other childhood influences enable people to develop more than one sexual preference.

Freud believed that all people are inherently bisexual, each sex being attracted to members of his or her own sex as well as to members of the opposite sex. This is the constitutional basis for homosexuality. In most people, socialization and evolutionary forces keep the homosexual drive latent. Freud saw proof of restraining social forces by pointing out that in those cultures that permit it, homosexuality is chosen by a significant number of people.

Despite the strength of homosexual attraction, evidenced by the deep emotional friendships adolescent boys and girls form with members of their own sex, Freud believed that the childhood experiences of both sexes directed them toward heterosexual attraction. For men, childhood memories of Mother's love and nurturing have a powerful effect that directs them to choose women as love objects. In addition, the infantile experience of competing with Father, who prevented them from expressing their sexuality toward Mother, helps divert their attraction away from members of their own sex.

The operation of these two forces can be seen in women as well. Since the sexual behavior of young girls is harshly criticized and penalized by their mothers, or at least it was in Freud's time, women develop hostility toward members of their own sex. This attitude helps direct them to the choice of men as love objects. In addition, competition with other women prevents them from being sexually attracted to them.

Nevertheless, Freud saw in the different sexual "deviations" and "perversions" a common and universal phenomenon, which testifies to the many different ways the human sexual drive seeks gratification. What is considered normal sexual response is the result of such restraining and directing forces as shame, disgust, pity, and the moral and legal norms that society enforces.

In other words, civilization controls and shapes the development and free expression of human sexuality. The sexual behavior we consider normal is an expression of these restraining societal forces. Freud was convinced that from the study of sexual deviations and perversions, it is possible to learn about the origins and development of normal human sexuality.

Let me summarize the key points in Freud's theory of romantic love. All of these points can be deduced from the preceding discussion.

- Romantic love is a socially accepted expression of the sexual drive, the libido, which includes both physical and emotional components.
- All people are inherently bisexual, each sex is attracted to members of its own sex as well as to members of the opposite sex. In most people, the homosexual drive remains latent as a result of socialization.
- The sexual drive, the libido of the person in love, directs the sexual and sublimated activity toward gratification.
- Romantic love and what seems to us the non-sexual love children feel toward their parents have the same roots. Adult romantic love is actually the equivalent of infantile love.
- The romantic and sexual experiences of adult men and women are related to early infantile experiences that take place during the Oedipal stage.
- The libido of adult men and women is displaced to people who are similar in some significant ways to their love objects during the Oedipal stage. For a man, this means a woman who resembles in some significant way his mother, for a woman, a man who resembles her father.
- The adult seeks a lover who represents an internal picture of his or her first love object—the male or female parent. This internal, infantile picture can be very different from the way the parent really is.
- When a person falls in love, he or she is reuniting with the first love object.

- Because the parental relationships of young children so strongly influence their adult, intimate relationships, it is understandable that a childhood disruption in the connection with the parent can have serious consequences for their adult sex lives and love lives.

If we accept Freud's contention that both son and daughter try to find in a romantic partner the love object on whom their libidos fixated in the Oedipal stage, and if we accept that the first object of a child's love and sexuality is a parent, then it is reasonable to ask, why don't adults choose their parents as love objects? The answer, according to Freud, is the incest taboo that is genetically imprinted. The incest taboo defends against sexual attraction to people who are family members and develops naturally toward people with whom we grow up. This is an important point. It explains, for example, why adults can be sexually attracted to their children—they didn't grow up with them—while children are not attracted sexually to their parents, despite what Freud thought. Beginning with adolescence, in which sexual maturity takes place and the Oedipal attraction toward the parent of the opposite sex is first re-enacted, the incest taboo teaches the individual to displace the libido in favor of love objects outside the family. But these new adult love objects always resemble or represent, in some important way, the first infantile love object.

In addition to *displacement*, Freud suggests yet another way in which we divert a forbidden love choice into one that is socially accepted—*sublimation*. As an example, he presents Leonardo da Vinci's paintings of the Madonna. These paintings, Freud argues, are a sublimated expression of Leonardo's longing for intimacy with his mother from whom he had been separated at a very young age (1910).

IDEALIZATION OF THE BELOVED IN ROMANTIC LOVE

Freud wrote, "The popular mind has from time immemorial paid homage" to the hypothesis that falling in love is akin to "intoxication" (Freud, 1917, 482). He admits freely that "we know nothing" about the "chemistry" of "sexual desire." He could not even decide whether we are to assume the existence of one or "two sexual substances which would then be named male and female."

Sexual arousal directs the sexual activity of the person in love and pushes for gratification and release of the accumulated sexual tension. The sexual drive is expressed in intense desire that is one of the most notable characteristics of falling in love. The sexual, physical, and instinctual drive receives in romantic love a pure emotional expression which renders it socially acceptable.

When we are in love, we tend to idealize our beloved. We see wonderful qualities, which may or may not be there, and are blind to faults that may be glaringly obvious to others. Freud called this love blindness "sexual overvaluation." In his article *On Narcissism* (1914), Freud described the tendency to idealize when in love as evidence of the flow of "libidinal narcissism" from the self to the beloved. The beloved becomes a substitute for an "ego ideal." Ego ideal is part of the "super ego" that includes traits and values the parents approved and rewarded. The person in love *projects* his or her ego ideal onto the beloved. The traits and values that are present in this part of one's super ego, values and traits the individual hopes to acquire and views as supreme, are projected onto the beloved and perceived as existing in the beloved.

Freud distinguished between two forms of romantic love: *narcissistic love,* or self-love; and *anaclitic love,* the love of a person who resembles a parent. In self-love the person falls in love with a "narcissistic object" that can be similar to oneself, similar to someone one would like to be, or had been, or someone who was part of oneself. An "anaclictic object" can be similar to the woman who fed and nurtured the child, Mother, or to the man who protected the child, Father. In some cases of narcissistic love the beloved becomes a substitute for an unachievable ego ideal. The admiration of the beloved enables the gratification of a "narcissistic need" for self-love. In extreme cases the "perfect" love object completely takes over the "modest and sacrificing" ego. In such cases the individual surrenders completely to the adored tyrant, the beloved.

Freud believed that falling in love with a person who resembles a parent, the anaclictic love object, is evidence of mature adult love, whereas the choice of someone who resembles oneself, a narcissistic object, is evidence of an infantile and regressive wish that should be overcome. In making the shift from narcissistic love to anaclictic love, the person changes from romantic love as the reflection in the beloved of one's own ego ideal, to loving the other for what the other really is. In mature love the person is enriched by internalizing the positive traits and ideals of an admired partner. These internalized values and traits become *introjects*, parts of the person's psyche, that help expand and enrich it.

It is interesting to note in this regard the *Michelangelo Phenomenon*—the partner as a sculptor of the ideal self (Drigonas et al., 1997). A paragraph from Lynn Sharon Schwartz's book *Rough Strife* explains this name:

> She thought often about Michelangelo's statues that they had seen years ago in Florence, in the first excitement of their love, figures hidden in block of stone, uncovered only by the artist's chipping away the excess, the superficial blur, till smooth and spare, the ideal shape was revealed. She and Ivan were hammer and chisel to each other.

The *Michelangelo Phenomenon* is a mutual pattern in which both partners sculpt each other in a way that moves each one of them closer to his or her ego ideal. Four different studies documented the existence of the phenomenon in romantic love relationships. These studies also showed that the presence of the phenomenon, when partners feel that they bring each other closer to each other's ideal, is related to feelings of satisfaction and vitality in the relationship (Drigonas et al., 1997).

EVALUATION OF FREUD'S THEORY OF ROMANTIC LOVE

Freud's theory made an important contribution to our understanding of the unconscious processes involved in falling in love. Later psychoanalytic thinkers, building on Freud's concepts, view the earliest experiences in a child's life as more important for the choice of a love object than the experiences in the Oedipal stage. Others object to the great emphasis Freud put on the child's sexual drive in the development of personality, and see primarily Mother, but also Father, as responsible for the romantic choice of both men and women. In addition, there are theorists as well as researchers who object to Freud's assumption that it is possible to learn about the normal and universal development of children from the phenomena and processes seen in adult pathologies. Some researchers went on to demonstrate that castration anxiety and penis envy are rare, not universal experiences that every child undergoes (Nathan, 1981). Other researchers showed that, when asked to determine a person's sex, children at the Oedipal stage pay more attention to hair length and clothes than to genitals.

The most consistent criticism of Freud's theory, however, came from the ranks of women psychoanalysts, including his students and followers, who criticized his ideas on female sexuality. These women analysts believed

Freud conceptualized as he did because he was a man and lived in the Victorian era. One of earliest and most prominent of those critics was Karen Horney (1922; 1967).

Horney perceived her ideas as falling within the framework of Freud's theory and wanted to correct the fallacies in his thinking about women's psychology, as well as other issues. She objected to Freud's idea that penis envy is the determining factor in the psychology of women. Horney believed, instead, that female psychology is based on lack of confidence and an overemphasis on love relationships, and has little to do with the anatomy of female sex organs. Unlike Freud, Horney believed that the transition girls made from Mother to Father as a love object arose from their attraction to the opposite sex, an attraction that has its roots in feminine sexuality.

Based on her observations of children, Horney contended that feminine sexuality is a primal experience that appears at an early age, and leads the girl to a unique sexual identity that is rooted in an awareness of her unique and preferred anatomy. She saw proof for this in girls' seductive behavior and enjoyment of dressing up. In other words, the attraction of a girl to her father is first and foremost an expression of her early feminine sexuality, and not a compensation for disappointment or for penis envy.

As for envy, Horney agreed that women envy men, not for their phallus however, but for the many rights and privileges that this organ entitles them to in a patriarchal society. She believed that the penis envy of girls results from the restrictions and prohibitions imposed on their ability to satisfy their sexual drives during the pre-Oedipal period, such as the strong prohibition against masturbation.

In her psychoanalytic work with men, Horney saw evidence for the existence of *womb envy*, men's envy of women's ability to give birth, parallel to women's penis envy. The tendency of men to underestimate women, to devalue them, and to express low opinions and disregard for them, was seen by Horney as rooted in their envy of a woman's ability to get pregnant, give birth, and nurse. In men's castration anxiety, she saw a fear of women. In men's strong need to be successful and conquer, she saw evidence of their overcompensation for this unconscious feeling of inferiority. This masculine need for power has been seen by many feminists as the psychological basis of patriarchy.

Postmodern feminist psychoanalysts argue with every idea suggested by Freud including his "anatomy is destiny" axiom. Here, for example, is Virginia Goldner:

Freud began with the so-called anatomical difference, a social distinction that fixated on the genitals, from which he derived, in what is now a suspect sequence, the normative dominance of homosexuality and the dichotomous, complementary division of gender into the polarity male/female . . . In this narrative of development, the genitals determine sexuality, which in turn, determines gender identity . . . Now, every term in that sentence has been disrupted by doubt (1998).

Despite these and other criticisms, there is no doubt that Freudian theory makes an important contribution to our understanding of the unconscious processes involved in falling in love. The most important conclusion we can derive from his theory is that *it is not by chance that we fall in love with a particular person*; we fall in love with careful, even if unconscious, consideration. Our romantic choices, even if we are not fully aware of them, are influenced by childhood experiences. And these childhood experiences are different for boys and for girls.

SUGGESTIONS FOR THOSE SEEKING LOVE

People who have a sense that there is something wrong with their romantic relationships, or the type of a person with whom they fall in love with over and over again, may want to consider the possibility that the cause of the problem is primarily in them, or more specifically in their romantic choices. This does not mean that the problems are their fault. After all, the original causes for their romantic choices are encored in early childhood experiences beyond their control. But, for this very reason, the problems are also not the fault of their partners.

Problems in romantic relationships are often related to people's romantic choices, even if these choices are unconscious, and therefore they are responsible for them. King Oedipus understood at the end of his life that although killing his father and marrying his mother were not his fault, still, he was responsible for his actions. We, too, need to take responsibility for our romantic choices even if they are not our fault. Taking responsibility is always a recommended strategy, because it is far more likely to bring about positive change than is blaming the partner. Once people decipher their romantic attraction codes, they can choose to follow the same scripts or alter them.

Freud's theory suggests one approach. Try to find similarities between your romantic partner and your opposite sex parent. When you make a list of all the notable characteristics—physical, emotional, behavioral, and mental—of your parent and compare it to a list of your romantic partner's characteristics, are there similarities between them? What does this say about you?

10

THE INTERNAL ROMANTIC IMAGE

This is why a man leaves his father and mother and is
united with is wife, and they become one.
  —Genesis

We will be happy together, drink deep, and lose
  ourselves in love.
My lover is mine and I am his.
  —*The Song of Songs,* Old Testament

"*I think he is like my father in the good ways, like he's very hard working, he's honest, he's on time, he's trustworthy. But he is also very affectionate that my father is not. He is very affectionate and my mother is very
affectionate. He cares a lot about me and supports me like my mother. He's
got a lot of my mom's qualities.*"

"*She is a good combination of both of my parents rolled into one. She
can be very compassionate, very loving, very tender, very understanding,
always smothering you with love and just patting you all the time like my
mother. Then like my dad she's got her really set ideas. You cannot make
her change her mind on some things.*"

"*I need to feel special and feel that the person I'm with is dedicated to
me. Actions speak louder than words proving that someone is dedicated to
me. With my dad, he always told me he loved me but he surely didn't act
it. With [my boyfriend] it's similar in that he tells it to me but things don't
add up to prove it to me. I question it because of the way he acts. With
both of them I hear it but it doesn't add up. Also it's easy for me to get into
the position of "you've hurt me," or "I'm being hurt." It's almost as if I'm
looking for it. Some day they'll realize what they've done to me. With my
parents I didn't talk about how I felt. I was afraid of conflict. I didn't
want to deal with the tension in my family. I still have a hard time defin-
ing my feelings and expressing them. When I was little I didn't let myself
feel things so I couldn't name them. I didn't have practice in saying what I*

feel and I can still see myself doing that."

"She's kind of similar to my dad in that she's as stubborn as hell. But she's a genuinely nice person and in that she's like my mom."

Is your romantic relationship similar to the relationship you had with your parents when you were growing up? The majority of the young men and women who were asked this question, 70 percent, responded affirmatively.[1] In some cases, people described a similarity in terms of the quality of the relationship. "The similarity between my relationship with him and with my parents is in the suffocating love." "[I have] the same sense of not quite living up to someone's expectations." In other cases, the young people described a similarity in the individual's appearance, personality, or behavior. "He is similar to my father in the way he's built, tall and skinny." "My mother is passive and he is passive." "She can be nice like my mother, and when she gets angry she gives me 'the look' that my mother used to give me."

It is not surprising that people who described an adult romantic relationship as similar to a childhood relationship with their parents were also likely to note a similarity between a partner and a parent. What is surprising is that noting this similarity has a positive impact on intimate relationships. The more similarity people saw between a childhood relationship with their parents and an adult romantic relationship, the more likely they were to describe themselves as feeling secure in the relationship, to be themselves in the relationship, to have fewer conflicts and to handle well the conflicts that came up.[2]

Clinical experience, mine as well as others', suggests that the childhood relationships with parents have a much a greater influence on people's adult romantic relationships than even these data, based on people's subjective perceptions, might suggest. One of the important revelations for couples in therapy is just how powerful and profound the connection is between their childhood relationships with their parents and their romantic relationship with each other. The discovery of this kind of a connection is helpful in getting people to understand qualities they may have had difficulty comprehending and accepting about each other and about their intimate relationships. Examples are presented in the next chapter in which four people describe their childhood stories and their adult romantic relationships. What becomes very clear when reading those stories is the lack of people's awareness of the obvious effect their childhood experiences have on their romantic relationships.

When I conduct an in-depth examination of a couple's relationship in therapy, I most often discover that the romantic choices are based to a large extent on the internal romantic images of both partners. The previous two chapters dealt with readiness for love and similarity between the romantic partner and the parent of the opposite sex. In the present chapter we will see how these subjects relate to the internal romantic image.

Falling in love is a powerful emotional experience. The dominant component in it is the feeling of togetherness, of bonding, of being like one. "My lover is mine and I am his" says the woman in the biblical *Song of Songs* and her words are echoed in love songs of all ages. Lovers feel as if their ego boundaries have melted away as they blend into one entity. In many respects it is possible to see in this melting-into-one a return to the primal symbiotic bond with mother. Both partners feel that all their emotional needs are totally satisfied, the way they were in their infantile Garden of Eden. Even the bible tells us that this is as it should be. "This is why a man leaves his father and mother and is united with his wife, and they become one" (Genesis, 2: 22). Man needs to leave his mother and father, and become an independent individual, before he can be united with, and have a truly intimate relationship with, his wife. We choose very carefully the person with whom we fall in love. Our main guide in making this choice is an internal, largely unconscious, romantic image.

We develop our internal romantic images very early. As we saw in the previous two chapters, the romantic image is based on powerful emotional experiences children have in their first years of life. Mother and Father, and anyone else who played a significant role during the childhood years, influence the development of the internal romantic image in two primary ways:

- by the way they expressed, or did not express, love toward the child. "My dad, he always told me he loved me but he surely didn't act it. With [my boyfriend] it's similar in that he tells it to me but things don't add up."
- by the way they expressed, or did not express, love toward each other. "Something in my relationship with him reminded me of the way my mother treated my father: A lot of patience, a lot of listening."

While Freud emphasized the role that the parent of the opposite sex plays in falling in love, in fact, the internal romantic image appears to be quite broad. It encompasses a reenactment of the positive and negative elements of both parents, their relationship, and the relationship each of them had with the child. As we will see, while the sex of the parent has an effect, unresolved issues with either parent have far greater impact.

There are several theories that explain how this reenactment happens. Amongst them are evolutionary theory that emphasizes the role of "imprinting"; Jungian theory that emphasizes the role of certain "archetypes"; and object relations theory that emphasizes the role of internal "objects," our relationships to them and to the people they represent. In the following pages, we will discuss these theories with an eye to how each contributes to the understanding of the central topic of this chapter: the influence of childhood experiences on the internal romantic image and, through it, on the experience of falling in love.

HOW WE CHOOSE WITH WHOM TO FALL IN LOVE ACCORDING TO OBJECT RELATIONS THEORY

More than the other theories, *Object Relations Theory* addresses falling in love. The word "object" conjures up an image of something inanimate. But the meaning of the word in object relations theory is very different. The *object* is an internal representation of a person, a thing, a relationship, or an event that has become part of an individual's psyche. The hungry baby has no internal picture of Mother and so it cries. Once Mother is "internalized," the baby can handle her temporary absence. Her internalized image says she will come back. In adults, the internalized mother object includes both a concrete representation of their own mothers, the way she was in different stages of their lives, and an abstract image that is influenced by cultural stereotypes and mythologies of motherhood.

The screen that filters objects is dictated by age, genetics, and past experiences. A baby perceives Mother differently than a person of fifty does. All internalized images are stored in the psyche simultaneously. This is why people are surprised when they notice how old and feeble their mothers or fathers look in old age. The new images contradict their childhood images of the parent as young and powerful.

Object relations theorists assume that our inner world consists of objects and *object relations*—our internal perception of the relationships between different objects. The relationships between romantic partners, as well as all other intimate relationships, are always "object relations."

One of the most prominent among object relations theorists is Margaret Mahler.[3] As noted in the detailed discussion of her work in chapter eight, Mahler (1974) believes that a newborn human infant has no personality.

Rather, the personality results from a developmental process she termed "psychological birth." The experience of *oneness* with mother, during the first symbiotic stage of the baby's development, is the building block for the ability to form romantic love relationships. Psychological birth happens in stages between the ages of six months and three years. When the child passes these stages successfully the result is "the first level of self-identity." The process of "separation-individuation" continues throughout life and is notable especially in adolescence, marriage, and parenthood. A person who passes through this process successfully is a person with a *differentiated* personality capable of stable love relationships. In other words, in order to be able to truly love and be intimate with another person, rather than some reflection of ourselves in that person, we need to be *individuated.* We all struggle to achieve a balance between a need to be part of something larger than ourselves—a couple—and a need to be separate, a struggle between togetherness and individuation (Blatt & Blass, 1996).

The "level of differentiation" that partners can achieve from their families of origin has a critical influence on the quality of their relationship. Actually, it can be said that if the early dyadic experience with mother is loving and warm, "the first, and perhaps essential step toward a good marriage will have been taken" (Dicks, 1967).

The Roots Of Obsessive Love

What happens when the initial bond with mother is not warm and loving? When the behavior of a parent is perceived by a child as rejection, abandonment, or persecution, the child cannot give up or change the "frustrating object" that is the parent. The child deals with the frustration by internalizing parts of the loved/hated parent and attempting to control the parent in his or her inner world. The frustrating object undergoes various "splits" that are repressed and remain as unconscious *introjects* that become part of the individual's personality structure (Givelber, 1990).

The introjects include both the remainders of infantile needs and the parent's response to these needs. The ego develops and gets organized around these introjects in different ways. The ego may develop a sense of inferiority and worthlessness, which reflects the baby's helplessness, as well as a sense of grandiosity and omnipotence that reflects the baby's perception of the parent's omnipotence. The self develops around these unconscious introjects and both their extremes can be found in it. When we see in the arrogant and snobbish behavior of a person, evidence for the presence of an introject of a grandiose self, we can safely assume that we are also going to find an introject of an insecure and inferior self that was repressed. When we see a person who always feels taken advantage of and abused, we can be sure that in addition to the introject of a victim, we are also going to find a hostile, aggressive, and destructive introject that has been repressed.

In most cases the individual is only aware of one part of this duality; in the last case, the individual is likely to be aware of the victimized self and unaware of the hostile aggressive self. In the familiar example of the paranoid, the introject of the persecuted victim controls the internal organization of the self, whereas the denied and repressed introject of the aggressive persecutor is projected onto other people. People with whom the individual has a relationship are perceived as fitting those unconscious introjects of aggressive, abandoning, or persecuting. In other words, the people a person comes in contact with are perceived and understood in the light of the person's internal world of objects and object relations.

Falling in love is an unconscious choice of a partner who fits a repressed, *split-off part* of the self (Dicks, 1967). Once the partner expresses, or is perceived as expressing, that repressed part in the self, there is no need to admit its existence in the self. A woman who feels unlovable, because she felt unlovable as a child, is likely to choose a man who does not show love. This way she can blame him for her bad feelings about herself. A man who feels inferior, because he felt that way as a child, is likely to choose a critical and judgmental woman. This way he can blame her for his feelings of inferiority. While the woman will continue to complain that her husband doesn't show her love and the man will continue to complain about his wife's cruel criticism, both are likely to remain with their partners. The reason? It is far easier to be with a partner who provides an external justification for your bad feelings about yourself than to confront those feelings directly in yourself. Furthermore, when partners are undifferentiated as a result of traumatic experiences of rejection, abandonment, or persecution in their childhoods, their feelings toward these suppressed and denied parts in themselves are especially negative or ambivalent. Because the need to deny the existence of these repressed parts is especially strong, so is the need to find a partner who will express them.

When they discover that part in a potential partner, they fall "madly in love." Their love may appear to others excessive, destructive, or even crazy, but it makes perfect sense given their unconscious needs. After having fallen in love, they unconsciously encourage their partners to express these repressed and denied parts. This enables them to criticize and try to control these split-off parts in their partners, not in themselves.

When both partners of a couple are differentiated and reasonably integrated people, their personality differences are perceived as complementary, valuable, and enjoyable. The slightly compulsive husband in such a couple may enjoy the spontaneity and impulsiveness of his wife, whereas the wife values her husband's attention to detail and careful planning.

Among the interviewees whose remarks appeared at the opening to this chapter, there was a listless and sad-faced man who said that he fell in love with his girlfriend because "she is full of joy, sure of herself, attractive. She is one of those people who always makes me happy when I see her. She is one of those optimistic people who always smiles." A slow-speaking and slow-moving woman said she fell in love with her boyfriend because he was "dynamic."

Contrary to the familiar dictum that in order to be able to love others we first need to love ourselves, psychoanalyst Theodore Reik observed that the more negative our self-perception, the more likely we are to fall in love. People sense something lacking in themselves and seek the missing quality or qualities in a mate. When they fall in love, writes Reik, they project onto the beloved their unfulfilled fantasies (1964).

The projection of split-off parts of the self, *split-off projection*, happens in both partners, with each partner trying to express denied and repressed parts through the partner. For example, a woman who has internalized traumatic, childhood experiences of violent conflict between a victim and an abuser, sees herself as a victim. She has split the two parts of the conflict, repressed the violent abuser part, and projected it onto her partner. The internalized conflict, in this case between abuse and victimization, becomes an ongoing conflict between the partners. The split self becomes a split couple. The woman needs a hostile and aggressive man in order to project onto him the unconscious and primitive, violent, repressed, split-off part of herself. The internalized conflict pushes her to find a partner who can fill that need, to the shock and dismay of her family and friends who cannot understand what a sweet and gentle woman finds in an aggressive and hostile brute. The answer is simple. She finds in him her split-off part.

Her lover has also internalized a violent conflict from childhood between an abuser and a victim. However, in his case the part that was split-off and repressed is the part of the victim. In his relationship with her he can experience this part and deal with it. In this way, undifferentiated partners import troubled early object relations into their romantic relationships (Dicks, 1967).

Since projection represents a primitive unconscious need, the individual who is projecting often "doesn't see" behaviors that do not fit the projection. Consequently, the woman is likely to see the man's behavior as hostile and aggressive even when it is not. Similarly, the man is likely to see the woman as a victim even when she is not.

As this example demonstrates, partners tend to have the same internalized conflicts and, in a mutual process, project onto each other the complementary, unconscious, and suppressed split-off parts of themselves. Furthermore, each partner identifies with the parts the other partner projects onto him or her. The result is a dynamic called *projective identification*.[4]

Projective identification is probably object relations theory's most important contribution to the understanding of falling-in-love and a couple's dynamic. The man, whose wife projects onto him her aggressive, powerful, parental, authoritative split-off part, internalizes this projection, identifies with it, and sees himself as his wife sees him. Similarly, the woman identifies with, and sees herself as, her husband's projection of his victimized, weak, infantile, and powerless split-off part. In this way, internal, unconscious conflicts in each partner become externalized as patterns of conflict in the couple. Stated differently, a couple's conflicts are a reenactment of internal conflicts in each one of the partners. The less integrated couples are, the more infantile their needs and the more intense their conflicts.

When two people fall in love, they project onto each other their split-off and repressed parts. A woman who learned to deny her urge for autonomy and independence projects it onto her husband. This causes him to appear even more independent than he really is. A man who learned to deny his dependence and need for intimacy projects them onto his wife who then seems even more needy and dependent than she really is. Projective identification makes both of them identify with the respective projections. In most cases, all we see is a traditional marriage in which the man and the woman are playing their so-called natural gender roles very comfortably. In a number of cases, however, these stereotyped sex roles can be rather costly for one or both of the partners. An example is a woman who as a result of such projective identification loses her ability to judge what is happening around her, especially her husband's behavior. Another example is a dominant husband who acts as if his wishes and needs ought to be the single most important basis for what his wife does (Low, 1990).

A similar process explains why certain women fall in love and stay with men who abuse them. Many of these women, says psychoanalyst and family therapist Virginia Goldner (1998a), grew up with the message that being loved and lovable is contingent upon feminine self-abnegation, so they split-off and disavow their "masculine" power and their rage. Such a woman tends to fall in love with the boy-man whose mix of vulnerability and masculine posturing is enormously gratifying to them. Being needed and adored by this "wounded soldier" creates the illusion of a new beginning that can completely overshadow the abuse that eventually explodes. The abusive man splits off and disavows his "feminine" vulnerable victimized self. Together such couples tie a Gordian knot around each other's hearts in a closed system of object addiction.

Family therapist Murray Bowen (1978) contends that people tend to fall in love with romantic partners at similar levels of differentiation but opposing defensive, or character, styles. *Defensive styles* are patterns of behavior that protect the self from awareness of anxiety; members of couples tend to compliment each other's styles. Let us take, for example, a man who copes with the anxiety of being flooded with emotions by suppressing his feelings. Bowen's theory predicts that this man would be attracted to women at similar levels of differentiation but whose defense mechanisms are the opposite of his—that is, women with hysterical tendencies to dramatize and excessively express emotions. A woman who deals with her anxieties by becoming phobic is likely to be attracted to men who defend against their anxieties by denying them and engaging in daredevil sports and adventures.

The different defensive or character styles mask the underlying similarity. Thus, one partner may appear dependent and the other quite independent, one active the other passive, one rational the other emotional. There are common patterns to couples' complementary defensive styles. The most common complementary patterns, according to Mittelman's pioneering work (1944), are:

- One of the partners in the couple is dominant and aggressive, the other is submissive and masochistic.
- One of the partners is emotionally distant, the other needs affection.
- One of the partners is helpless and needs to be taken care of, the other is omnipotent.
- Both partners are in a continuous and hostile struggle for control.

Despite the ubiquity of certain patterns, every couple relationship has a unique emotional pattern that is based on the interplay between conscious and unconscious, internalized, repressed, and projected parts of both partners.

When romantic partners are differentiated, the intimacy between them happens without the loss of individuality. These couples feel very close to each other and encourage each other's personal growth. This is almost impossible when partners are undifferentiated. When a couple's level of differentiation is low, every effort to develop an independent identity by one of the partners is perceived as a threat to the relationship. Partners respond by feeling hurt and either attack or withdraw; emotional flooding is frequent and communication is poor. The lack of security from an undifferentiated identity prevents the partners in such a couple from taking responsibility for their feelings of insecurity and inadequacy. Instead, they tend to blame each other in the utter conviction that if only the partner were different the feelings of insecurity, inadequacy, and pain would be relieved (Meissner, 1978).

Since undifferentiated partners are trying to satisfy unconscious infantile needs and frustrations through a partner who cannot possibly satisfy them, the inevitable result is hurt, despair, disappointment, frustration, hostility, and endless conflicts. A pattern of angry, frustrated, hurt love develops when neither one of the partners is willing to give in. A hostile life and death dependence develops. Every conflict, even the most trivial, is escalated and imbued with great significance. These couples say that they love each other desperately, that they can't live without each other, but they also can't live with the pain they cause each other.

A failure of differentiation can also result in an inability to disconnect from the family of origin and has serious consequences for romantic love relationships. Because the sense of a separate and independent self is missing, all the emotional energy is focused on the family. This can be expressed in an invisible loyalty to the family; a "ledger of unpaid debts" binds the individual to the parents, so that a full investment in the partner is perceived as a disloyalty to the family (Boszormeny-Nagy & Ulrich, 1980). For example, a man can feel compelled to visit his mother every day, call her several times a day, and eat at her house, despite the protests of his wife. The fact that the wife complains but stays with him suggests that her level of differentiation is similar to his, but probably manifests itself by completely severing contact with her family of origin. In other words, she has a good reason, even if unconscious, to stay with him.

Another example of a failure in the process of differentiation is an individual who feels like the "deprived child" in the family of origin. This person expects romantic partners to compensate for all childhood injuries and deprivations and provide the love that was not given as a child. It is clear to see that this person is in fact "collecting from the wrong source," trying to settle a childhood debt within the romantic relationship (Boszormeny-Nagy and Ulrich, 1980). Such a "deprived child" is likely to fall in love with a person who sees him- or herself as a "a kind and nurturing parent."

The level of differentiation in a couple reflects, of course, the level of differentiation in the childhood relationships of both partners. When the level of differentiation is low, both partners bring with them to the relationship problematic object relations that carry over from their childhoods. An undifferentiated man is likely to attract and be attracted to similarly undifferentiated women. He creates, with all the women with whom he falls in love, relationships that are characterized by the same conflicts and stresses that he had with his mother as a child.

Problematic internalized objects, *pathogenic introjects,* can result from relationships with both parents and the relationship between them. For example, a woman who as a child witnessed her father's infidelity and her mother's pain and helpless rage, internalizes both the role of the "betrayed victim" and the role of the "unfaithful villain." As an adult, both these introjects play a significant role in her romantic relationships. She can play one role in one relationship, the other role in another relationship, or, play both in a relationship and never notice the paradox between being unfaithful to her partner and having jealous tantrums at his suspected infidelities.

Pathogenic introjects and unconscious motivations help explain behaviors that are otherwise difficult to understand—such as why people fall in love with romantic partners who seem so inappropriate for them. The reason? The partner represents a repressed part of the self. Or why a person stays with a partner who makes life an apparent living nightmare. The reason? It is easier to blame the suffering on the partner than to look inside and touch the pain. Both these concepts help explain obsessive loves in which a romantic partner becomes a drug for an individual's addiction. Such obsessive love relationships generate an intensity of feeling and a seeming irrationality in the romantic choice. Despite tremendous pain, rage, disappointment, and never-ending conflicts, the lovers insist that they are madly in love with each other and seem unable to let go of the relationship.

In summary, according to object relations theory:

- People actively, albeit unconsciously, create their romantic relationships. Childhood experiences, especially those of deprivation, rejection, and abandonment, exert the greatest influence on the choice of a romantic partner. The explanation is linear: childhood experiences are reenacted in adult love relationships.

- A couple's relationships are "object relations" that are most powerfully influenced by the childhood relationships both partners had with their parents. Falling in love does not happen by chance. People choose a person who fits an internalized "object" and "object relation." The reason? Only such a person can help them re-enact childhood experiences and gratify needs that were not satisfied in their childhood. When they find such a person, they experience tremendous excitement, joy, and hope—and fall in love.

- The unconscious needs of couples reflect the introjects of both partners and tend to complement each other. Couples collude in gratifying these unconscious, complementary, psychological needs by creating such unwritten contracts as: "I will express your anxiety if you will keep me calm"; and, "I will think for you, if you will express my emotions."

- The ability to love and function successfully in a romantic love relationship reflects an individual's level of differentiation, which depends on childhood love experiences. When the childhood relationships with the parents were warm and loving, the person will become a differentiated individual capable of mature and satisfying love relationships. When the childhood relationships with the parents were frustrating or injurious, the person will grow up with a low level of differentiation capable only of immature love relationships. Relationships in which both partners are undifferentiated tend to arouse very powerful emotions, both positive and negative, and be experienced as obsessive love.

- People tend to fall in love with partners who are in a level of differentiation similar to their own, but whose defensive style is opposite—abuser and victim, sadist and masochist. When a certain conflict or pathology is found in one of the partners, it can be assumed that it is also found in the other.

Criticism of Object Relations Theory and the contribution of Heinz Kohut

A number of theorists have criticized object relations theory for positing an ideal of autonomy, differentiation, and individuation, and suggest instead, the importance of affiliation and connectedness for a healthy development and ability to love (e.g., Klein, 1976; Josselson, 1992).

Self-psychologist Heinz Kohut (1977) also believes that people's self-esteem and well-being are derived from and embedded in relationships. The need for the affirming echo of the mother's approval is never outgrown, says Kohut, but transferred to a lover. Kohut views falling in love as a state in which the beloved is a perfect, primal "self-object" and gratifies completely the lover's narcissistic needs. At the beginning of life, parents are experienced as parts of the self, or "self-objects." Once the child's empathy and identification needs are satisfied, the child gradually experiences the parents and other people as separate. If these basic needs are not satisfied, other people will always remain self-objects, viewed as parts of the self. For this kind of person, someone new triggers no curiosity about who that person is and what is special and unique about him or her. Rather, what effect will that person have on one's self image? The idealization of the beloved fills the desperate need for experiencing oneself as part of an admired self-object. All the traits of power, wisdom, and beauty that the person feels lacking in him- or herself are attributed to the beloved. Merging with the beloved provides security and peace. The merging that couples in love experience results from their being self-objects for each other (Kohut, 1971).

HOW WE CHOOSE WITH WHOM TO FALL IN LOVE ACCORDING TO JUNGIAN THEORY

> I seem to have loved you in numberless forms,
>   numberless times,
> In life after life, in age after age forever . . .
> Today it is heaped at your feet, it has found its end
>   in you,
> The love of all man's days both past and forever:
> Universal joy, universal sorrow, universal life,
> The memories of all loves merging with this one love
>   of ours—
> And songs of every poet past and forever.
> —Rabindranath Tagore, *Unending Love*

Carl Gustav Jung was a brilliant Swiss psychiatrist that Freud considered for many years his successor. Their relationship cooled and eventually terminated when Jung rejected key concepts in Freud's theory. While Freud believed that human behavior is conditioned by biological drives and personal history, Jung (1964) believed that it is conditioned by both individual and racial history, goals, and aspirations. In the human psyche, Jung saw not a drive to satisfy biological needs but a constant development in the search for wholeness. And unlike Freud, Jung saw in the individual's personality the product and container of all ancestral history, shaped and molded into its present form by the cumulative experiences of all past generations.

Based on his vast knowledge of mysticism, religion, mythology, anthropology, and the classics, Jung formulated his ideas of a *collective unconscious* that is deeper and more powerful than the personal unconscious. While the individual unconscious houses the impulses and experiences of the individual, the collective unconscious houses the memories and experiences of the entire human race extending far back into its dim and unknown origins. These memories and experiences have been transferred from one generation to the next from the dawn of history. It is possible to learn about them from the appearance of similar images or symbols in different cultures. Jung called these images *archetypes*.

Archetypes are universal "thought forms" common to all human beings. The archetypes are based on the collective experience of all of humankind and are expressed as the universal symbols of myths, rituals, visions, works of art, and dreams. Archetypes can be human, such as the "earth mother" or "the old wise man"; they can be places, such as the perfect home in which we would have liked to have lived, or the perfect place, such as the Garden of Eden, in which humans lived in the past; or states of being, such as the archetype of "perfection," the image of the perfect life. All of us share innate archetypes of birth, rebirth, death, God, the demon, unity, energy, the hero, the child, as well as an archetype of a mother and an archetype of a father. These last two archetypes are universal symbols. Jung believed that our relationships with our actual mother and father are formed on the basis of these innate archetypes.

Jung emphasized some archetypes more than others because, among other reasons, he saw evidence for their existence in his clinical work. He believed that these archetypes evolve into separate systems within the personality. One of them is the "shadow," the most powerful and dangerous archetype, which includes the most primitive and bestial instincts. This is the "dark side" in ourselves, which we don't like, or were taught to hide. The shadow is also the source of creativity, vitality, and spontaneity.

Among the most important archetypes in Jung's theory are the *anima* and the *animus*. Jung believed that the psyche is androgynous and includes complementary masculine and feminine elements. In the psyche of every man there exists an inner woman, the *anima*, and in the psyche of every woman there exists an inner man, the *animus*. The combination and integration of the masculine and the feminine elements serve the adaptation and survival needs of the human race, both because of the roles they play in the development of the individual and because they enable romantic love, communication, and understanding between the sexes.

The *animus*, Latin for the male psyche, is the personification of the masculine archetype, "the masculine principle" in the female unconscious. Jung believed that all women hid a latent masculine personality beneath their conscious feminine personality. The animus is the product of the universal experience of women with men. By living with men throughout the ages, women have developed an internal "masculine voice." The animus expresses such masculine traits as power, ambition, initiative, courage, objectivity, and wisdom; it propels the woman toward a dedication to a "sacred mission." The internal voice of the animus is forceful, persistent, and, at times, cold and distant. It is a voice that emphasizes the ability to be assertive and to control people and situations.

The positive animus helps a woman build "a bridge to the self" through creative work and activities in the outside world. The positive animus is represented in legends and folk tales by Prince Charming who comes riding in shining armor on a white horse and rescues the beautiful maiden from a terrible danger. The animus is seen in different stages of development in the muscle man, such as Tarzan, the romantic hero, such as the British poet Shelley, the man of action, such as Ernest Hemingway, or the spiritual guide, such as Mahatma Gandhi.

The negative animus, represented by death, pushes a woman to abandon her human ties, especially those with men. A famous negative animus figure is the murderous and seductive Bluebeard. As the story goes, the rich and mysterious Count Bluebeard marries a young innocent woman and brings her to his castle. The castle is full of treasures and Bluebeard assures his wife that they are all hers. One day he tells her that he has to leave for a few days. He brings a giant key ring that holds the keys to all the rooms and closets in the castle. He tells his wife that she can use all the keys except for one little key. She is not to use this key under any circumstance. His young wife cannot withstand the temptation, and her curiosity drives her to try and find the door opened by the forbidden key. Only after a long and extensive search does she find the lock in a door to a room hidden in the castle's basement. Her heart pounding, she opens the secret door with the little key and discovers the murdered bodies of Bluebeard's former wives.

The animus causes women to manifest masculine traits and acts as a collective image that motivates women to respond to and understand men. A woman can truly comprehend the nature of a man by virtue of her animus. But she can also misunderstand him if she projects her animus onto a man without regard for his real personality. Well-adjusted women are able to make a distinction and compromise between the demands of their collective unconscious as represented in their animus, and the reality of the external world as represented by the real man of a romantic relationship.

The *anima*, Latin for the female psyche, is the personification of the feminine archetype, "the feminine principle," the feminine psychological tendencies in the male unconscious. It is the latent feminine personality hidden underneath the conscious masculine personality and very different from it. The anima is the product of all the universal experiences of men with women. By living with women throughout the ages, men have developed an internal "feminine voice." It expresses itself through feelings and moods, intuitions about future occurrences, sensitivities to nature and the irrational, and the ability to love. It propels men to connect with people and especially with women.

The positive anima is sometimes represented in folk tales and fairy tales by the beautiful princess who needs a brave hero to rescue her; at other times, in legends of a spiritual, glowing, female figure who helps the hero on his dangerous journey by lighting the road ahead of him.

The negative anima is represented by witches and dark sorceresses—the dangerous all-knowing priestesses—who connect with the "spirit world" and the "forces of darkness" that represent the dark side of the unconscious. The negative anima is also represented by dangerous and evil beauties that tempt men to their death, such as the sirens of Greek mythology, or the Lorelei of ancient German mythology, beautiful female water creatures whose enchanting voices seduced and drew sailors into the deadly waves. (See an artist's portrayal of the Lorelei in Figure 11.)

The anima causes men to manifest feminine traits and it acts as a collective image that motivates men to respond to and understand women. A man can truly comprehend the nature of a woman by virtue of his anima. And, it is possible to get to know a man's anima by the type of women he falls in love with. But a man can also misunderstand women if he projects his anima onto them without regard for their true personalities. Well-adjusted men, just like well-adjusted women, are capable of compromising the demands of their collective unconscious, represented by their anima, with the demands of the real woman in a romantic relationship.

The anima and the animus can be positive or negative, problematic or wonderful. The feminine side can correct a one-sided masculinity in a man and make him softer, more sensitive, and more communicative. Similarly, the masculine side can correct a one-sided femininity in a woman and make her more assertive, self-expressive, and active.

Jung's notion that the anima and the animus are archetypes and part of the collective unconscious helps explain a curious phenomenon that neither object relations theory nor evolutionary theory can account for—the fact that there are some men and women that many people fall madly in love with. These are people who represent archetypal masculinity and femininity. Two famous examples of such anima figures are Marilyn Monroe, the sexy woman, and Greta Garbo, the mystery woman.

Since the anima and the animus are archetypes, they can be similar in different people. But since they are also part of the unconscious of an individual, they appear in dreams in the symbolic expression that is appropriate for that individual. Jung believed that a man's anima is shaped by his mother and a woman's animus is shaped by her father. The anima and the animus play central roles in the life of the individual and the survival of the human race because of their influence on falling in love. Every man carries in him the eternal image of a woman, not a particular woman but a defined feminine image that is fundamentally unconscious; so too, for the woman

FIGURE 11. *The Lorelei.* The beautiful Lorelei seduce men to their deaths with their sweet singing.

and her innate image of a man. Since the image is unconscious, it is always unconsciously projected onto the beloved and is one of the primary reasons for romantic attraction.

When a man meets a woman who reminds him in some significant way of his anima, his response is immediate and powerful. He projects onto her his unconscious image and then he no longer sees the real woman, the way she is, but only his projection. If, as is often the case, this man reminds the woman in some significant way of her animus, she too projects onto him her unconscious image. This mutual projection is experienced by both of them as falling in love.

If the anima helps men find an appropriate romantic partner, what about homosexual men? Well, it has been suggested that the anima figure for homosexual men can be a male rather than a female figure (Hopcke, 1992). And, it can similarly be argued, the animus figure for lesbian women can be a female rather than a male figure.

When a man's anima is projected onto a certain woman, or man, this person is perceived as possessing the traits of his anima. The perceived presence of these anima traits in the woman causes the man to fall in love with her with complete certainty that "she is the one"—the ideal woman he has been looking and longing for.

Since the anima is part of a man's psyche, even if an unconscious part, finding a woman who resembles his anima makes him feel as if he has known her, intimately, all his life. And in a sense he has known her all his life through the image that is engraved in his psyche. He falls in love with her so totally and so helplessly that it appears sheer madness to the people around him. In men who are lacking psychological awareness, projection onto a woman is the only way they ever come to know their anima. Women who are introverted, "mysterious," and "like fairies," tend to attract such anima projections more than other types of women do. Men find that they can project almost anything, weave endless fantasies around creatures so fascinating in their vagueness and mystery. This scenario is equally fitting for a woman in search of her internal image of a man.

HOW WE CHOOSE WITH WHOM TO FALL IN LOVE ACCORDING TO EVOLUTIONARY THEORY

Just like Jungian theory and object relations theory, evolutionary theory assumes that early childhood experiences of love play a critical role in adult romantic relationships. The key concept, however, that explains the reenactment of childhood's love bonds in adult romantic relationships is not "archetypes," or "object relations," but *positive imprints*.

According to evolutionary theory, humans develop according to a program constantly exposed to environmental influences. There are "critical periods" in which environmental forces can shape and mold us. This molding process is termed *imprinting*. Imprinting happens very fast during a critical period in the life of the young of every species, causes neural changes in the brain, and is probably irreversible. It has significant long-term effects on behavior. Every new stimulus, in order to give it meaning and significance, is compared to the pattern that already exists in the brain.

Concepts such as love are created in the brain in a network of neural wiring. Once a concept is imprinted in the brain, we continue to use it in order to make sense of the world around us. Ada Lumpert (1997) gives a most appropriate example of the effect of the childhood experience of maternal love on adult romantic attraction. The first love is imprinted on the brain of a child, writes Lumpert, and is engraved on it for better or for worse for the rest of life. A boy who grew up with a cold and hostile mother has such a pattern of love relationships imprinted on his brain. When he grows up and becomes a gifted and good-looking young man, he enjoys the advances of many young women, and can choose the most attractive and sweetest amongst them. But, instead, he chooses the meanest and coldest. When his best friend asks him why he has done such a stupid thing, our young man has an interesting answer: "I know she's cold and mean-spirited, but only with her do I feel a spark." And he knows what he says. The mean-hearted woman is the one to whom his brain imprintings respond. The response of brain cells is electric, this is why they generate a spark. A kind-hearted, sweet girl cannot spark any of his "romantic love" imprintings; this is why he does not find such a girl attractive.

When the young man marries his mean and cold sweetheart, other imprintings are sparked in his brain. His hostile and cold mother hurt, humiliated, and angered him as a child. As a result, brain imprintings of love, humiliation, pain, and anger are combined, and all of them come to life when sparked in his adult relationships. Later in the couple's relationship, many old imprintings are likely to reappear and be enforced on the realities of the couple's life. She may say something as insignificant as "Do you mind taking out the garbage?" and he will respond with rage, pain, and humiliation, "You are always sending me out with the garbage. This is all I am for you, a garbage disposal." He was first attracted to the landscape of his childhood, but later, that very same landscape brings up his childhood pain.

Childhood experiences are imprinted on our brains and become the familiar worlds that we seek to recapture for the rest our lives. These are the positive imprints that childhood landscapes, smells, tastes, and people we grew up with leave engraved on our brains. Such positive imprints also direct attraction. Every element of physical shape, color, personality, behavior, and attitude can become imprinted and, in adulthood, desired. This, claims Lumpert, is the reason for the high frequency of romantic partners who remind us in some important way of our parents, whether in their features, personality traits, or abilities.

A mechanism similar to positive imprinting is *lovemapping* that sex researcher John Money (1986) talks about. A *lovemap*, according to Money, is a mental map, a template, replete with brain circuitry, that determines the people with whom you will fall in love and what arouses you sexually. Children develop these love maps between ages five and eight, or even earlier, in response to their parents, family, friends, and life experiences. As children grow up, their unconscious maps create subliminal templates of the image of the ideal lover including details about physiognomy, build, and color, not to mention temperament and manners. Lovemaps include the kinds of places people find sexually arousing as well as the kinds of interactions and erotic activities most exciting to them. Since most people are surrounded during their childhoods by members of their biological family, it is only natural that, as adults, they will be attracted to people who are similar to their families.

If the greater the similarity, the greater the romantic attraction, why aren't we attracted to our family members? The answer evolutionary theorists offer is the same as the answer provided by Freud to the same question, namely the incest taboo. Incestual mating would have decreased the genetic variability that is necessary in order to assure new solutions for problems and challenges the human race might face in the future. The universality of the incest taboo, which exists in some form in all human societies, suggests to evolutionary scientists that it must be the result of natural selection and is well encoded in our genetic makeup. While the attraction to the similar is aided by positive imprinting, the avoidance, and repulsion, of the too-similar is guaranteed by "negative imprinting." Negative imprinting guarantees that we will not be sexually attracted to people we grew up with. Such people are negatively imprinted in our brain and don't arouse our passion. It cancels the effect of the attraction to the similar and prevents sexual attraction towards parents and siblings.

An example of the operation of such a negative imprinting is described in the doctoral dissertation of Joseph Shefer (1971). In his research, Shefer examined marriage records of 2,679 Israeli Kibbutz members. Out of all these married couples, only 14 had grown up together in the same Kibbutz. Out of those 14, only 5 couples had lived together in the "children's home" before they were six years old. But even among those five couples, not even one couple had spent all first six years of life together. Shefer explained this phenomenon as the extension of the incest taboo. Kibbutz children who spend their early years together, develop toward their "potty siblings" a negative imprinting of the kind children develop towards parents and biological siblings. As a result of the combined effect of these two mechanisms—positive imprinting and negative imprinting—we tend to fall in love with someone who is similar to us but is not a member of our immediate family.

THE PHYSIOLOGY OF FALLING IN LOVE

Once we identify someone as the "right person," a certain chemical process is activated. Anthropologist Helen Fisher (1992) says that the chemistry of falling in love starts in a tiny molecule with a very long name—Phenylethylamine—or PEA for short.[5] The PEA molecule, a natural amphetamine produced in the brain, is responsible for feelings of excitement, joy, ecstasy, and delight. When the amount of PEA in the brain neurons goes up, it produces a feeling of excitement and emotional uplift. This is the chemical reason why couples in love can spend whole nights making love and having deep heart-to-heart talks, why they tend to be absent-minded, and why they feel so sexually aroused and so optimistic, full of life and vitality.

Fisher also emphasizes the role of brain wiring in early childhood and the special effect of smell in lovemaps. Every person's smell is a little different, says Fisher, and each one of us has a "personal smell signature." A baby identifies Mother by her smell. Smells cause a reaction in the part of the brain that controls strong emotions and stores long-term memories. This is why we can remember smells many years after having smelled them. Because of this brain connection, smells can arouse powerful emotions including erotic feelings.

During adolescence, glands located under the arms, around the nipples, and in the sex organs start exuding a smell that attracts the opposite sex. When people meet someone whose smell they enjoy, the smell arouses a passion that enhances their romantic attraction. When the smell, the lovemap, and other conditions, such as the right amount of similarity, challenge, and mystery, happen simultaneously, the chemical reaction involving the PEA molecule takes place in the brain and is experienced as falling in love.

The well-known work of brain researcher Paul MacLean (1973) enables the identification of the physical location of the lovemap in the brain. MacLean distinguishes among "three brains," or more accurately, among three layers in the human brain:

The brain stem—the most primitive part of the human brain, a part that humans share with reptiles. It is responsible for instinctive behaviors such as aggression, territoriality, self-defense, rituals, including mating rituals, and reproduction. This brain layer is also responsible for automatic physical activity including breathing, sleep, and blood flow.

The limbic system—the layer that surrounds the brainstem and is shared by humans and primates. This brain layer is responsible for strong emotions including rage, fear, happiness, sadness, disgust, hatred, and passionate love.

The cortex—the newest brain layer to evolve, covers the limbic system, and is unique to humans. This brain is responsible for cognitive functioning. It is conscious, awake, rational, and in contact with the environment and with reality. It enables us to make decisions, think, plan, respond, and create. It is the brain layer that helps us find logic, order, and causality in things, the part of us we call "I".

According to this analysis it is clear, as Helen Fisher also notes, that *the emotional ecstasy of falling in love happens in the limbic system.* While Paul MacLean points to the physical location where falling in love happens and Helen Fisher points to the chemical changes in the brain that are responsible for the experience of falling in love, John Money's lovemaps explain why we fall in love with a particular person.

In summary, whether we are talking about a "love object" of the object relations theorists, or an "archetype" of the Jungian theorists, an "imprint" or a "lovemap" of the evolutionary theorists, it seems clear that we are discussing the same thing—*an internal romantic image* that plays a key role in the choice of a person with whom we fall in love.

THE INTERNAL ROMANTIC IMAGE AND FALLING IN LOVE

My beautiful love as yet unknown
you are living and breathing
somewhere far away or perhaps quite close to me,
but still I know nothing
of the threads that form the fabric of your life

or the pattern which makes your face distinctive.
My beautiful love as yet unknown,
I would like you to think of me tonight
as I am thinking of you –
not in a golden dream that is far from the real self,
but as I really am, a living person
that cannot be invented without distorting the truth.
    —Michel Quoist,
      My beautiful love as yet unknown

Lovers: the one whom you seek
is with you
Search within and without,
He is with you.
    —Shah Nimattuffah,
      The One Whom You Seek Is With You

While most clinical theories emphasize the role of the negative and unconscious elements, when people talk about their romantic relationships, they tend to emphasize the positive aspects of the romantic image. Many of these positive aspects are conscious and direct us to find a romantic partner with whom we can replicate the positive aspects of our childhood relationships with our parents.

> *"The similarity is in the safety. The fact that the person is always there for you with open arms."*
> *"I try to make him fatherly toward me. I made him spoil me like my dad did. He's like my dad in being vulnerable and trusting people. But he can also be like my mom in opening up to people and being warm and loving."*
> *"The really high communication, the high verbal factor is similar. It was real warm, real close. We didn't hide it from anyone. The way I interacted with her is similar to my parents."*
> *"He's very similar to my mother, caring, intelligent, that's probably the reason why we got along so well. I'm closer to my mother than to my father and he's more like her."*
> *"They [husband and parents] are all dependable and they all accept me the way I am."*
> *"Many of the words I would use to describe our relationship are also*

words I would use to describe my relationship with my mother: full of laughter, fun, mutually respectful, honest, secure. . . . I see the way my mother treated me as an ideal. Honesty, trust, independence, my mother gave me those things, and in all my good relationships these things are present."

While the positive aspects of our romantic models help us reenact the good parts of our childhood relationships with our parents, the negative aspects direct us to find a partner who can compensate us for negative, early-childhood experiences and things we wanted but did not get:

"He is similar to my father in his love and concern for me, but he is not stingy like my father, he spoils me more. And he listens to everything I have to say without screening like my father does. He is similar to my mother in his concern for me, but he doesn't tell me what to do like she does. He only suggests things."

"I felt totally comfortable with her. I never felt totally open with my parents. I was more open with her."

"We understand each other much more and he's more interested in understanding me. He doesn't disapprove or approve whereas they do."

"He's the same odd mix of emotion and rational thinking, but I think he's more sensitive and tuned to people than my father ever was, very attuned. When he listens you're the most important person in the room."

At times the relationship with the parent was rejecting or abusive. This, of course, has a major effect on the choice of a romantic partner.

"He was physically scary. There was a great deal of aggression in him, which is similar to the way my father was when I was a girl. No self control."

"One negative pattern that I've got is trying to provoke him to get really angry. Because he is really calm and diplomatic and doesn't fly off the handle, but I can make him crazy. And I find that I do it. It's also a pattern that I had with my dad. A sense of relief that I get from seeing him get so angry."

"She would tell me to do stuff in a similar way to the way my mother told me to do things. I wanted someone to dominate me. I wanted someone who will unconditionally love me. For some reason I thought that my mother didn't."

"Having a difficulty being open because I don't want to hurt anyone, and feeling like the Mom, the one who needs to nurture even if it causes me harm. I'm afraid of anger and rejection. I felt those things growing up."

While our romantic images are influenced by the positive and the negative traits of our parents and other important people in our childhoods, there is a significant difference between the impact of the positive and the impact of the negative traits. Sadly, or luckily, which is the way I choose to see it, negative traits have a greater influence on our romantic image. The reason is not, as some psychologists believe, that we choose to marry our worst nightmares, but that with these traits we are far more likely to have unresolved issues. The person who fits our romantic image is the person who can best help us resolve this unresolved issue. This is why we choose to fall in love with people who share the negative traits of our parents (Hendrix, 1992).

In the example of a woman whose father was unfaithful to her mother, while reason will direct her to find a man whose fidelity she can trust, in most cases, she is far more likely to choose a Don Juan like her father. Not because she wants to repeat her childhood trauma, but because only a man like her father can give her what she didn't get from her father—the fidelity of a Don Juan. The paradox is that this woman chooses to fall in love and marry a Don Juan because he is similar to her father, but what she wants more than anything is for him to treat her, and only her, differently than her father. She wants her husband, a sexy and attractive man who loves women and is always surrounded by adoring women, to be a faithful and loving husband. Only a faithful Don Juan can give her the security that her mother did not get as a wife, and that she, because of her identification with her mother, did not get as a child. Even if she can't satisfy this unconscious need, because her Don Juan husband is unfaithful, the adult repetition of her childhood trauma with the greater sense of control of herself and her life, many times, has a healing effect.

At other times a romantic image can dictate the choice of a romantic partner who is the exact opposite of a parent with whom the person has an unresolved issue. A man who as a child witnessed the unfaithfulness of his mother can choose to fall in love with a woman whose most notable trait is her fidelity. He can then either enjoy this fidelity and the security it provides directly or else be pathologically jealous and, without any basis, accuse her of being unfaithful. Her repeated declarations and proofs of fidelity can help heal his childhood wound. They prove to him again and again that contrary to his cuckolded father, his wife is faithful (Pines, 1998).

We are attracted to people who fit our romantic images in some significant way. The fit can be in personality, in appearance, in social background, or in behavior. When we meet such a person we project onto him or her our romantic image. If our beloved projects onto us his or her romantic image, and both of us identify with the projection, the mutual projection and identification is experienced as falling in love. This is why when couples fall in love they feel that they have known each other their entire lives.

Because the person with whom we fall in love plays such an important role in the dynamics of our psychological lives, the discovery of such a person is a very powerful experience. When people are in love and their love is reciprocated, it generates a feeling of complete and total happiness. They are convinced that this perfect love will last forever and they will never again feel loneliness, pain, or sorrow. Love paints everything pink and gives life a sense of meaning (Pines, 1997).

SUGGESTIONS FOR PEOPLE SEEKING LOVE

The romantic image explains how people choose with whom to fall in love. How can you bring your unconscious romantic image to a conscious level? The easiest way is by looking at the projection of your romantic image onto the people with whom you were in love in the past. These people represent your love objects, your anima or animus, your imprinting, and your lovemap. Take time for the wonderful task of remembering—with as much detail and clarity as possible—each and every one of the people with whom you have ever been passionately in love. Make a list of their most endearing traits—physical, emotional, behavioral—the traits that made you fall in love with them. Are there traits that several of your beloveds share? Are there traits that your beloveds share with one or both of your parents? These shared traits represent your romantic image. If you have had hundreds of falling-in-love experiences and none of the people with whom you were in love showed any similarity to each other or the people who were significant in your childhood, it may mean that you are falling in love with falling-in-love more than with a particular person.

If your past love experiences have been frustrating, and you decide that you don't like the prescription of your romantic image, you have two main options. One is to avoid people to whom you are attracted and choose instead people with whom you are comfortable, people who can be close and trusted friends, but never bring you to either the height of passion or the depth of despair. The other option, rather than assuming that your problematic past relationships were bad accidents, is to take responsibility for your romantic choices, analyze your romantic image, and try to turn it from a script for disaster into an opportunity for growth. People who choose this option will find suggestions for how to undertake this difficult and exciting task in the last chapter.

FOUR STORIES

Asleep on my bed, night after night
I dreamed of the one I love . . .
As soon as I . . . found him
I held him and wouldn't let him go
Until I took him to my mother's house,
To the room where I was born.
    —*Song of Songs,* Old Testament

After reading various quoted remarks throughout the book, the reader may feel a certain curiosity about the man or woman speaking or the particular relationships they describe. In this chapter, I hope to satisfy a portion of this curiosity. The first ten chapters of this book used the remarks from different interviews to demonstrate aspects of falling in love. In this chapter, in the manner of a clinical interview, we will learn the backgrounds and romantic relationships of four of the people interviewed.

Out of all the participants in my clinical studies, 93 Americans and 87 Israelis, I chose the following four interviews for in-depth analysis. Two, a man and a woman, were chosen because they received the highest score possible for the levels of intimacy they described in their romantic relationships. At age twenty-three they were either married or about to get married to someone with whom they were very much in love, someone they described as a best friend, with whom they had had a long-term, deep, intimate, and highly satisfying relationship. The other two, also a man and a woman, were chosen because they received the lowest possible score in the same category. At age twenty-three, neither has had an intimate relationship.

These four young people's romantic relationships will be described, preceded by descriptions of their childhood relationships with their parents. Let me emphasize that, before analyzing their romantic relationships, I did not know anything about their childhood experiences; I learned about them *after* I had chosen the four interviewees from their very different experiences in intimate relationships. It is amazing to see in these four case studies just how powerful the influence of childhood experiences is on romantic attraction, and how unaware of it people are.

Each story begins with a description of the childhood relationship the person had with his or her mother and father and proceeds to describe the person's most significant intimate relationship. At the end of each story a table displays a numerical analysis of the romantic relationship.[1]

JILL

Jill was an only child and a very loved child. As long as she can remember, she felt very close to her mother. Mother used to take her with her everywhere she went, and Jill had a hard time separating from her even for a short time. She was a little less close to her father who was very busy with his work, but her relationship with him was also very loving and physically expressive. Father was very interested in what Jill thought and gave her a feeling that her opinion was important to him.

Jill's father was better in his parental role than in his role as a breadwinner. He used to kiss Jill a lot and tell her often that he loved her. She used to sit on his lap when he watched television and loved it when he would tell funny, amusing stories. But her father had a hard time keeping a steady job and her mother, who carried everything on her shoulders, often lost her temper. She almost always had a good reason, but still felt terrible afterwards. She and Jill would talk about it at great length. Because of their financial difficulties, Jill and her parents lived in a one-bedroom apartment, enclosed in their own little world.

The most traumatic experience of Jill's childhood was a temporary sense of abandonment when she was about four years old. Jill and her parents drove to visit relatives many miles away. After the long and exhausting drive, Jill's father carried his fast-asleep daughter from the car to the relatives' guest room in their home. Convinced that Jill would never wake up in her state of exhaustion, her parents went out with their relatives to a nearby café. When they returned after about an hour, they found Jill in the middle of the living room screaming, almost paralyzed with fear and exhaustion.

Other experiences, that could have been traumatic, such as falling off a swing and breaking her arm, cutting her forehead, or having one of her many severe ear infections, were not that traumatic for Jill because her mother was always there, nurturing, assuring, and comforting. When she was sick, her parents let her stay home; her mother would make soup and let her watch television. One time, when Jill was humiliated in school and was certain she would never be able to show her face there again, her mother assured her that by the next day no one would remember. And she was right! Jill thought that was amazing—how did her mother know?

While Jill is very aware of the many benefits she had as an only child in terms of the respect she received from her parents as well as the love and attention showered on her, she is also aware of the price she paid. The price was being alone a lot and having to grow up too fast. She thinks it would have been wonderful if she had had a brother or a sister. As an only child Jill had to deal with adults and adult issues when she felt she was still supposed to be a child and behave like a child. Since her parents couldn't afford baby sitters they took her with them everywhere they went. She saw the games adults play, their dishonesties, and it made her cynical about them.

When she was young, Jill was sure she was very different from her parents, but every day as a young adult, she notices more of the similarities between herself and them. "We are so similar," she says, "I am half my father and half my mother. There's no doubt about that."

What kind of a romantic relationship is a young woman who was the apple of her parents' eyes likely to develop? Well, Jill is married and describes herself as very close to her husband. "He's definitely my best friend. I've never been that close to someone. It sounds so corny, but it's true. I never have a feeling with him that I can't say something. He always knows how I mean something and I know exactly what he means. We argue sometimes, but we are really in sync. We know what the other person thinks before he even says it." (This last comment is a sign of a symbiotic relationship.)

When they first met, Jill thought her husband was "a jerk". The second time they actually talked, she thought she'd like to go out with him, but didn't think it was going to last because, since he came from a small town, she thought he wanted to play around and be wild. But she discovered that she was wrong. When asked what attracted her she says, "Physically I was attracted to him. He had sort of a carefree attitude. He was fresh, not jaded." When they first started spending time together, they would apologize: "Is it okay if I come over?" Then it avalanched into spending every moment together. In the last two years they have been "inseparable."

Jill describes her marriage as close, secure, loving, inspirational, and constantly growing. "I am not worrying about what I'm saying," she explains. "This aspect of my life is totally taken care of, so I can take care of other aspects of my life without worrying about it. We love each other very much and we show it often. Through being together, being able to have this support system, we can be more creative and explore other aspects. It gives more options. I feel able to try new things, and to change, and to grow spiritually, sexually, mentally."

Despite the obvious similarity between the close, secure, and loving relationship Jill has with her husband and the close, secure and loving childhood relationship she had with her parents, when she is asked about it, she doesn't see the similarity. "I don't know. . . . We understand each other much more and he is more interested in understanding me. [Like father?] He doesn't disapprove or approve, whereas they do. He doesn't let me get away with as much as they do. I have a tendency to like to have things my way. They would indulge me. He confronts me on this. [Like mother?]" As for similarity, Jill notes "being close and being incredibly honest with each other. We agree on the basic things. We have the same values."

What are likely to be the areas of conflict in the marriage of a woman who thought that her father was "useless as a breadwinner"? The answer, "He's not as ambitious as I am, and I don't understand this. So we made this deal. I go to school full-time and he works, and after I graduate, he goes to school and I support him. We argue about that a lot. We have an argument and then go into a pep talk. I hate it. I hate arguing. But I think it's healthy." It is clear that not only the content of the fights Jill has with her husband—why aren't you ambitious?—but their pattern —first fight, then reconcile through talking—is similar to the fights between Jill's parents and her fights with her mother.

And what is the approach to separation of a woman who was "very close" to her mother, who had a difficult time being away from her even for a very short time, and for whom a one-hour "abandonment" was the most traumatic childhood experience? It turns out that Jill and her husband have never been apart for longer than a day since they got married. "If we were, I'm sure we'd be on the phone all the time. For short periods it's okay because we are both very busy, but we have withdrawal symptoms."

Jill is an example of a secure attachment style. In her highly intimate, somewhat symbiotic, relationship with her husband, Jill reenacts her childhood highly intimate, somewhat symbiotic relationship with her mother. The equality, security, respect, and total openness of her marital relationship is also similar to her childhood relationships with her parents. In addition to replicating the emotional tone of her relationship with her parents, Jill replicates their unresolved issue—a dominant, explosive, woman and a loving non-ambitious man.

AN ANALYSIS OF JILL'S ROMANTIC RELATIONSHIP

Dating frequency: 4 (average number of dates)

Number of significant intimate relationships: 1 (the relationship with the husband)

Length of this relationship: 30 months

Commitment to the relationship: 7 (happily married)

Sense of security in the relationship: 7 (very high, feels totally secure)

Ability to be oneself in the relationship: 7 (definitely yes, can be totally herself)

Intimacy in the relationship: 7 (very high, symbiosis, know what each other thinks)

Power in the relationship: 4 (both partners have equal power)

Pursuer/Distancer: 4 (both partners have equal involvement in the relationship)

Physical attraction to partner: 5 (physical attraction mentioned)

Friendship before romance: 3 (knew each other a little beforehand)

Stereotyped sex roles: 2 (sex role stereotypes are not mentioned and are not an issue)

Frequency of conflicts: 4 (fighting some times)

Ability to deal with conflicts: 6 (talking about everything and trying to resolve)

How are conflicts resolved: talking

Ability to stand separation: 3 (suffers withdrawal symptoms)

Jealousy is a problem in the relationship: 2 (jealousy was not mentioned at all)

Jealousy is a personal problem: 2 (jealousy was not mentioned at all)

Arousal played a role in the initial attraction: no

Propinquity played a role in the initial attraction: no

Similarity played a role in the initial attraction: yes

Partner's attraction played a role in the initial attraction: no

Physical attraction played a role in the initial attraction: yes

Personality traits of the partner played a role in the initial attraction: yes

Status of partner played a role in the initial attraction: no
Is/was partner satisfying an important need? yes
Is the partner described as the "best friend"? yes
Was it love at first sight? no
Is the interviewee showing psychological understanding? yes
Is partner similar to father? yes
Is partner similar to mother? yes
Is partner different from father? yes
Is partner different from mother: yes
Are the relationships with partner and parents similar? yes, both are close
    and honest
Number of children: none
Sexual preference: heterosexual
Abuse in the relationship: definitely not

STEVE

Steve was also an only child. His parents divorced when he was a baby
and he hardly ever saw his father. His mother had different boyfriends
throughout his childhood; some of them lived with her. But neither she
nor they were adequate as parents, so Steve spent most of his time at his
grandparents' house. As a child he thought his mother was his sister. She
would come for visits, stay for a while, and then leave. It was only when
he started going to school that Steve moved in with her. He discovered
that she could be demanding, moody, cruel, and had a very unconven-
tional circle of friends, some of them drug dealers, who were involved in
crazy and scary things. Steve was sure that his mother never did things
the way other people did them. She always tried to evade the system
even if it meant cheating and lying. She didn't like working and preferred to stay at home and do nothing. She seemed incapable of taking
care of things. Often she was out of the house, leaving Steve alone, mis-
erable, and terrified. Knowing how cruel and vindictive she could be, he
was terrified of being caught in the crossfire between some of the shady
characters she knew.

In comparison to the difficult and complex relationship Steve had
with his mother, his relationship with his grandparents was wonderful.
In their house he had a taste of normal life. His grandfather took him

fishing and took him to amusement parks and bowling. After he moved to his mother's place, Steve would often wake himself before sunrise, get dressed, and sneak out of the house. He wanted to get to his grandparents' house, have breakfast with them, and see his grandfather work.

While Steve's father abandoned him, and his mother's boyfriends terrified him, his grandfather was a positive and significant masculine figure in Steve's life. He was wise and knowledgeable, caring and strong. No one would ever tell him what to do except grandmother. He once got a loud obnoxious person to shut up just by going over and asking him very calmly to please be quiet. His size had a lot to do with it. Steve's grandfather was a very big man, big hands, big arms. Even people who were eager to get into a fight calmed down quickly when they saw him approach.

Steve's grandfather was always doing something, always busy with some project. He loved repairing things, building things with his hands. And he was a very caring person. He took care of his own mother even though she was never much of a mother to him. Probably identifying with Steve's plight, his grandfather took good care of Steve as a child. He gave Steve everything he wanted: an electric train, bicycles, trips. Christmas was wonderful because Steve would get a ton of gifts. He loved sitting and watching sport programs with his grandfather. At night Steve would sneak out of bed and get into bed with his grandfather and grandmother. Grandmother was the one who took care of the kind of things his mother ignored. She took care of Steve's needs, cooked for him, cleaned, took him to the doctor. She was always asking what he was doing, what was troubling him, how he was managing. He loved her dearly and felt very close to her, but he felt closer to his grandfather. Even as a young adult he described himself as feeling very close to his grandparents. "Everything they ask of me I do, if I only can," he says.

What kind of intimate relationships is a man like Steve likely to have? A man who had such a complex and non-nurturing relationship with his mother? A man who hardly knew his father, and whose most stable, deep, and significant male bonding was with his grandfather? Whose most significant nurturing figure was his grandmother? In response to the question of whether he is currently in an intimate relationship, Steve says, "no." Has he ever been in a romantic relationship? "No, not really." "It's tough, cause I can be guessing wrong. When you finally meet someone you want to go out with, they don't always want to go out with you."

Steve was in love once. "One of the only women I really fell in love with is this girl I was going out with a year ago. I knew her a lot of years. She hung around the group that I hung around. I'd always see her around, and one night we were at the same club and started looking at each other. Then we talked and stuff. She had just broken up with a boyfriend. We [I?] liked each other but we [I?] were waiting to make a move. She's a big girl, about six-foot. From the moment I saw her, I liked her, red hair, good family, and she's interesting, very independent. I liked everything about her. She was at the center, everybody knew her. Many of the women in our group found themselves a boyfriend and adjusted themselves to his pattern. She didn't do it.

I sent her flowers every Friday. I would arrive at her door with wine and cheese, the whole routine. She was special and I wanted to make it special. I gave her a lot of space. I didn't call her every night. I didn't tell her 'I love you' the way boys love girls. That's one of the problems. I'm one of these guys who don't say what they feel, and it's hard. Because maybe I'm guessing wrong. Once, on her birthday, she had a date with me. Then she changed it to a breakfast, and then to a lunch, and then she gave me a talk on how she's not ready for a relationship. So I moved back. I don't think I'm ready for the kind of relationship she wanted. I have a bad problem with the physical aspect of the relationship, the whole boy-girl thing. She was comfortable with the physical part in her relationship with other men. But with me she could see that it was more than that. I saw her regularly and tried to spend time with her for four months. She was very busy, all the time."

Steve found the relationship exciting, enjoyable, and fascinating, but also scary. "I liked to talk to her about stuff. I was amazed at the things that she was doing. Just being around her was pleasurable. I liked giving her things, just thinking about places that I could take her to. I was awfully happy but also scared, not knowing the game of relationships. I didn't know what she wants. It scared the hell out of me, a lot of feelings I wasn't used to feeling. It's tough to deal with someone when you feel like that. There was nothing that she could do wrong. I put her on a pedestal."

In response to the question about possible similarity to his mother, Steve says: "I'm trying not to see a similarity, but I could see similarities. I can easily do it, but it would spoil the picture in my brain of what I wanted her to be. She was definitely a woman of the 90s, very sure of herself. She ran her life, knew how to be on top. She would tell me to do stuff in a similar way to the way my mother told me to do things. I wanted someone to dominate over me." It is significant that the woman Steve chose to fall in love with is similar to his mother and not to his grandparents.

Steve is an example of an anxious-ambivalent attachment style. After the relationship ended, Steve went out with only two other women. One seemed interested in him, but he wasn't sure he was interested in her (probably because of her obvious interest in him). Actually, Steve is not sure what he wants. It seems that what he wants, consciously or unconsciously, is yet another strong and dominant woman with whom he can re-enact his frustrating, painful childhood experience with his mother.

AN ANALYSIS OF STEVE'S ROMANTIC RELATIONSHIP

Dating frequency: 3 (very small number of dates)

Number of significant intimate relationships: 1 (the relationship was significant but not intimate)

Length of this relationship: 4 months

Commitment to the relationship: 2 ("actually, nothing really happened")

Sense of security in the relationship: 2 (very low, "I felt scared.")

Ability to be oneself in the relationship: 2 (not really)

Intimacy in the relationship: 2 (very low, "I don't know the dating game.")

Power in the relationship: 2 (partner had most of the power, "I wanted to be controlled")

Pursuer/Distances: 2 (interviewee is the pursuer in the relationship)

Physical attraction to partner: 5 (physical attraction mentioned)

Friendship before romance: 3 (knew each other a little before the romance started)

Stereotyped sex roles: 5 (sex roles mentioned: "She's a woman of the 90s.")

Frequency of conflicts: 3 (low frequency, didn't dare to object)

Ability to deal with conflicts: 2 (issues don't get discussed and are not resolved)

How are conflicts resolved: escaping

Ability to stand separation: 3 (suffers)

Jealousy is a problem in the relationship: 2 (jealousy was not mentioned at all)

Jealousy is a personal problem: 2 (jealousy was not mentioned at all)

Arousal played a role in the initial attraction: yes

Propinquity played a role in the initial attraction: yes

Similarity played a role in the initial attraction: no

Partner's attraction played a role in the initial attraction: no

Physical attraction played a role in the initial attraction: yes

Personality traits of the partner played a role in the initial attraction: yes
Status of partner played a role in the initial attraction: yes
Is/was partner satisfying an important need? yes
Is the partner described as the "best friend"? no
Was it love at first sight? no
Is the interviewee showing psychological understanding? no
Is partner similar to father: not clear
Is partner similar to mother: yes
Is partner different from father: not clear
Is partner different from mother: not clear
Are the relationships with partner and the parent similar? yes
Sexual preference: heterosexual
Number of children: none
Abuse in the relationship: possibly (emotional abuse in the form of
   rejection)

MARY

Like Steve's parents, Mary's parents separated when she was a young girl. Her father remarried, but her mother did not. Her father was a successful businessman, her mother was a housewife, and Mary, too, hardly saw her father even before her parents broke up. He would leave for work very early in the morning and come back very late at night. He was often away on business, at times for months. After the divorce there was a period in which he took his children out for dinner often, and they thought it was weird; when he lived with them they never saw him eat.

Mary was the second of four children. She spent more time with her siblings than with her mother. The mother's way of teaching them to cope was to let them take care of things on their own. Mary felt that other children were much closer to their mothers than she was. When she would have a fight with one of her siblings, her mother refused to hear about it and told them to figure it out on their own. Knowing that this was going to be her answer, her children avoided approaching her. Mary remembers her mother's favorite saying: "Take care of number one." She didn't understand what it meant. Mary's mother was nonjudgmental of other people but very critical of her own children. For example, she criticized Mary's sister because she got a B in a class, and unjustly assumed that she hadn't worked hard enough. She was also critical of Mary's appearance. One time, when Mary was a young girl sitting on her mother's lap, her mother told her she could lose some weight. It made Mary feel very bad.

As an adult recounting this event, Mary noted that she should not have been bothered by weight at that age. Her mother used to look at Mary's hair and tell her she needed a hair cut or that her hair was too thin. They often had fights about how much Mary weighed and how she looked. But the most painful incident happened when Mary sat on her mother's lap and told her that she loved her. Her mother's cool response was to correct her and say that Mary didn't love her but needed her, and, as a child, was dependent on her. Years later, Mary still remembered painfully how hurt and rejected she had felt.

Mary's father was a very closed and emotionally distant man and his children never understood him. Before the divorce, he bought himself a car. The family had a family car that was quite adequate, and all of a sudden there was another car parked next to the house. At first, the children assumed that it belonged to a neighbor. Then one day they saw their father drive it and thought it was very strange. When they asked him about it, he said, "I decided that we need another car." Then, saying that he needed a place to work because his desk stood in a corner in the living room, he showed them an apartment that he had rented. All this seemed reasonable, but, of course, was the way he chose to gradually introduce the children to the idea that he was leaving the house. And they didn't get it. It was Mary's mother who told them about the divorce. Long before that Mary had felt that something bad was happening, but didn't know what.

Mary never felt close to her father. She describes her relationship with him as distant and "heavy." A big part of her father's relationship with his children involved his bringing gifts and their receiving them. When he came back from business trips he would bring them all sorts of gifts. The children liked the gifts but it didn't seem to them like the normal relationship most children had with their fathers.

Father would do nice things such as take them to an amusement park, something their mother refused to do, but would never go on rides. He would stand on the side taking pictures. When the children came off the rides, they often couldn't find him anywhere. They would run around looking for him. It didn't seem normal. He would do nice things but he himself wasn't there. His heart wasn't in it.

Mary's father didn't like children in general and was uncomfortable around them. He was patient with his own children, and always seemed happy to help them with their school work. He hated pets and found it difficult that his kids had pets. He had little in common with his children, but made an effort. Mary felt closer to her mother only because she was around more. When Mary was hurt or sick, mother was the one who took care of her. Father simply "wasn't there."

What effect does a father have if he doesn't like children and maintains a relationship with his own children that is "distant" and "heavy"? What effect does a mother have if her children experience her as uninvolved, critical, and, at least on one occasion, rejecting? When asked about romantic relationships, Mary says "Well, I'm single and I don't have a boyfriend and I haven't had a boyfriend. I would say I have never had a boyfriend.

"I never dated in High School. When I went to college I dated some. In five years I probably went out with about ten people. That's not very much. And most of those people I didn't see ever again. Since I've been in college, here's my terrible bias, I have even more of a distrust for guys at that age. I feel like it's a heartache for a lot of people. Other people are more excited about just being with someone than being with someone in particular. I had a few good male friends, well, two, but as far as a romantic relationship goes, I just was not ready emotionally for it. I was just not used to it. Most people were moving faster than I was and I just wasn't very comfortable, so I would get out of the romantic relationship. For a while that really bothered me, especially in the first and second years. I thought, what's wrong with me? Then I decided that if it takes me longer, it takes me longer, and that's okay."

Even with the two men she dated several times, "There was always a sense that the relationship wasn't my idea. I have no problem being friends with men, but it's sort of a struggle getting into a romantic thing . . . something about it just didn't feel right to me. Often I didn't even feel like I had a chance to become attracted to someone. At least with two, two I liked, I could see that I could become romantically attracted to them, but they just moved so fast that I suddenly felt like I was uncomfortable. The whole idea just scared me and so it ended for me, and so it ended that way.

"I kind of felt bad about it though. I don't know why I should have. I guess there were just a lot of unsaid assumed things. I assumed that it was going to be a friendship longer, and I was amazed that it wasn't, so that was the problem I had. A lot of my female friends had boyfriends or had a steady boyfriend or they just dated a lot. And so, in comparison, I felt like I was doing something wrong, but it didn't outweigh how uncomfortable I felt. So I decided, well, I guess I'm just different.

"I remember with one person, I knew he had a girlfriend so I just thought we were friends and I was kind of attracted to him, but we were just friends. When he made a move to be more than that, I kind of lost respect for him. The next day I saw him. He was kind of mad, but I don't think he was mad because of anything that didn't happen. I think his pride was hurt. I have a hard time seeing men mistreat their girlfriends.

"Another guy was in one of my classes and he said 'Do you want to meet after class and talk?' I thought that was weird but I said okay. I guess I knew him as a friend for about a week and then he showed this romantic interest that I didn't think was there. I didn't even feel like I knew him well enough to be attracted to him yet. I just said look, things are going too fast. I'm not used to this. He didn't like me after that."

When analyzing her experiences with men, Mary says,

"I think it may have been partly my fault. I don't trust a guy until I really know him, and if he shows too much interest and just gets physical, then I'm not the right person for him to be with. I have a lot of friends who like to go to parties and when a guy would show interest it would just be a one-night thing, and they would never see him again. I didn't want to deal with that at all, so I just kind of said no. I'm sure that I could have made it work, if I really wanted to work at the relationship. But I know I do get scared real fast.

"I think that someday I would like to get married and have kids, but I really would like it to start with a friendship first." When asked what kind of a person she imagines getting involved with Mary says: "Someone who, I was just going to say someone who likes kids. I don't know why. I don't have this great need to have children, but for some reason, a man who likes children and animals appeals to me, someone who cares about living things, aside from any sexual relationship, and someone who is smart.

"I don't think I could live with anyone who was terribly clingy. I'm probably too standoffish right now, so I know I would have to work at being less so. But I still think that I'm going to need someone who doesn't have to do everything together . . . . For some reason I just keep thinking it is going to be scary, but it shouldn't be. It should be just friends, so what does it matter if it's tomorrow or ten years from now? I don't think it would be in the immediate future. I have to take everything slow and I can't work fast. I just feel that the slower the better."

Mary doesn't know why she wants a romantic partner who likes kids and animals. But we do; we know that her father disliked children and hated pets. The anxiety aroused in Mary at the mere thought of an intimate relationship suggests an avoidant attachment style. Mary was pushed to be independent too early, before she achieved a sense of security in her early love relationship with her parents, especially her mother. Mary has no model of a warm and loving intimate relationship, and she has no faith in her own lovability because she did not feel loved and cherished as a child.

AN ANALYSIS OF MARY'S ROMANTIC RELATIONSHIP

Dating frequency: 1 (very low number of dates)
Number of significant intimate relationships: 0
Commitment to a relationship: 1 (has never been in an intimate
    relationship)
All questions about the intimate relationship: not relevant.
All questions about the initial attraction: not relevant.
All questions about partner's similarity/dissimilarity to parents: not relevant
Is the interviewee showing psychological understanding? Not clear
Number of children: none
Sexual preference: heterosexual

JACK

Like Jill, Jack was a beloved only child. He grew up in a small college town. His father taught at the college and his mother was a housewife. Jack's relationship with his parents was always very warm, and he can't remember ever having bad feelings towards them. He was often hugged and held in his parents' arms as a child. The three of them often did things together such as eat in restaurants or go on trips related to his father's work. His parents treated him as an equal from a very young age. They raised him the way they wished they had been raised. Jack had no brothers or sisters, and aunts and uncles lived far away. Yet his father and mother were always there for him. When Jack wanted to do some father-son thing with his father, such as play baseball, his father always found the time, despite being a very busy man. While Jack's father was strict and demanding, his mother was sweet and understanding. She was the one who said "it's okay." She was always around the house, doing all the "motherly" things like putting on a Band-Aid when Jack hurt himself, cooking, and taking care of the family, the house, and the dog. She was always busy and seemed happy and contented.

Jack's father was the disciplinarian. He would punish Jack by withholding his pocket money, which worked very well. His mother removed herself from it. Father would get very angry when Jack's grades weren't what he expected or when Jack did things he wasn't supposed to do, such as taking a short-cut through the yard and stepping on plants. He was very strict about things like that. Jack's father was an imposing man with a strong personality, who expressed his opinion in a forceful way. Jack always knew that his father really loved him and was concerned about him, that when he got angry and punished him, it was for a good reason.

Jack's father seemed scary, but was not really. He was the kind of teacher students are scared to go to, but after they do, say to themselves, "Why didn't I do this earlier?" Jack always tried to please his father. Father was his role model and Jack wanted to be like him. Jack's father was very busy with his work, but was always doing things with Jack, or his mother, or the dog, and on weekends, he worked in the yard.

Despite his admiration of his father, Jack felt closer to his mother because they spent much more time together. As a young child, Jack was always with his mother, rather than in child-care. When his father came home, they were a family. On weekends they would do things together as a family.

Jack never felt rejected by his parents; if anything, he says, it was the opposite. Their love and their concern for him were almost too much. His parents were very protective and always wanted to know where he was. They were also very strict and did not allow Jack to do some of the things he loved doing, which, sometimes, he did anyway.

What kind of a romantic relationship is a man likely to have if he was so close to his mother and his father during his childhood? The answer, according to Jack is, "a wonderful relationship."

"We've been going out, officially, just us, for four years. But we went out for a year before that, so it's five years. It's pretty serious. We'll probably get married in a couple of years. It depends on our jobs and such things. If we knew everything, we'd get married tomorrow.

"We met at the beginning of school in my sophomore year when she was a freshman. I used to hang out with a friend that lived right next to her and we started to hang out together. It's really funny, because I had the wrong idea about her. First it was this blond who is living next to my friend Bob. I had the image that she was a party girl, which is totally wrong. When I got to know her I realized that that's not her. I helped her with her Italian, and I found out later that she didn't need any help with her Italian at all! The relationship kind of happened. We started going out, going to movies and hanging out.

"She's really cute. That's the first thing. And she's fun to be with. She's funny. She has this naive streak that is amusing some times. We got along really well together. We asked each other advice on writing papers and things like that. We used to correct each other's papers. When we had problems with friends we talked about it with each other. We are at the point now that we'd rather be together than with anybody else. Both of us know that we are there for each other.

"She knows how I work and I know how she works, so we can always tell how the other one is feeling. And there's always warmth there. When I'm with her, I'm always happy. Stuff that I'm doing with her, even if just watching TV, is more fun with her than with other friends or when I'm alone. Even doing stupid things, like washing dishes with her, is so much better. Things are never boring. We never do the same old thing. There's always something that is different. Little things that change it from being a lull."

When asked about similarity between his romantic relationship and his relationship with his parents Jack says: "I know she loves me and I know that my parents love me. They all care for me and that's that. And I care for all of them, so there's that kind of similarity. She's kind of similar to my dad in that she's stubborn as hell. But she's a genuinely nice person, and in that she's like my Mom. I'm really stubborn too. We both make compromises, but we both want it our way and we're both stubborn." As for differences: "certain things that she hasn't experienced that I've experienced and that then we've experienced together, like experimenting with things such as cooking, which we did a lot when I was growing up. She didn't grow up that way. It's neat to see her try new things that are not her way. My parents who are older have experienced everything that I've experienced. So it's neat to be close to someone who hasn't experienced everything and being able to re-experience things with them."

Separations are difficult for Jack. "I get really sad. I try to immerse myself in doing things. I miss her a lot. We talk a lot on the phone, at least half an hour every day, sometimes more than once a day. Something is missing. I can't explain it."

Conflicts in the relationship are few. "We've had some discussions, but not blatant screaming and yelling type of thing. Both of us are stubborn. But there is nothing we fight over. Recently both of us have been stressed out, so both of us felt a little left out. I felt that she wasn't giving me much attention and she felt that I wasn't giving her much attention, so there was that kind of tension. But both of us realized what was going on. We talked about it. We sit down and talk everything out. We're close so we bring everything out right away."

Jack's description of his relationship suggests a secure attachment style.

AN ANALYSIS OF JACK'S ROMANTIC RELATIONSHIP

Dating frequency: 4 (average number of dates)

Number of significant intimate relationships: 2

Length of this relationship: 48 months

Commitment to the relationship: 6 (very good relationship with marriage plans)

Sense of security in the relationship: 7 (very high, feels totally secure)

Ability to be oneself in the relationship: 7 (definitely yes, can be totally himself)

Intimacy in the relationship: 7 (very high, symbiosis, know what each other feels)

Power in the relationship: 4 (both partners have equal power)

Pursuer/Distances: 4 (both partners have equal involvement in the relationship)

Physical attraction to partner: 5 (physical attraction mentioned)

Friendship before romance: 4 (were friends before the romance started)

Stereotyped sex roles: 2 (sex role stereotypes are not mentioned and are not an issue)

Frequency of conflicts: 3 (low frequency)

Ability to deal with conflicts: 6 (talking about everything, trying to resolve things)

How are conflicts resolved: talking

Ability to stand separation: 3 (feels very sad)

Jealousy is a problem in the relationship: 2 (jealousy was not mentioned at
     all)
Jealousy is a personal problem: 2 (jealousy was not mentioned at all)
Arousal played a role in the initial attraction: no
Propinquity played a role in the initial attraction: yes
Similarity played a role in the initial attraction: yes
Partner's attraction played a role in the initial attraction: no
Physical attraction played a role in the initial attraction: yes
Personality traits of the partner played a role in the initial attraction: yes
Status of partner played a role in the initial attraction: no
Is partner satisfying an important need? yes
Is the partner described as the "best friend"? yes
Was it love at first sight? no
Is the interviewee showing psychological understanding? yes
Are there signs of abuse in the relationship? no
Is partner similar to father: yes
Is partner similar to mother: yes
Is partner different from father: yes
Is partner different from mother: yes
Are the relationships with partner and parents similar? yes
Sexual preference: heterosexual
Number of children: none

IN SUMMARY

We see that at age twenty-three, both Jack and Jill, who were loved and respected as children, are in long-term, intimate, loving, and egalitarian relationships; whereas Mary and Steve, whose parents were separated and who
felt rejected by their parents, have never been in intimate relationships. A
coincidence? Maybe. But a more likely explanation is that the childhood
experiences and observations of love, affected the internal romantic images
of all four.

Jack and Jill reenact in their intimate relationships the loving childhood
relationships they had with their parents. Mary and Steve reenact in their
relationships with the opposite sex the rejecting and hurtful childhood
experiences that they had with their parents.

The fact that family relationships in childhood predict the romantic intimacy of young adults was demonstrated in other studies as well (e.g., Feldman et al., 1998). It was also true for every single one of the hundreds of people I have worked with in individual and couple therapy. But, as we will see in the next chapter, this is not a simple reenactment, a kind of repetition compulsion of childhood experiences, but an occasion to repeat the positive and overcome the negative. And there is no human relationship that is more appropriate for healing childhood wounds than an intimate romantic relationship.

SUGGESTIONS FOR THOSE SEEKING LOVE

Like the four young people described in this chapter, most people are not aware of the effect their childhood experiences with their parents have on their love relationships. Tragically, people who were unloved or even rejected as children continue to suffer in unsatisfying love relationships as adults. People with a history of such unsatisfying relationships, who are willing to abandon the comfort of blaming their inappropriate partners, can try to break free of their familial scripts. How this difficult task can be undertaken and carried out is the subject of the next chapter.

Part Three

ROMANTIC LOVE
IN LONG-TERM RELATIONSHIPS

People use each other
as a healing for their pain. They put each other
on their existential wounds,
on eye, on cunt, on mouth and open hand.
They hold each other hard and won't let go.
　　　—Yehuda Amichai, "People use each other,"
　　　　Love Poems

Let me under your wing
and be for me mother and sister
and let your bosom be a refuge for my head
nest for my banished prayers.

I will confess a secret to you:
My soul burned in a flame;
They say there is love in the world—
What is love?
　　　—Chaim Nachman Bialik,
　　　　"Let me under your wing," *Songs*

What, if any, is the role of falling in love in a couple's long-term relationship? While the previous two parts of the book are based on studies, theories, and analyses of clinical interviews, this third and last part is based primarily on clinical experience, mine and those of others. This part shifts the perspective from the individual to the couple and addresses the relationship between falling in love and the issues a couple is likely to struggle with later on. It is based on my strong belief that an intimate relationship provides us with one of the best opportunities for mastering unresolved childhood issues and achieving existential significance in our lives.

Most people choose a therapist because they heard about him or her from a person they trust, or because they read a book the therapist wrote, and liked the things he or she said. Which is to say the choice is based on logical considerations. The unconscious, however, more than anything else, dictates with whom we fall in love. Falling in love is an intense emotional and physical experience that seems quite illogical because it is not our faculties of reason that dictate it. The electrical activity in the brain of a person in love is not in the cortex, the seat of logical thinking, but in the limbic system, the seat of powerful emotions.

Although not logical, in most cases, the unconscious romantic choice is a wise one because it directs people to choose the person most appropriate to helping them master an unresolved childhood issue. This is why finding such a person ignites the romantic spark and why it causes such elation and great excitement. Even when the choice is dangerous, as it is when the unresolved issue involves physical abuse, still, in principle, it is a wise choice because it is aimed at healing the trauma, not merely repeating it.

When a couple is in love, the unconscious of both partners dictates their mutual selection. The interweaving of both their core issues creates their core issue as a couple. When, after many years of marriage, a couple comes for therapy and disentangles what seems like an endless morass of problems, conflicts, hurts, and disappointments, what emerges is the core issue at the center of most of their problems.

As we will see next, understanding the connection between unresolved childhood issues and the problems experienced in an intimate relationship is only the first step. Both partners need to take responsibility for their own contributions to the problem, express empathy for their partner's core issue, and—the hardest part—change those behaviors that are most problematic for the other. This kind of effort, even more than individual therapy, is what enables couples to change their problems into opportunities for personal and couple growth.

Such an opportunity for growth is imbued with great existential significance for modern men and women who expect to derive their existential significance, or part of it, from their intimate relationships. All of us need to express our unique individuality and make a significant contribution to the world in order to feel that our lives matter; this is our way of defending against the fear of death. We also need to belong, to feel cared for and loved; this is our way of defending against the fear of life (Yalom, 1980). Couples who continue growing in their intimate relationships and feel that the relationship is a safe base from which they can face all the challenges in the world, are couples who derive a sense of existential significance from their relationships. They are also the couples who are able to keep alive indefinitely the romantic spark of the falling-in-love stage (Pines, 1996).

TURNING LOVE PROBLEMS INTO OPPORTUNITIES FOR GROWTH

"A wrestling match." He laughs. "Yes, you could
    describe life that way."
So which side wins, I ask?
"Which side wins?"
He smiles at me, the crinkled eyes, the crooked teeth.
"Love wins. Love always wins."
    —Mitch Albom, *Tuesdays with Morrie*

At first she was attracted to "his sense of humor. He's really funny, always has a joke." Later his humor came to annoy her. "I have difficulty talking to him seriously about what's going on in my life."

At first he was attracted to her shyness and sensitivity: "She's a really neat person . . . really shy and reserved. Really sensitive to what other people think." Later these very traits became a problem. "It began to bother me just how sensitive she was to others in the sense that she was hyperaware of what others were thinking about her. It bothered me that she was so shy and reserved."

At first she was attracted to his calm and impressed by his reserve. "I had a crush on him . . . He was very quiet and didn't open up at all. Because he was so quiet I thought he was on a social level above me and I thought he'd never like me." Now she resents his reserve and sees in it evidence of his lack of interest in her. "He doesn't ask me about myself and about my life, he isn't interested. I don't feel it's a two-way thing."

At first he was attracted to her nuttiness. "She was very, very active, and funny and quick. She always seemed to be thinking up something nutty to do." Later, her nuttiness terminated the relationship. "She had serious emotional problems."

At first his lack of ambition attracted her. "He was at school but wasn't obsessive about it." Later his lack of ambition became a problem. "He talks

about going back to school, but he's not sure. We already had a few confrontations about that."

"He comes off as being very confident, almost cocky. That's what attracted me to him, but that's also what upsets me."

What is missing in these remarks is the partner's perspective on both the
attraction and the conflict. As we already know, for couples in love, the
causes of attraction are most often complementary. If she was attracted to
his care-free attitude, he was probably attracted to her intense involvement
with things. And if she later complains that "He's not as ambitious as I am,"
it is likely that he complains about her excessive intensity and "pushiness."
The poles of carefree attitude versus intense involvement exist in both of
them and reflect the core issue in their characters and the relationship. We
can see two such poles in the example of Susan and Robert.

SUSAN AND ROBERT

One of Susan's most painful childhood memories was of being sent out of
the house when her mother's friends would come for a visit. Susan enjoyed
participating in their conversation, which drove her mother crazy. Deaf to
Susan's tears and pleas, her mother would send her out and slam the door in
her face. Susan can remember herself standing on the wooden balcony,
banging on the locked door, sobbing and begging to be let in. One of
Robert's most painful memories is escaping from the endless demands of his
beautiful mother. Robert used to hide in his room and imagine that the little carpet he was sitting on was a raft in the middle of the ocean. His
mother's angry, demanding voice sounded like a faraway thunder storm. It
no longer intimidated him.

Susan and Robert met when they were both in their early forties, the
veterans of many destructive and unsatisfying relationships. It was the holi-
day season, a time for new resolutions and new beginnings. Robert had just
completed a year-long journey around the world on a small boat and Susan
had gone back to college, determined this time to graduate no matter what.
They met at a mutual friend's dinner party. There was something about
Robert's quiet masculinity, his independence and adventurous spirit that
sparked Susan's imagination. His admiration flattered her. He was calm and
reassuring and he made her feel safe. Susan's beauty and poise left Robert
breathless. The strength of her personality and the sophistication of her interests dazzled him. He could not believe that a woman like her would pay

attention to a primitive brute like himself. Her warm response excited him and made him happier than he ever believed possible.

Robert and Susan fell madly in love with each other. Both of them felt that this time they had chosen the right person, someone with whom they could spend the rest of their lives. Several months later, Robert bought a house, and shortly thereafter, Susan moved in with him. A year after they first met, Susan and Robert got married. Despite the wonderful beginning, Susan and Robert's relationship was full of frustrating confrontations. The hardest thing for Susan was Robert's tendency to "disappear" when she was in an emotional turmoil and needed him. When she sensed his distancing, she would create "scenes" to engage him. But nothing she said, nothing she did helped. Robert would distance himself even further, hiding "like a turtle." The hardest thing for Robert were Susan's angry, unprovoked "attacks" on him. He would distance himself from her, hoping that the angry storm would pass, but nothing he did seemed to help; his distancing only made things worse. When they came for couple therapy, both Susan and Robert felt deeply hurt by each other and very disappointed in their relationship.

In therapy Robert and Susan came to understand their core issues, and how they combined to create their core issue as a couple. Susan understood that like the hurt, rejected girl that she had been, she is banging on Robert's door, feeling left out and begging to be let in. But on the other side of the "door" is not a rejecting parent but a scared boy who is terrified by the banging, and anxious that he will not be able to satisfy her demands. Robert, for his part, understood that like the anxious, hiding, little boy that he had been, he is escaping Susan's demands, "sailing on the little carpet in the middle of the ocean" of his room. But on the other side of the "door" is not a demanding parent who is insensitive to his feelings, but a hurt girl who needs his love. The image of the scared boy hiding away and the hurt left out girl helped Robert and Susan change their behavior. Susan understood that when she needs Robert's love and support she cannot demand it from him in a loud voice or by attack, because the louder the demand, the less Robert will be able to respond to it as a mature adult. But if she can express her need for him calmly, he will always be there for her. Robert understood that his distancing himself from Susan is not a way to prevent the storm, but a sure way to make it happen with greater force. But if he can respond to Susan's feelings and express his own, her anger will evaporate.

This seemingly very simple change in behavior—in fact, a very difficult change for both of them to implement—enabled Susan and Robert to mas-

ter a painful childhood experience, an experience they were both still strug-
gling with as adults. After all, it is not by accident that Susan fell in love
with a man whose primary strategy for coping with demands is withdrawal,
a strategy that helped him survive as a child and thus became imbued with
existential significance. And, it is not by accident that Robert fell in love
with a strong and awe-inspiring woman who learned to demand forcefully
what she needs, a strategy that helped her survive as a child and thus had existential significance for her.

Susan's heroic struggle to control the impulse to demand loudly, and
Robert's response to her distress when she expressed it directly and quietly,
helped heal her childhood wound. Robert's heroic struggle with the impulse
to escape, and Susan's gratitude and love when he was able to stay connected to her, helped heal his childhood wound. These changes, difficult at
first but increasingly easier with time and practice, helped turn their marriage into a very rewarding relationship that enhances both their personal
and couple growth.

The reason their behavioral changes had such a powerful effect has to
do, once again, with the unconscious forces that directed them to fall in
love with each other. As is almost always the case in intimate relationships,
the thing that Susan needed most from Robert in order to heal her childhood wound was the very thing that Robert needed to give in order to grow
emotionally. Instead of turning into a scared little boy, running away and
hiding, he needed to learn to stay an adult and face whatever is demanded
of him as an adult. In the same way, the thing that Robert needed most
from Susan in order to heal his childhood wound of helplessness was the
very thing that Susan needed to give in order to grow emotionally. Instead
of turning into a rejected little girl that needs to pound on people's doors to
be heard, she needed to learn to stay an adult and ask for what she wants in
a way that will increase her likelihood of getting it. The magic of a couple's
relationship is that when two people fall in love, whatever they need to do
for themselves in order to grow emotionally is most often the very thing
that the partner needs from them. Whatever efforts they invest in their own
growth are the most valuable healing gifts to their partners.

FATAL ATTRACTION OR WISE UNCONSCIOUS CHOICES?

Very few studies dealt with the connection between what makes couples fall
in love with each other and what causes their problems, sometimes even
their breakup, later on. One of the few, which included 60 married couples,

showed that the most annoying trait was very often an exaggeration, implication, or the exact opposite of the trait that was first described as the main reason for attraction (Whitehouse, 1981).

In another study, Diane Felmlee (1995) examined the hypothesis that the same traits that cause dissatisfaction in the partner are a negative translation of the traits that caused the original attraction. Felmlee termed this phenomenon "fatal attraction," fatal "in the sense that it foretells a sequence that ends in future disillusionment" (296). She assumed that "the characteristic responsible for the initial attraction to a romantic partner and a characteristic that is later disliked, are often dimensions of the same overall attribute" (297). Felmlee suggested three primary conditions under which such "fatal attraction" may occur. First, it is more likely in a state of infatuation or intense passionate love, when people are blinded by love and thus likely to underestimate the importance of negative traits. Second, it is likely to occur when an initial attracting quality is a characteristic that stands out and is readily noticed. Such a quality, therefore, may be possessed to an extreme, and extreme positive attributes may be especially likely to have negative dimensions. For example, a partner who is attractive because he is very successful may soon be viewed as workaholic, since it's usually difficult to attain success without a great deal of work. Third, some qualities that may be attractive and rewarding in the short run, such as spontaneity, may prove problematic in an extended committed relationship.

In order to investigate the extent of "fatal attraction," Felmlee asked students to describe their most recent romantic relationships that had ended. Then the students were asked specific questions about the relationships and the breakups. Among the questions about the relationship, students were asked to describe the features that attracted them. Among the questions about the breakup, they were asked what they found least attractive. Key words, such as *nice*, and phrases, such as *treated me well*, were put into categories. Results showed that in 29.2% of the cases, the reason for the breakup was the same quality that originally attracted.

My own clinical experience leads me to believe that the phenomenon is far more common than Felmlee's data suggest. In almost every case of the hundreds I have worked with in therapy and in couple groups, if the relationship was based on romantic love, it was possible to find a connection between the traits that attracted the members of a couple to each other and the traits that later became the focus of their problems (Pines, 1997).

When a couple comes to therapy for the first time, one of the questions I always ask is, "What attracted you to each other when you first met?" I then show the couple the connection between their original attraction and the problem that has brought them to therapy. Similarly, one exercise I do in every couple group is to ask participants what attracted them to their mates initially, and then ask what they find most stressful. There is almost always some connection between the two (Pines, 1996). But contrary to Felmlee who views this as "fatal attraction," the dark side of every human virtue, I view it as a "wise unconscious choice" (Pines, 1997).

Like other psychodynamic therapists,[1] I believe that unconscious forces operate in both romantic attraction and relationship problems. The unconscious dictates the choice of a partner who can help the individual master a "core issue" that is the manifestation of an unresolved childhood problem. If a person's core issue is fear of abandonment, this person's unconscious will direct the choice of a partner who can help him or her master this fear. And who is more appropriate for the task than a person whose core issue is a fear of engulfment? This is the why couples fall in love with each other. Since their choice is complementary, they jointly create their core issue as a couple. Ann and Ed are an example. They would not have been included in Felmlee's "fatal attraction" category, yet there is an obvious connection between the traits that made them fall in love with each other and the traits that turned their relationship into a living hell.

ANN AND ED

A professional couple in their late thirties, Ann and Ed came to couple therapy as the last resort before applying for divorce. Ann's main complaint was Ed's "total lack of sensitivity and consideration" toward her and other people. Ed's main complaint was Ann's angry outbursts that always came as a big surprise to him and were "incomprehensible and totally unjustified."

When they first met, in addition to Ann's "obvious good looks and sharp intelligence," Ed says he was attracted to her powerful and dynamic personality. "She was direct and cynical and funny," he explains with a smile. For her part, Ann liked "Ed's mind and the way he thinks," as well as his "laid-back personality. He knew how to enjoy life, and was pleasant and easy-going, no complexes or complications."

Both Ann and Ed came from homes where there was no love between the parents. Ann's parents divorced when she was a young girl, and Ed's parents fought frequently. Ed's father, who was a very religious man, forced Ed to attend services with him and demanded a show of respect. But hardest for Ed as a child were his father's angry outbursts, which included screaming and, at times, even beatings. Ed's mother did not love or respect his father, but was warm, loving, and nurturing toward Ed. Ann's hardest experience as a child was the loss of her beloved father who, disregarding her love and need for him, moved to another state after the divorce. Her mother, who was "very conscientious" about her duties as a mother, was insensitive to Ann's feelings and unresponsive to her wishes.

Ed's core issue was a fear of his father's angry outbursts, and a bitter resentment of being forced to attend religious services and show respect, which Ed felt his father did not deserve. Ann's core issue was the painful feeling that people close to her were not responsive to her needs and wishes. Her eagerness to read her beloved father's feeling and her longing for him developed into her great sensitivity to people.

These same issues combined to create the core issue of Ann and Ed's problems as a couple. Ed cannot stand it when people "force him" to behave in a way they consider proper and which doesn't suit him. He responds by being "dense and inconsiderate." Ann responds to his insensitivity with anger and rage. Ed "doesn't understand" her "uncalled-for, angry attacks"; Ann sees his lack of understanding as yet another demonstration of his lack of sensitivity and consideration of her feelings. This way both of them reenact their childhood trauma in the relationship.

By analyzing what they found most attractive about each other when they first met and fell in love, it is possible to identify early signs that, at some level, Ann and Ed were well aware of the opportunity they presented to each other to master their unresolved childhood issues. At that time, Ed was attracted to Ann's "powerful personality," "directness," "cynicism" and "sharp intelligence." He found those traits exciting and enjoyable. Now the sharp intelligence and cynicism have turned into "unfair criticism" and the powerful direct personality has turned into threatening "outbursts." At first, Ann was attracted to Ed's easy-going, uncomplicated way of being, and to his ability to enjoy life. Now she views him as "insensitive and dense" and "totally focused on himself." Despite the clear connection between Ann and Ed's original attraction and their distress, they would not have been included in the "fatal attraction" category because they used different words and phrases to describe their attraction and distress.

Ed and Ann are an example of the wisdom of unconscious romantic choices in directing people to choose partners with whom they have an opportunity to master psychological issues. When a man such as Ed learns to show sensitivity to his partner's needs, it will enable him to grow tremendously as a person; he will get out of the dense armor he has constructed around himself as a defense against the outbursts and demands of his father. This kind of change in Ed will, of course, be a healing experience for Ann. And when a woman such as Ann learns to respond without exploding in anger, it will enable her to grow tremendously as a person; she will learn to express herself in a way that keeps others connected rather than pushing them away as a defense against her fear of abandonment.[2] This kind of change in Ann will, of course, be a healing experience for Ed.

According to Felmlee, "fatal attraction" is more likely to happen during infatuation, which can lead to a situation in which "love is blind." Clinical experience with couples such as Ed and Ann suggests that like the "blind" in Greek mythology that see better than sighted people, and like "winged Cupid painted blind" in Shakespeare's *Midsummer Night's Dream*, love is very wise in its choice (see Figure 12).

Since one example is hardly enough, see the box "Initial Attraction and Subsequent Stress." Ten brief examples represent couples chosen randomly from 100 with whom I have worked in recent years. In each case I describe the main attractions that made the couple fall in love with each other, and what later became their major sources of stress.[3] In every one of the cases presented, there is an obvious connection between the cause of the couple's attraction to each other and the cause of their later distress. In addition

FIGURE 12. Love looks not with the eyes, but with the mind,
And therefore is winged Cupid painted blind
—William Shakespeare, *A Midsummer Night's Dream*

INITIAL ATTRACTION AND SUBSEQUENT STRESS

Attraction

Wife: He was a very persistent pursuer, made me feel desirable and adored.

Husband: She seemed like a dream come true, unapproachable.

Stress

Wife: He doesn't let me breathe; he is always in my face.

Husband: She never lets me feel like she wants me.

Attraction

Wife: He gave me a sense of security, was always there, always reliable.

Husband: There was something mysterious about her.

Stress

Wife: He is boring.

Husband: She is never completely there, there's no true intimacy.

Attraction

Wife: He seemed like the kind of a man who would reach high, be a success.

Husband: She seemed like someone who could build a home for me.

Stress

Wife: He travels a lot, meets all kinds of people, is never home.

Husband: She is too homely, not exciting.

Attraction

Wife: He seemed very easy-going.

Husband: I liked her energy. She was very active, things were always happening around her.

Stress

Wife: He doesn't stand up for his own rights, is not assertive.

Husband: She explodes at the slightest provocation, has tantrums.

Attraction

Wife: He seemed very smart, very capable.

Husband: She respected me. I felt accepted and appreciated.

Stress

Wife: He makes me feel stupid and incompetent.

Husband: She feels bad about herself and blames me.

Attraction

Wife: He was like a rock, strong, someone you can lean on.

Husband: She seemed very sensitive, good "wife" material.

Stress

Wife: He is like a block, you can't convince him of anything.

Husband: She is too sensitive, too involved with the home and the children.

Attraction

Wife: He seemed fatherly and wise, someone you can rely on.

Husband: She was like a little girl who needs protection, vulnerable, sensitive.

Stress

Wife: His fatherly calm can drive me nuts, I try to shake him up.

Husband: Her childish tantrums are very hard to take.

Attraction

Wife: He seemed very wise, mature, and knowledgeable about life.

Husband: She seemed full of life, loved nature, was open to the world.

Stress

Wife: He tries to teach me all the time, and wants to tie me to the house.

Husband: She doesn't take care of the house, is not a housewife.

Attraction

Husband: I was impressed by her. She seemed very competent and very confident.

Wife: He was adoring and tried to impress me. I liked it. It made me feel special.

Stress

Husband: I feel put down by her. She doesn't respect my wishes, is withholding.

Wife: He behaves like an irresponsible child and forces me to be the bad mother.

Attraction

Wife: He adored me. I was the center of his world.

Husband: She was beautiful and smart, all my friends envied me.

Stress

Wife: He is jealous and possessive. His insecurity drives me nuts.

Husband: She criticizes me and puts me down. It hurts my feelings.

there is an obvious complementarity between the causes of attraction and stress mentioned by the husband and those mentioned by the wife.

It is possible to argue that couples who come to therapy are a select group; they are more likely to experience this type of disillusionment; and unconscious, unresolved issues are more common among these couples.

However, the experiences of people who participate in workshops as part of their professional training, or as part of an enrichment program for employees, seem to suggest that this is not the case. Unlike couples in therapy, these people do not choose to learn about themselves and their relationships. Yet, to their great amazement, they, too, find the connection between what made them fall in love and what later became the focus of their stress, disappointment, and annoyance.

In my work on couple burnout, a work that involved hundreds of couples, I also found that the qualities that initially attract partners to each other eventually cause their burnout. A woman who was attracted to her husband because he was "the strong silent type," which she saw as "very romantic," later feels burned out in her marriage because "he doesn't communicate." A man who fell in love with his wife because of her strong personality, later feels burned out because she argues with him about everything (Pines, 1996).

Another possible criticism of the finding of the 100 "wise unconscious choices" is that they were not subjected to objective coding criteria; that, as a clinician, it is possible that I looked for evidence to fit the theory and influenced people to see a pattern that wasn't there. I have two answers to this criticism. First, when people hear about the connection between the qualities that attracted them and the qualities that have become stresses in the relationship, they are quick to agree with it. Second, as we will see next, seeing that connection has a very positive effect on couples.

VARIATIONS ON THE THEME

Some people fall in love, marry the person with whom they fell in love, and remain happily married ever after. Some people repeat over and over again the same pattern of frustrating romantic relationships. They leave one partner because he or she is too suffocating, or too withdrawn and withholding, only to fall in love with another, very similar to the first. Other people, aware of their childhood deprivations and frustrations and determined to avoid them at all costs, choose a partner who is the exact opposite of the parent with whom they had an unresolved issue. However, choosing the opposite still means engagement with the issue, but in its opposite version. As we can see in the following two examples, even in such cases, things that were at first attractive later turn into frustrations.

Gary was born to a large, close-knit Italian family on the East Coast. He felt suffocated by the family's constant pressures and intrusions into every aspect of his life, and hated the endless, never-ending, crowded, noisy family events. He moved to the West Coast to escape the family, especially his "suffocating" mother. He started dating women who were the exact opposite of his mother. While his mother was short, fat, dark, loud, as well as very warm and nurturing, the women he fell in love with were all tall, skinny blonds with long straight hair and reserved demeanors. They also didn't like cooking, the exact opposite of his mother whose kitchen was her acknowledged empire. Again and again Gary would fall in love with one of these "cool blonds," but after a while his enthusiasm would stall. The reason, in every case, was that the tall, skinny blond wasn't warm enough, wasn't loving and nurturing enough.

Joan met her husband after the painful termination of a stormy love affair in which she felt like she was constantly "swinging wildly, tied to a dragon's tail." Her husband who was "a wonderful person," the exact opposite of her father, promised her a life of calm security. And he kept his promise. He was a doting husband and a wonderful father to their three children. Joan, whose primitive, violent father used to beat her and her brother viciously, appreciated her husband and his warm family who accepted her with open arms; she loved the home that she and her husband created for their children. Her husband believed in her and his faith helped build her self-confidence. Her new self-confidence helped her succeed in the world of business and her business success helped enhance her self-confidence even further.

With the increase in her self-confidence there was a decrease in her need for her husband's support and admiration. The calm and security he provided, so appealing and so significant to her at the beginning of the relationship, turned to boredom. The lack of drama and excitement that she craved after the excessive drama of her abusive childhood and previous relationship, so important to her at the beginning of her relationship with her husband, a calm that had helped build her sense of security and confidence, now became an intolerable deprivation.

There are cases in which people are able to resolve a childhood issue through a romantic relationship, through therapy, or through other significant life changes. As a result, they are ready for a truly different type of relationship. These are often cases in which the unresolved childhood issue was less traumatic and did not involve severe abuse, neglect, or rejection. George is an example.

George was the middle child in a large and very poor family. He had six brothers and sisters. His father, who was a hard working farmer, was a gentle and kind man. His mother was a powerful dominant woman who constantly criticized the father for his incompetence as a breadwinner. While the atmosphere in the home was warm and loving, the economic hardship was oppressive. George remembers with great pain the times he was unable to attend friends' birthday parties because his parents couldn't afford to buy a birthday gift.

George fell in love with a woman who came from a wealthy middle-class family. He admired her "class" and superior manners and felt grateful when she agreed to be his wife. His wife's superior attitude toward him and his family, which she expressed in such "little" ways as constantly correcting his language, helped reenact George's parents' marriage.

The significant life change that prepared George for a different type of relationship was his economic success as a businessman. The respect and prominence that he achieved as a result of this success, built George's self-confidence. While his wife continued her efforts to keep the status difference between them, George felt that her superior attitude toward him was no longer appropriate. Indeed, his next romantic relationship started as a friendship based on deep professional respect. It was with a successful career woman with whom he had a business relationship. The woman adored George and saw him as a brilliant businessman and a very exciting man. Her perception, and the relationship with her, felt much more "right" for the new George, the George who had freed himself from the feelings of inferiority and vulnerability that were a legacy from his childhood.

The assumption that unconscious romantic choices are inherently wise is most easily challenged in the cases of people, most often women, who suffered serious abuse in their childhoods, and who are attracted to partners who exhibit behavioral patterns similar to those of their abusive parents. Such a romantic choice seems, for obvious reasons, extremely unwise. It is possible to argue, however, that even in these difficult and, at times even tragic, cases, the attraction is based on an unconscious drive to overcome the early trauma, and in that sense is wise. Often times, in such cases, unless the abusive partner is willing to work on the issues at the root of the abusive behavior, the only way to avoid abusive relationships for a woman who was abused as a child is to avoid people she is extremely attracted to.[4]

At times, people who are aware of the destructive and frustrating patterns they have internalized, especially if they have had painful intimate relationships that repeated these patterns, decide to ignore them and choose a person who is a soul mate and a kindred spirit. Such a person tends to be a close friend who comes from a similar background, and has similar attitudes and interests, someone who is kind and considerate and can be trusted. Typically, such a person is also not very exciting sexually. Such friendship relationships tend to be very warm, very pleasant, very comfortable and easy, but lack "insane" passion.

Every choice has advantages and disadvantages. A romantic choice directed by unconscious forces, in an attempt to overcome a childhood trauma, is characterized by powerful, electrifying, physical attraction, intense emotional excitement and obsessive love—the more serious the early trauma the more obsessive the love. A conscious romantic choice, in an attempt to ignore the past and build a relationship with a close, kind, and understanding friend assures an easy, comfortable, pleasant relationship with fewer highs and fewer lows.

RELATIONSHIP PROBLEMS AS OPPORTUNITIES FOR GROWTH

The existence of a relationship between the original attraction and the cause of couple distress has an important and very practical implication. It suggests that an intimate relationship provides one of the best opportunities to work on unresolved family-of-origin issues. When a couple realizes how the things that made them fall in love with each other later become the core issue in their relationship, feelings of guilt and blame are reduced. Breaking the "blame frame" makes people much more willing to take responsibility for their parts in their relationship problems. This is very important, because issues related to the family of origin are almost always at the heart of a couple's issues.[5]

A couple's problems are very often repeated attempts to correct, overcome, cope, reenact, or erase old conflicts that originated in infantile relationships. These conflicts are transferred to adult intimate relationships. A couple copes with old anxieties and frustrations through their intimate relationship. The partners work to resolve their own intrapsychic conflicts (occurring within their psyches) through interpersonal conflicts with each other.

People cope with conflicts that originated in frustrating or threatening experiences in their childhood by shaping their intimate relationships to fit patterns similar to the ones they experienced in their families of origin. They typically do it in one of the following three ways. They fall in love with a person who resembles in a significant way the parent with whom they have an unresolved issue. Or, they unconsciously push a partner to act the way that parent acted. Or, they project an internal romantic image onto a partner and perceive the partner as similar to the parent even when no real similarity exists.[6]

The feelings generated in such intimate relationships, and in intimate relationships in general, have the kind of powerful intensity that is not usually found in other human relationships such as friendship, work, or neighborhood. A romantic partner who is capable of generating intense positive emotions at the beginning of the relationship is capable later in the relationship of generating equally intense negative emotions. A couple's conflicts, even when they are supposedly centered on trivial issues, are perceived as having existential significance. And, indeed, a couple's conflict is in the deepest sense an existential struggle. Couple therapists describe it jokingly when they say that marriage is the battleground to which two families of origin send their representatives to fight a war that will determine which family will direct the couple's lives.

In therapy, couples learn to identify the errors they make in their perceptions of each other. A woman, after checking repeatedly with her husband, realizes that when she thinks he is angry, he is actually hurt. And they learn to recognize feelings they did not admit to in themselves but, instead, projected onto their partners. In the case of this woman, she recognized her own anger that she had denied. This recognition helps develop a more complete, integrated, and secure sense of self in both partners and a perception of the other as different, independent, and non-threatening.

Working on couple conflicts enables the resolution of individual issues. This does not necessarily mean that couples get over their infantile feelings and needs. In a mature and healthy intimate relationship they don't have to. In such relationships, partners can tolerate each other's infantile needs and are willing to make an effort to satisfy them.

Couples who learn to accept each other also learn to accept themselves, including those denied and suppressed parts of themselves which they had worked so hard to ignore. Total acceptance of the other, especially of infantile and needy parts, requires empathy. Empathy implies feeling what the other feels. This can be very scary for undifferentiated individuals who don't have firm ego boundaries. Such a person does not feel a secure sense of self or psychological independence. Feeling what the partner feels means denying or giving up personal feelings. Here, once again, the ability to listen to an intimate partner and express empathy not only testifies to the existence of a separated and individuated self but also helps develop it.

HOW TO TURN COUPLE PROBLEMS INTO
OPPORTUNITIES FOR GROWTH

The first step is developing awareness. It starts with an exploration of the things that made the couple fall in love with each other, the things that are most problematic for them in each other, and the connection between the two. Both families of origin need to be examined, with an emphasis on the relationship each partner had with each parent, the relationship between the parents, the connections among these three relationships for each partner, and the couple's core issue. At the end of this step both partners should understand why they chose to be in the relationship and be willing to take responsibility for their part in their couple problems.

Awareness of the role they played by falling in love and taking responsibility for their romantic choice helps people better control its outcome. This taking of responsibility, or "self-focus," requires changing the direction of the flashlight of awareness to point away from the partner and toward the self; thus, it forgoes the far easier solution of blaming the partner for disappointments in the relationship.

The second step, and the harder step for many, is *expressing empathy*. Couples can be taught to listen to each other and to express empathy, although the lower the level of differentiation of a couple, the harder this is. *Mirroring*—one of the most basic and important techniques in behavioral marital therapy—is a good way to start. Here is how it is done.

With clear instruction to talk about oneself, without judging, criticizing, or attacking the other, each partner is asked, in turn, to talk about an important problem or issue. The other partner is instructed to listen, is permitted to ask clarification questions, but make no other response, and then "mirror," or reflect back in his or her own words, what was heard and understood. If it seems to the speaking partner that the listening partner "didn't get it," the speaker can explain again and again, until the listener understands.

Harville Hendrix (1992) adds to this classic exercise the crucial component of empathy. In his version of the exercise, after it is clear that the listener understood fully what the speaker tried to say, all the aspects of the problem are raised and discussed by using such questions as, "Is that all?" or "Is there anything else?" Then the listener is encouraged to express empathy by explaining how the personality, history, and experiences of the speaker, make the speaker's feelings perfectly understandable. The expression of empathy is wonderful for the person receiving it, and is a powerful impetus for personal growth in the person expressing it.

The third step is *behavioral change*. After both partners understand the deeper dynamic of their relationship and are able to express empathy for each other's feelings and needs, it is easier for them to give each other the gift of the thing each most desires (Hendrix, 1988). Given the special dynamic of couple relationships, the effort to grant the partner's wish is the most effective way to bring about personal growth. After all, the partner is asking for the expression of parts in the self that have been repressed or projected onto the partner. And so, when a woman behaves in a more rational manner as a gift to her husband and when a man expresses his deep emotions as a gift to his wife, both the husband and the wife as well as their marriage grow.

SUMMARY AND CONCLUSIONS

From everything said so far in this chapter and throughout the book, it is possible to draw a number of conclusions.

- An intimate relationship provides one of the best opportunities for mastering unresolved childhood issues.
- Unconscious forces more than logical considerations dictate those with whom we fall in love.
- The unconscious choice is of the most appropriate person with whom the individual can reenact childhood experiences. Such a person combines the most significant traits of both parents.
- Negative traits have more of an impact on romantic choices, especially in obsessive loves, than do positive traits, because the injury or deprivation caused by them needs healing.
- The more traumatic the childhood injury, and the greater the similarity between the partner and the injuring parent, the more intense the experience of falling in love.
- In falling in love there is a return to the primal symbiosis with Mother, a perfect union with no ego boundaries. This is why we only fall in love with one person at a time. The return to the lost paradise recreates the expectation that the lover will fill all infantile needs.
- Since falling in love is dictated by an internal romantic image, lovers feel as if they have known each other forever. And since it involves a reenactment of very specific and very powerful

childhood experiences, lovers feel that the beloved is "the one and only" and that the loss of the beloved is unbearable.

- When a couple falls in love, their unconscious choice is mutual and complementary, enabling both partners to express their own "core issues." Together they create their "core issue" as a couple, the issue around which most of their later conflicts center.

- Understanding the connection between unresolved childhood issues and later problems reduces feelings of guilt and blame, and helps both partners take responsibility for their parts in the relationship problems. It helps couples turn problems into opportunities for personal and couple growth.

- Couples who listen to each other's feelings and needs, express empathy, and give each other the things they ask for, can keep the romantic spark alive indefinitely. The reason for this is that expressing empathy and granting the partner's wishes that grow out of the connection between the couple dynamic and childhood issues, is the best way to bring about personal and couple growth. As the partners grow psychologically, their relationship grows. And growth is the antithesis of burnout (Pines & Aronson, 1988).

And finally, once again, on the many perspectives on love:

> As there are as many
> minds as there are heads,
> so there are as many kinds
> of love as there are hearts.
> —Leo Tolstoy, *Anna Karenina*

As I noted in the introductory chapter, this book addresses only one of the many forms of love—romantic love. It addresses only the romantic love between two people who actually have a relationship and excludes those cases in which love is one-sided or unrequited. And it only addresses one stage of romantic love—falling in love. Only in this last chapter do we refer to problems that couples have later on in the relationships, but even this discussion ties the problems to the falling-in-love stage. From the many perspectives on falling in love, this book focuses on the psychological perspective, with brief mentions of the biological, historical, social, and cultural perspectives. It argues that every experience of falling in love has a unique emotional and psychological dynamic based on an interaction between the conscious and unconscious, repressed and projected, parts of both partners. In a combination unique to each partner, those parts are influenced by two parents and the relationship between them. Because falling in love is such a unique experience, a definition of falling in love is never offered. Readers are invited to contemplate their own unique definition.

The emphasis on the unconscious influences on falling in love may leave the impression that the past, especially early childhood, has complete influence on romantic choices. This is definitely not the case. As we saw in the first part of the book, environmental, situational, dispositional, social, cultural, and even genetic factors also play a role in falling in love, even more so in mate selection. In addition, logical considerations, social and familial pressures, plans for the future, spiritual quests, and romantic ideals affect romantic choices.

Studies show that people's expectations of love relationships and their romantic ideals affect their experiences in romantic relationships (Morrow & O'Sullivan, 1998). People who believe in romantic destiny, that potential romantic partners are either meant for each other or they are not, have a stronger connection between their initial satisfaction with a romantic relationship and that relationship's longevity, than people who don't. They also tend to use avoidance strategies in dealing with relationship problems and take more responsibility for ending the relationship by describing it as wrong from the beginning. On the other hand, people who believe that successful relationships are cultivated and developed have more long-term approaches to dating, use more relationship-maintaining coping strategies, and, even if a relationship has ended, disagree that it was wrong from the start (Knee, 1998).

So romantic ideals and expectations about romantic relationships have an impact. But do they tell us the specific person with whom we are going to fall in love or why? The answer is no. The best answer to this most fascinating of questions about romantic love is offered by clinical theories that describe, each using its own terminology, the internal romantic image. The theories suggest that people fall in love with a person who reminds them of their parents, especially a parent with whom they have an unresolved issue. The more intense the unresolved issue, the more intense the experience of falling in love, with incredible highs when the infantile needs are satisfied, and incredible lows when the infantile needs are frustrated the way they were in childhood.

Because parents are complex people whose traits are both positive and negative and with whom the relationship is multi-layered and complex, because our childhoods include a huge number of experiences some positive and some negative, and because our romantic images continue evolving throughout our lives—our internal romantic images are complex and applicable to more than one person. The same person creates with every romantic partner a unique pattern of interaction. At times, a person will fall in love with one lover who satisfies a core issue such as a need for security, but once that need is satisfied, the person will fall in love with another lover who will satisfy the opposite need for drama and excitement. At times people don't see the beloved at all, but fall in love with the projection of a romantic image.

Despite the unique emotional pattern of every romantic relationship, all romantic relationships share one dynamic—a constant battle between forces pulling for symbiosis and forces pulling for individuation. The forces pulling for symbiosis are fueled by the longing to get back to the safety of the primal symbiosis with Mother. The forces pulling for individuation are fueled by the desire to do something unique and significant that will give meaning to life. When people fall in love, the forces pulling for merging and symbiosis win. But in most relationships, after a period of time that can be days, months, or years, the forces pulling for individuation become stronger. When a relationship remains stuck in the symbiotic stage, the result is a suffocating relationship in which people have little sense of their individual selves as separate from the other (Bader & Pearson, 1988).

Intimate relationships that keep the romantic spark alive are characterized by a balance between the need for intimacy and security and the need for individuation and self-actualization. In these relationships both partners feel secure enough in their individuality and ego boundaries that intimacy and closeness are not perceived as threatening and dangerous. Experiences of fusion when they happen, for example, during orgasm, are experienced as pleasurable rather than as scary. This type of relationship can be described by the metaphor of "roots and wings" (Pines, 1996).

In *roots and wings* relationships, the *roots* symbolize intimacy, togetherness, security, and commitment. The *wings* symbolize individuation, self-actualization, and self-expression. The togetherness supports self-actualization, and self-actualization strengthens the togetherness. But what is more important, in the context of a book about falling in love, is that in "roots and wings" relationships, couples manage to keep, indefinitely, the romantic spark of the falling-in-love stage.

Falling in love and having a romantic involvement have a positive effect on people's psychological well-being. People in romantic relationships feel closer to their ideal selves and feel better about themselves (Campbell et al., 1994). In other words, falling in love is not only a positive experience in and of itself, it is an important experience within the context of people's emotional life and within the life of their romantic relationship.

In *Ethics of the Fathers* (Mishna 15), it is said that "All is foreseen, yet freedom of choice is granted; and by grace is the universe judged, yet all is according to the amount of work." This Mishna (Oral Law) is usually interpreted as meaning that everything is predetermined by God, yet a person still has free will. As a psychologist I choose to interpret it differently: while our genetic makeups and childhood experiences are engraved in us, by influencing the way we look, our personalities, and our basic attitudes toward ourselves, toward others, and toward love, we can still choose whether, or how, to follow the scripts in our romantic love relationships.

Appendix

ATTRACTION DATA

An Analysis of a Romantic Relationship

Dating frequency (7 = non-stop dating to 1 = never dated):_____

Number of significant intimate relationships:_____

Length of this relationship:_____

Commitment to a/the relationship (7 = happily married to 1 = never was in a relationship): _____

Sense of security in the relationship (7 = very high to 1 = very low):_____

Ability to be oneself in the relationship (7 = definitely yes):_____

Level of intimacy in the relationship (7 = very high):_____

Power in the relationship (7 = the interviewee has all the power to 1 = the partner has all the power):_____

Pursuer/Distances (1 = the interviewee is the pursuer to 7 = interviewee is the distancer):_____

Physical attraction to partner (7 = very strong attraction):_____

Friendship before romance (7 = great friendship): _____

Stereotyped sex roles (7 = very stereotyped):_____

Frequency of conflicts (7 = fighting all the time to 1 = never fight):_____

Ability to deal with conflicts (7 = very high)_____

How are conflicts resolved (fight/flight/talk):_____

Ability to stand separation (7 = very high ability to 1 = very low ability):_____

Jealousy is a problem in the relationship (7 = a serious problem):_____

Jealousy is a personal problem (7 = a serious problem):_____

Arousal played a role in the initial attraction (yes/no):_____

Propinquity played a role in the initial attraction (yes/no):_____

Similarity played a role in the initial attraction (yes/no):_____

Partner's attraction played a role in the initial attraction (yes/no):_____

Physical attraction played a role in the initial attraction (yes/no):_____

Personality traits of the partner played a role in the initial attraction (yes/no):_____

Status of partner played a role in the initial attraction (yes/no):_____

Is/was partner satisfying an important need? (yes/no): _____

Is the partner described as the "best friend"? (yes/no):_____

Was it love at first sight? (yes/no): _____

Is the interviewee showing psychological understanding? (yes/no/not clear): _____
Is partner similar to father (yes/no/not clear):_____
Is partner similar to mother (yes/no/not clear):_____
Is partner different from father (yes/no/not clear):_____
Is partner different from mother (yes/no/not clear):_____
Are the relationships with partner and parents similar? (yes/no/not clear)_____

Sexual preference:_____
Number of children:_____
Abuse in the relationship (definitely not, possibly, probably, definitely): _____

TABLE ONE

Attraction Variables by Sex and Country: Percentages

(Pearson Chi-Square. df = 1)

	SEX		COUNTRY	
	MEN	WOMEN	USA	ISRAEL
Arousal	16%	30%	22%	25%
Chi-Square	4.6 p = .04		.3	
Propinquity	52%	57%	63%	46%
Chi-Square	.4		4.8 p = .03	
Similarity	19%	20%	29.5%	8%
Chi-Square	.1		12.2 p = .001	
Need Fulfillment	56%	58%	54%	60%
Chi-Square	.1		.7	
Best Friends	21%	34%	25%	31%
Chi-Square	3.6 p = .06		.9	
Mate's Attraction	35%	46 %	41%	40%
Chi-Square	2.2		.03	
Appearance	80%	53 %	63%	70%
Chi-Square	13.8 p = .000		1.04	
Personality	89%	97%	92%	94%
Chi-Square	4.0 p = .07		.2	
Love at First Sight	7%	12%	11%	8%
Chi-Square	1.1		.4	
Status	4%	4%	8%	0%
Chi-Square	.1		6.9 p = .014	

TABLE TWO

Analysis of Variance

Attraction Variables by Sex and Country: Means

	USA		ISRAEL				
	MEANS				ANOVA		
	MEN	WOMEN	MEN	WOMEN	COUNTRY	SEX	INTER.
					F p	F p	F p
Physical Attraction	4.2	2.8	4.5	3.4	3.8*	26***	
Status or Dominance	2.6	2.5	2.1	2.3		5.6*	
Friendship Preceded	3.2	3.5	2.9	2.8			
Significant Relationships	1.2	1.5	1.5	1.8	4.5*	4.1*	
Dating Frequency	3.5	3.4	3.7	3.1		8.3**	5.2*

TABLE THREE

Analysis of Variance

Relationship Variables by Sex and Country

	USA		ISRAEL				
	MEANS				ANOVA		
	MEN	WOMEN	MEN	WOMEN	COUNTRY	SEX	INTER.
					F p	F p	F p
Relationship Length	17	25	24	24			
Being Oneself	4.3	4.9	5.0	4.9			
Handling Separation	4.2	3.9	4.0	3.7		3.2*	
Pursuer/Distancer	4.2	4.1	4.1	3.9			
Security	4.1	4.7	4.9	4.8	4.8*		
Power in Relationship	4.0	4.0	4.1	3.9			
Frequency of Conflicts	4.0	4.2	4.0	3.9			
Intimacy	3.9	4.9	4.8	4.8	3.0*	10.0**	6.0*
Commitment	3.5	4.4	3.9	4.2		9.4**	
Self-Understanding	3.5	3.8	3.5	3.5			
Handling of Conflicts	3.4	3.9	4.3	4.4	10.9**		
Sex-Role Stereotyping	3.3	2.6	2.3	2.6	5.8*		
Understanding Mate	3.0	3.4	3.3	3.4		bn 4.8*	
Relationship Jealousy	3.0	3.2	2.8	2.7			
Personal Jealousy	2.4	2.8	2.6	2.3			4.3*

TABLE FOUR

Pearson Correlation Coefficients with Relationship Variables

(only significant correlations are noted)

	MEN & WOMEN		MEN		WOMEN	
WITH RELATIONSHIP LENGTH	r	p	r	p	r	p
Commitment	.46	.0001	.74	.0001		
Security	.42	.0001	.57	.0001		
Intimacy	.39	.0002	.37	.015	.32	.03
Being Oneself	.39	.0002	.38	.01	.34	.02
Understanding Mate	.37	.0004	.36	.02	.30	.04
Self-Understanding	.33	.002	.36	.02		
Jealousy in the Relationship	.29	.006	.37	.01		
Frequency of Conflicts	.25	.02				
WITH COMMITMENT	r	p	r	p	r	p
Security	.65	.0001	.71	.0001	.56	.0001
Understanding Mate	.60	.0001	.51	.0004	.65	.0001
Intimacy	.57	.0001	.51	.0004	.54	.0001
Being Oneself	.57	.0001	.53	.0003	.54	.0001
Handling Conflicts	.53	.0001	.36	.02	.64	.0001
Relationship Length	.46	.0001	.74	.0001		
Self-Understanding	.43	.0001	.38	.01	.41	.004
Dating Frequency	.27	.009			.34	.02
Significant Relationships	.24	.03				
Frequency of Conflicts	-.23	.03			-.48	.0008
Friendship before Romance	.22	.03				
Power	.22	.04				
Attraction to Dominance	-.22	.04				
Physical Attraction	-.21	.04				
WITH POWER	r	p	r	p	r	p
Being the Distancer	.80	.0001	.86	.0001	.71	.0001
Security	.54	.0001	.59	.0001	.49	.0005
Handling Separation	.51	.0001	.43	.004	.66	.0001
Attraction to Dominance	-.22	.04	-.46	.0020		
Commitment	.22	.04				
Number of Relationships	.22	.04				
Sex Role Stereotyping			.44	.004	-.39	.007
Dating Frequency			.33	.03		

	MEN & WOMEN		MEN		WOMEN	
WITH BEING THE DISTANCER	r	p	r	p	r	p
Power in the Relationship	.80	.0001	.86	.0001	.71	.0001
Handling Separation	.68	.0001	.66	.0001	.71	.0001
Security	.48	.0001	.57	.0001		
Attraction to Dominance	-.27	.01	-.48	.001		
Sex Role Stereotyping			.40	.01	-.37	.01
Dating Frequency					-.42	.003
WITH INTIMACY	r	p	r	p	r	p
Being Oneself	.82	.0001	.87	.0001	.73	.0001
Understanding Mate	.71	.0001	.78	.0001	.51	.0003
Handling Conflicts	.65	.0001	.70	.0001	.60	.0001
Security	.62	.0001	.56	.0001	.70	.0001
Commitment	.57	.0001	.51	.0004	.54	.0001
Self-Understanding	.44	.0001	.56	.0001		
Friendship before Romance	.41	.0001	.49	.0008		
Relationship Length	.39	.0002	.37	.015	.32	.03
Sex-Role Stereotyping	-.38	.0002	-.31	.04	-.37	.01
WITH SEX-ROLE STEREOTYPING	r	p	r	p	r	p
Understanding Mate	-.43	.0001	-.32	.04	-.51	.0003
Intimacy	-.38	.0002	-.31	.04	-.37	.01
Handling Conflicts	-.35	.0009	-.30	.05	-.35	.02
Physical Attraction	.34	.001	.34	.03		
Friendship before Romance	-.31	.004	-.42	.005		
Being Oneself	-.28	.008			-.54	.0001
Self-Understanding	-.25	.02			-.34	.02
Significant Relationships			.50	.002		
Power			.44	.004	-.39	.007
Being the Distancer			.40	.01	-.37	.01
Security					-.49	.0005
Handling Separation					-.45	.002
Attraction to Dominance					.44	.003
Commitment					-.33	.03
Jealousy as a Personal Problem					.29	.05

Notes

INTRODUCTION: About Falling In Love And About This Book

1. This clinical study is part of a longitudinal study carried out at the University of California, Berkeley, by developmental psychologists Jeanne and Jack Block. The study was initiated over twenty years ago by Jeanne Block who, besides being a pioneer and a leading scholar on the influence of differential socialization on the personality development of boys and girls, was a remarkable human being, a real *mensch,* and a lady. Jeanne died an untimely death of cancer. Like almost everyone who knew her, I loved and admired Jeanne. I hope I can make in this book a small contribution toward keeping her memory alive.

Jeanne and Jack Block followed 103 children from age 3 and until age 23. In one of the parts of the follow-up study that took place at age 23, 93 of the young men and women were interviewed extensively about their romantic relationships. (During the 20 years of the research some of the original 103 subjects dropped out of the study, and others, for one reason or another, were not interviewed in this final stage.) I transcribed these interviews and analyzed them. Some of the 93 interviewees had never been in a romantic relationship while others were already married and had a child. Some even managed to get divorced by age 23.

The data gathered in the study were supported by a National Institute of Mental Health Grant M11 16080. I wish to thank Adam Kreman for his computer implementations and Jack Block for his permission to use this data.

Some of the results of the study were presented in a paper entitled "A prospective study of personality and gender differences in romantic attraction" (Pines, 1998b).

2. The Israeli part of the cross-cultural study was carried out at Tel-Aviv University and The Institute of Technology Arts and Sciences, with the help of my psychology students, Liat Bernstein, Keren Adir, Dana Talmor, Shalhevet Cohen, Michal Katz, Irit Noiberg, Rachel Radsevski, Sarit Reisman, Ruti Sharf, and Dalit Shoshan. Results of the study, "Gender and culture in romantic attraction" (Pines, 1998a), were presented at the 24th International Congress of Applied Psychology.

3. This study is described in the third part of the book as well as in the article entitled "Fatal attraction or wise unconscious choices: The relationship between causes for entering and breaking intimate relationships" (Pines, 1997).

4. I also examined various aspects of the relationships. Who has more power in the relationship? Who is the pursuer and who is the distancer? How rigidly defined are the sex roles in the relationship? Does the relationship provide a sense of security? Can one be oneself in it? What is the frequency of conflicts? What are the conflicts about? How, and how successfully, are conflicts handled? Is jealousy a problem either for the person

or in the relationship? How difficult are temporary separations? Is there any evidence of physical or emotional abuse or of drug use? Is the relationship heterosexual, bisexual, or homosexual? What are the plans for the future? People who were not currently in a relationship were asked with what kind of a person they would like to be involved.

The Appendix presents some of the data based on these analyses.

5. I elaborate on this point in my book *Couple Burnout*.

6. The Greek names for the six styles of love were *storge* (best friends), *agape* (unselfish), *mania* (possessive), *pragma* (practical), *lodus* (playful), and *eros* (romantic).

LOVE STYLES
(adapted from Lasswell & Lobsenz, 1980)

Passionate love: You are in love with love and willing to tolerate anything for love.
Game-playing love: You view a relationship as a challenge without a need for commitment.
Friendship love: You enjoy a comfortable non-romantic intimacy in which sex is secondary.
Logical love: You are concerned with a mutual compatibility in which reason rules.
Possessive love: You are consumed by the need to possess and be possessed.
Selfless love: You subordinate yourself to others and are devoted and sacrificing.

---

7. In Robert Sternberg's "triangular model of love," when none of the three basic components of love—intimacy, passion, and commitment—is present, the result is non-love. A relationship with passion and commitment is "Hollywood style" fatuous love. A relationship with intimacy and commitment but no passion is companionate love. (Sternberg, 1986)

8. My book *Couple Burnout* is devoted to a discussion of what happens to intimate relationships after the falling-in-love stage.

1   Proximity, The Hidden Matchmaker

1. In 63 percent of the interviews, propinquity was mentioned as a cause of attraction. It may also be worth noting that despite the somewhat larger effect that acquaintance had on women, the gender difference in this case was small and insignificant (67 percent of the women as compared to 58 percent of the men).

2   Arousal, The Elixir Of Love

1. In 22 percent of the interviews, the romantic relationship started in a period of great emotional turmoil. While women were more likely than men to describe a state of arousal at the start of the relationship, 24 percent of the women vs. 19 percent of the men, the sex difference was not significant. In several cases the woman wasn't attracted to the man at first. But he was there for her in her hour of need, and with time her feelings of gratitude and appreciation turned to love.

2. A study showed that even in a laboratory setting, misattribution can generate in

subjects feelings of love and excitement within two minutes of acquaintance (Keller-man, 1989). Also, a recent metaanalysis that summarized the results of 33 studies on the effect of arousal on romantic attraction suggests that arousal exerts a stronger influ-ence on attraction when it is ambiguous. Ambiguity refers to an inability to perceive the arousal as caused by its true source (Foster et al., 1998).

3. The study was done in Israel and included 240 men and 253 women, of whom 56 percent said they believe in love at first sight, 37 percent said they did not, and 7 percent said they didn't know. In addition, 60 percent said they believe that love can last forever, and 40 percent said they believe that everyone has a twin romantic soul.

3   Beauty and Character

1. In 92 percent of the American interviews and 94 percent of the Israeli inter-views, the subject mentioned some aspect of the partner's character when trying to ex-plain why he or she fell in love. Women mentioned personality traits more often than men; in the American interviews, 96 percent of the women and 88 percent of the men. However, the sex difference was small and insignificant. A smaller percentage, 63 per-cent of the Americans and 70 percent of the Israelis, mentioned appearance. Here, however, the sex difference was very large and statistically significant. Specifically, 81 percent of the American men, as compared to 44 percent of the women, mentioned be-ing attracted to the physical appearance of the partner.

2. The first four explanations and the studies supporting them are discussed by Sharon Brehm in her book *Intimate Relationships* (1992).

3. The six styles of love are: *storge* (best friends' love), *agape* (unselfish and sacrific-ing love), *mania* (possessive love), *pragma* (practical love), *lodus* (playful and game-play-ing love), and *eros* (romantic, erotic love). They were mentioned and discussed in the introduction.

4   Birds Of A Feather Or Opposites Attract?

1. Analysis of the romantic attachment interviews suggests that 28 percent of the men and 31 percent of the women mentioned similarity as playing a role in the initial attraction. For some reason, possibly greater social homogeneity, similarity was men-tioned significantly less frequently in the Israeli sample than it was in the American sample.

2. Literature reviews on the effect of similarity on mate selection can be found in Pines, A. M. (1996); Brehm, S. (1992); Berscheid & Hartfield–Walster (1978).

3. A third study done in Hawaii showed that the couples were similar in level of ed-ucation, verbal ability, and professional success (Nagoshi et al., 1987). The participants in the study were couples and their siblings. The researchers compared the siblings, the couples, and the couples to the siblings. They concluded that the similarities of the couples were due to both attraction to the similar and a similar social environment.

4. See, for example, Byrne & Blaylock (1963), and Levinger & Breedlove (1966), as well as Berscheid and Hartfield–Walster (1978).

5   Satisfying Needs And Reciprocating Love

1. Analysis of the romantic attraction interviews shows that in 54 percent of the American interviews, and 60 percent of the Israeli interviews, the subject mentioned that the beloved satisfied an important need.

2. See, for example, the classic works of Homans (1961) as well as Thibaut and Kelley (1959).

3. See, for example, the study by Aronson and Linder (1965) as well as the series of studies by Jones (1964).

4. Analysis of the romantic attraction interviews shows that in 40 percent of the American interviews, and 41 percent of the Israeli interviews, an indication of attraction by the beloved played an important role in the initial attraction. For women the rate was 47 percent, a bit higher than the 35 percent rate for men.

6   Falling In Love As A Process

1. In 33 percent of the cases, falling in love was gradual. In 11 percent of interviews, love was at first sight.

2. In 30 percent of the men's stories and 35 percent of the women's stories, there was a description of falling in love as a process.

7   On Gender And Love, Status And Beauty

1. There was no gender difference in the effect of geographic proximity; 58 percent of the men as compared to 67 percent of the women were influenced by it. There was no gender difference in the effect of arousal; 19 percent of the men as compared to 24 percent of the women were influenced. There was no gender difference in the effect of attractive personality traits; 88 percent of the men as compared to 96 percent of the women were influenced. There was no gender difference in the effect of similarity; 28 percent of the men as compared to 31 percent of the women were influenced. And there was no gender difference in either the effect of reciprocity in attraction, 35 percent of the men and 47 percent of the women were influenced; or the effect of satisfying needs, 53 percent of the men and 54 percent of the women were influenced.

2. The only variable in which there was a significant gender difference (in both the Israeli and the American samples) was physical attraction—81 percent of the American men as compared to 44 percent of the women mentioned it as a significant cause of attraction (Chi Sq. = 12.8, df = 1, p = .000). In addition, when describing the things that made them fall in love with their mates, men described physical attraction as having played a more significant role. On a 7-point scale, the average for men was 4.2 and for women 2.8 (t = 4.0, p = .0001).

The emphasis on physical appearance was especially pronounced in men who define sex-roles rigidly and stereotypically. The correlation between mentioning physical attraction as an important variable at the beginning of the relationship and the tendency to define sex-roles in a rigid and stereotypic way is r = .34 (p = .001).

3. The study by Alan Feingold was a "metaanalysis." For the interested reader, I'd like to add a few words about what a metaanalysis is. As the quantity of information in different areas of science exploded in recent years, an accompanying need arose to develop statistical techniques that would enable a significant summary of large volumes of research data. Metaanalysis is just such a summary. It is a sort of statistical summation of research findings, akin to a literature review. It provides in a *single number* a summary of many studies that were done on a certain subject. Metaanalysis takes into account the size of the samples when evaluating the significance of their findings. Thus, one general finding, based on a large number of studies, can include a huge number of subjects.

4. See for example, Buss & Schmitt (1993), Trievers (1972), Trost & Alberts (1998).

5. In recent years a huge number of studies were done on the psychology of gender differences. Metaanalyses involving hundreds of studies and thousands of subjects were done on such topics as gender differences in mathematical ability, verbal ability, spatial orientation, and aggression, most of them showing very small gender differences.

For example, a metaanalysis of 143 studies that investigated gender differences in aggression revealed that gender accounts for only 5 percent of the explained variance in aggression (Hyde, 1984). Similarly, a metaanalysis of 165 studies (and 1,418,899 subjects) that investigated gender differences in verbal ability showed that over 99 percent of a given score is influenced by things other than gender (Hyde & Lynn, 1988). A metaanalysis of 100 studies (involving 3,985,682 subjects) revealed an even smaller gender difference—close to zero—in mathematical ability (Hyde & Lynn, 1986). And a metaanalysis of 172 studies that examined gender differences in spatial orientation revealed that less than 5 percent of the variance is explained by gender (Hyde, 1981).

Given these consistent findings that show no gender difference in various areas, the results of a metaanalysis showing a large and significant gender difference in attitudes toward sexual intimacy is especially notable. The study showed that the difference between men and women regarding sex and intimacy are among the largest gender differences found. It is far greater than the gender differences in verbal ability, mathematical ability, and spatial orientation, and similar in size to the difference in the ability to throw to a distance (Hyde, 1993).

6. See for example, Nancy Chodorow (1978); Dorothy Dinnerstein (1976); Lillian Rubin (1983), and Jean Baker Miller (1976).

7. Results of the study showed that, significantly more so than men, women were likely to describe a partner as a best friend, and, furthermore, to describe higher levels of intimacy, commitment, and security in their intimate relationships. More than men, women were themselves in their relationships and expressed a greater understanding of a partner than men did. On the other hand, men's relationships tended to be shorter in duration and more sex-role stereotyped.

Here are the numbers: Women were more likely to describe a partner as a best friend (21 percent of the men and 34 percent of the women described a partner as a best friend; Chi Square = 9.2; p=.01) and their descriptions of their relationships indicated higher levels of intimacy (men's mean = 3.9, women's = 4.9; t = 3.5; p = .0009), commitment (men's mean = 3.5, women's mean = 4.4; t = 3.1; p = .02), and security (men's mean = 4.1, women's = 4.7). Women felt more themselves in their relationships (men's mean = 4.3, women's mean = 4.9; t = 3.1; p = .002) and women showed greater understanding of a partner than men did (men's mean = 2.9, women's mean = 3.4; t = 3.1; p = .002).

On the other hand, men described relationships that were more sex-role stereotyped (men's mean = 3.3, women's = 2.6; t = 2.3; p=.02). Women's intimate relationships tended to last longer than the relationships of men. The average length of a relationship for men was 18 months, for women 26 (t = 2.1; p = .03).

In most cases, when men described an intimate relationship, they were describing a relationship with a woman. By the same token, when women described an intimate relationship, they were describing a relationship with a man. How, then, can these descriptions be so different? It is as if there are two relationships: "his relationship" marked by physical attraction and sex role stereotyping and "her relationship" marked by intimacy, commitment, security, and a sense that intimate partners are each other's best friends.

One explanation for this puzzling finding is that it is an artifact, a result of the difference in emotional maturity between men and women at the tender age of 23. Another possible interpretation is that the men and women are describing the same relationships, but their perceptions of these relationships are different, the result of different socialization and/or different evolutionary programming. Because of these differences, deep friendship, intimacy, commitment, and security are more important to women causing them to notice these factors more in their love relationships. On the other hand, because physical attraction is more important to men, it causes them to notice it more.

8. See Beall & Sternberg (1995); Benjamin (1998); deLamater & Hyde (1998); Eagly (1987); Goldner (1998); Hyde (1990); Tavris (1992).

9. The table on page 249 presents the results of the gender by culture comparison.

8   Openness To Love

1. 12 percent of the American interviewees and 5 percent of the Israeli said that at age 23 they still had never had a romantic relationship.

2. The relationship between self-confidence and different love styles was first noted at the end of chapter three.

3. It is important to note that Kernberg's view of personality development/organization varies somewhat from traditional object-relations theory. It is also somewhat idiosyncratic diagnostically. For example, there is no diagnosis of narcissistic schizophrenic personality in the DSM IV. (One is Axis I the other Axis II.)

4. Masterson is another theoretician who talks about difficulties with intimacy that arise out of different types of personality disorders—particularly the Borderline Person-

ATTRACTION VARIABLES BY SEX AND COUNTRY

	PERCENTAGES			
	SEX		COUNTRY	
	MEN	WOMEN	USA	ISRAEL
Appearance	80%	53%	63%	70%
Chi-Square		13.8 (p = .000)	1.04	
Status	4%	4%	8%	0%
Chi-Square		.1	6.9 (p = .014)	
Arousal	16%	30%	22%	25%
Chi-Square		4.6 (p = .04)	.3	
Propinquity	52%	57%	63%	46%
Chi-Square		.4	4.8 (p = .03)	
Similarity	19%	20%	29.5%	8%
Chi-Square		.1	12.2 (p = .001)	
Need Fulfillment	56%	58%	54%	60%
Chi-Square		.1	.7	
Mate's Attraction	35%	46%	41%	40%
Chi-Square		2.2	.03	
Personality	89%	97%	92%	94%
Chi-Square		4.0 (p = .07)	.2	

ality Disorder (a need to merge, rage, and withdraw), and the Narcissistic Personality Disorder (a self-absorption that only connects in the mirror of the other person by seeing the self reflected in a positive way). Masterson makes an interesting point of how often the Borderline woman marries a Narcissistic man and how these relationships erupt in major drama. Or how two Narcissists essentially exist for each other in the mirror each holds up for the other's reflection.

5. When the mother cannot stand the baby's withdrawal, when the baby's move away from the symbiosis with her causes her anxiety, the baby internalizes symbiotic remnants such as narcissistic needs, infantile dependence, and ambivalence about them. The self develops around these pathological internalizations (called "introjects") and both their extremes can be found in the adult: feelings of inadequacy and inferiority together with grandiosity, submission, and aggression. When we see in a person evidence of a grandiose self, we can be sure to also find evidence for an inferior self. When we find the submissive self of a victim, we can be sure to also find evidence of aggression, hostility, and destructiveness.

6. For example, Benjamin (1998); Goldner (1998); Tavris (1992).

7. See for example, Chodorow (1978); Dinnerstein (1976).

8. Fairbairn (1952/1992). Fairbairn believes that the study of the schizoid personality is the most fascinating and productive in the area of psychopathology. While the

schizoid condition is among the most difficult psychopathological conditions, still, because of his introversion, the schizoid has an ability for self-examination that far ex-
ceeds that of the average person. Fairbairn also believes that everyone has schizoid
episodes. Examples of such episodes that are familiar to all of us are the strange feeling
we sometimes have in the presence of a familiar person or environment, or the feeling
of *déjà vu,* of having experienced an event before.

9   The Son Falls In Love With "Mother," The Daughter With "Father"

1. A significantly higher percentage of women than men described their partners as
similar to their fathers, 78 percent of the women as compared to 31 percent of the
men; and in the Israeli sample, 27 percent of the women as compared to 3 percent of
the men. A significantly higher percentage of men than women described their partners
as similar to their mothers, 50 percent of the men as compared to 43 percent of the
women; and in the Israeli sample, 21 percent of the men as compared to 11 percent of
the women.

The cross-cultural differences between the Israelis and the Americans can be attributed to the greater psychological sophistication of the American sample and their
greater familiarity with Freud's ideas in their popular version.

2. It should be noted that most people, both men and women, view sexuality and
motherhood as mutually exclusive. If a woman is described as sexual they don't see her
as a mother, and if they are told she is in fact a mother they assume she is a bad mother.
See Friedman, A., Weinberg, H., & Pines, A. M. (1998). Sexuality and Motherhood:
Mutually exclusive in perception of women. *Sex Roles,* 38, 781–800.

3. Anna Freud lived with a woman called Dorothy Burlington for over thirty years
and there has been ample speculation as to the nature of that relationship, but without
doubt, sexual or not, it was a primary attachment.

10   The Internal Romantic Image

1. Seventy percent of the interviewees (83 percent of the women and 55 percent of
the men) answered yes when asked if there was a similarity between their relationship
with their parents and their most significant romantic relationship. Since we can assume that the gender difference found does not mean that women's relationships are
more similar to their relationships with their parents than men's are, then another explanation is needed. One possible explanation is that women are more familiar with
psychological thinking than men are, in part because they read more psychological
books, and thus see the similarity between a childhood and adult relationship more
clearly than men do. Support for this interpretation is provided by the cross-cultural
comparison between the Americans and the Israelis. Only 30 percent of the Israeli interviewees, 38 percent of the women and 21 percent of the men, noticed a similarity
between their childhood relationship with their parents and their current romantic relationship. Once again it is far easier to explain both these cultural and gender differ-

ences as a result of differences in psychological sophistication than it is to explain them in terms of the different dynamics of intimate relationships in the two cultures.

2. People who described their childhood relationship with their parents as more similar to the relationship they had with their romantic partner also described their partner as more similar to their mother (r = .31 p = .004) and their father (r = .41 p = .000). They described themselves as feeling more secure in the relationship (r = .24 p = .03), as more able to be themselves in the relationship (r = 22 p = .047), and as more able to handle conflicts in the relationship (r = .29 p = .009). The romantic relationships they described had fewer conflicts than relationships described by people who did not notice a similarity between their partner and parents (r = .23 p = .036).

3. Other notable theoreticians of object relations theory, in addition to Margaret Mahler (1974), are Melanie Klein (1959), Ronald Fairbairn (1952) and Donald Winnicott (1965).

4. See for example: Dicks (1967), Framo (1990), Meissner (1978), Ogden (1979).

5. Helen Fisher (1998) distinguishes three primary emotion categories for mating and reproduction that can be found in humans as well as other mammals: the sex drive, attraction, and attachment. Each emotion category is associated with a discrete constellation of neural correlates and each has evolved to direct a specific aspect of reproduction. The sex drive is associated primarily with the sex hormones estrogen, the female hormone, and androgen, the male hormone. It evolved to motivate individuals to seek sexual union. The attraction system is associated primarily with the catecholamines, neurotransmitters that activate various systems in the brain. This system evolved to facilitate mate choice and enable individuals to focus their mating efforts on preferred partners. The attachment system is associated primarily with peptides, amino acids that regulate various systems in the brain including the reproductive system. The attachment system evolved in order to motivate individuals to engage in positive social behaviors and assume parental duties.

11   Four Stories

1. The four tables demonstrate how the romantic interviews presented throughout the book have been analyzed. They serve to help interested readers understand the research appendix and how the numbers presented in it were obtained. They can also help interested readers to analyze their own relationships. It is recommended that couples do this kind of analysis separately, by using copies of the form presented in the appendix, and then compare their scores.

12   Turning Love Problems Into Opportunities For Growth

1. See, for example, Bowen (1978); Dicks (1967); Freud (1921); Hendrix (1992); Kernberg (1974); and Meissner (1978). The psychodynamic perspective was presented in chapter ten as part of the discussion on object relations theory.

2. A woman like Ann is likely to push intimate partners away with her angry out-

bursts because in this way, rather than be as helpless as she felt as a child when her father abandoned her and her mother, she can control the desertion.

3. See Pines (1997) for details. I worked with the 100 couples during the years 1995–1996.

4. When the abusive partner is willing to work on the issues at the root of the abusive behavior, feminist psychoanalytic theory has some profound insights about the early childhood determinants of this behavior. Some of these were described in chapter ten of this book. For an especially deep and profound article, see Virginia Goldner's paper entitled "Violence and Victimization in Intimate Relationship: A Feminist Intersubjective Perspective" (1998).

5. This point was made by many leading couple therapists, among them Bowen (1978); Dicks (1967); Framo (1980); Givelber (1990); Meissner (1978).

6. As noted in chapter ten, when these dynamics were first mentioned, most people didn't see their partners the way they really were because old family ghosts obscured their views.

References

Ainsworth, M. D. S. (1989). Attachment beyond infancy. *American Psychologist*, 44, 709–716.

Ainsworth, M. D. S., Blehar, M., Waters, E., & Wall, S. (1978). *Patterns of Attachment*. Hillsdale, NJ: Erlbaum.

Alberoni, F. (1983). *Falling in Love*. New York: Random House.

Alicke, M. D., Smith, R. H., & Klotz, M. L. (1986). Judgments of physical attractiveness: The roles of faces and bodies. *Personality and Social Psychology Bulletin*, 12, 381–389.

Allen, J. B., Kenrick, D. T., Linder, D. E., McCall, M. A. (1989). Arousal and Attribution: A response facilitation alternative to misattribution and negative reinforcement models. *Journal of Personality and Social Psychology*, 57, 261–270.

Amabille, T. (1983). Brilliant but cruel: Perceptions of negative evaluators. *Journal of Experimental Social Psychology*, 19, 146–156.

Anderson, N. H. (1981). *Foundations of Information Integration Theory*. New York: Academic Press.

Archer, R. P., & Cash, T. F. (1985). Physical attractiveness and maladjustment among psychiatric inpatients. *Journal of Social and Clinical Psychology*, 3, 170–180.

Aron, A., & Aron, E. N. (1986). *Love and the Expansion of Self*. New York: Hemisphere.

Aron, A., & Aron, E. N. (1989). *The Heart of Social Psychology*. Lexington, MA: Lexington Books.

Aron, A., Dutton, D. G., Aron, E. A., & Iverson, A. (1989). Experiences of falling in love. *Journal of Social and Personal Relationships*, 6, 243–257.

Aron, A., Paris, M., & Aron, E. N. (1995). Falling in love: Prospective studies of self-concept change. *Journal of Personality and Social Psychology*, 69, 1102–1112.

Aronson, E. (1998). *The Social Animal*. (7th Ed.) San Francisco: Freeman.

Aronson, E., & Linder, D. (1965). Gain and loss of esteem as determinants of interpersonal attractiveness. *Journal of Experimental Social Psychology*, 1, 156–171.

Aronson, E., & Mills, J. (1972). The effect of severity of initiation on liking for a group. *Journal of Personality and Social Psychology*, 59, 177–181.

Backman, C. W. (1981). Attraction in interpersonal relationships. In R. Turner and M. Rosenberg (Eds.) *Sociological Perspective in Social Psychology*. New York: Basic Books, 235–268.

Bader, E., & Pearson, P. T. (1988). *In Quest of the Mythical Mate*. New York: Brunner/Mazel.

Banner, L. W. (1983). *American Beauty*. New York: Knopf.

Barclay, A. M., & Haber, R. N., (1965). The relation of aggressive to sexual motivation. *Journal of Personality*, 33, 462–475.

Barnett, R. (1993). Multiple roles, gender, and psychological distress. In L. Goldberger and S. Breznitz (Eds.) *Handbook of Stress.* (2nd Ed.) New York: Free Press.

Bartholomew, K. (1990). Avoidance of intimacy: An attachment perspective. *Journal of Social and Personal Relationships*, 7, 147–178.

Bartholomew, K., & Horowitz, L. M. (1991). Attachment styles among young adults: A test of a four-category model. *Journal of Personality and Social Psychology*, 61, 226–244.

Basow, S. (1992). *Gender stereotypes and roles.* Pacific Grove, CA: Brooks/Cole.

Beall, A. E., & Sternberg, R. J. (1995). The social construction of love. *Journal of Social and Personal Relationships*, 12, 417–438.

Becker, E. (1973). *The Denial of Death.* New York: Free Press.

Benjamin, J. (1998). How was it for you? How intersubjective is sex. Keynote address presented at the American Psychological Association convention. Boston: August.

Benton, C., Hernandez, A., Schmidt, A., Schmitz, M., Stone, A., & Weiner, B. (1983). Is hostility linked with affiliation among males and with achievement among females? A critique of Pollak and Gilligan. *Journal of Personality and Social Psychology*, 45, 1167–1171.

Berkowitz, L., & Frodi, N. (1979). Reactions to a child's mistake as affected by his/her looks. *Psychiatry* 42, 420–425.

Berscheid, E., & Hartfield-Walster, E. (1978). *Interpersonal Attraction.* (2nd Ed.) New York: Random House.

Berscheid, E., & Reis, H. T. (1998). Attraction and close relationships. In D. T. Gilbert et al., (Eds.) *The Handbook of Social Psychology*, 2, 193–281. New York: McGraw–Hill.

Blatt, S. J., & Blass, R. B. (1996). Relatedness and self definition: A dialectic model of personality development. In G. G. Noam & K. W. Fischer (Eds.) *Development and Vulnerabilities in Close Relationships.* Hillsdale, NJ: Elbaum.

Bornstein, R. F., Leone, D. R., & Galley, D. J. (1987). The generalizability of subliminal mere exposure effects: Influence of stimuli perceived without awareness on social behavior. *Journal of Personality and Social Psychology*, 53, 1070–1079.

Bossard, J. H. S. (1932). Residential propinquity as a factor in mate selection. *American Journal of Sociology.* 38, 219–224.

Boszormeny-Nagy, I., & Ulrich, D. (1980). Contextual family therapy. In A. S. Gurman and D. P. Kniskern (Eds.) *Handbook of Family Therapy.* New York: Brunner/Mazel, 159–186.

Bowen, M. (1978). *Family Therapy in Clinical Practice.* New York: Jason Aronson.

Bowlby, J. (1982). *Attachment and loss:* Vol. I. Attachment (2nd Ed.) New York: Basic Books.

Brehm, S. (1992). *Intimate Relationships.* New York: McGraw-Hill.

Brehm, S. S., & Brehm, J. W. (1981). *Psychological Reactance: A Theory of Freedom and Control.* New York: Academic Press.

Brennan, K. A., & Shaver, P. R. (1995). Dimensions of adult attachment, affect regulation, and romantic relationship functioning. *Personality and Social Psychology Bulletin*, 21, 267–283.

Brickman, P., Redfield, J. Harrison, A. A., & Crandall, R. (1972). Drive and predisposition in the attitudinal effects of mere exposure. *Experimental Social Psychology*, 8, 31– 44.

Brinberg, D., & Castel, P. A. (1982). A resource theory approach to interpersonal interactions: A test of Foa's theory. *Journal of Experimental Social Psychology*, 43, 260–269.

Burgess, R. L., & Huston, T. L. (1979). *Social Exchange in Developing Relationships*. New York: Academic Press.

Burleson, B. R., & Denton, W. H. (1992). A new look at similarity and attraction in marriage: Similarities in social-cognitive and communication skills as predictors of attraction and satisfaction. *Communication Monographs*, 59, 268–287.

Burleson B. R., Kunkel, A. W., & Szolwinski, J. B. (1997). Similarity in cognitive complexity and attraction to friends and lovers. *Journal of Constructivist Psychology*, 10, 221–248.

Buss, D. M. (1994). *The Evolution of Desire: Strategies of Human Mating*. New York: Basic Books.

Buss, D. (1985). Human mate selection. *American Scientist*, 73, 47–51.

Buss, D. M., Abbott, M., Angleitner, A., & Asherian, A. (1990). International preferences in mate selection: Evolutionary hypothesis tested in 37 cultures. *Behavioral and Brain Sciences*, 12, 1–49.

Buss, D. M., & Angleitner, A. (1988). Mate selection preferences in Germany and the United States. *Personality and Individual Differences*, 10, 1269–1280.

Buss, D. & Barnes, M. (1986). Preference in human mate selection. *Journal of Personality and Social Psychology*, 50, 559–570.

Buss, D. M., & Schmitt, D. P. (1993). Sexual strategies theory: An evolutionary perspective on human mating. *Psychological Review*, 100, 204–232.

Byrne, D. (1971). *The Attraction Paradigm*. New York: Academic Press.

Byrne, D. (1997). An overview (and underview) of research and theory within the attraction paradigm. *Journal of Social and Personal Relationships*, 14, 417–431.

Byrne, D., & Blaylock, B. (1963). Similarity and assumed similarity of attitudes between husbands and wives. *Journal of Abnormal and Social Psychology*, 67, 636–640.

Byrne, D., Ervin, C. E., & Lamberth, J. (1970). Continuity between the experimental study of attraction and real life computer dating. *Journal of Personality and Social Psychology*, 16, 157–165.

Calvert, J. D. (1988). Physical attractiveness: A review and reevaluation of its role in social skill research. *Behavioral Assessment*, 10, 29–42.

Campbell, W., Sedikides, C., & Bosson, J. (1994). Romantic involvement, self discrepancy and psychological well-being. *Personal Relationships*, 1, 399–404.

Carnegie, D. (1982). *How to Win Friends and Influence People*. New York: Pocket Books.

Cash, T. F., & Duncan, N. C. (1984). Physical attractiveness stereotyping among black American college students. *Journal of Social Psychology*, 122, 71–77.

Cashdan, E. (1993). Attracting mates: Effects of parental investment on mate attraction strategies. *Ethology and Sociobiology*, 14, 1–23.

Caspi, A., & Harbener, E. S. (1990). Continuity and change: Assortive marriage and the consistency of personality in adulthood. *Journal of Personality and Social Psychology*, 58, 250–258.

Chafetz, J. S. (1975). *Masculine/Feminine or Human?* Itasca, IL: Peacock.

Chodorow, N. (1978). *The Reproduction of Mothering.* Berkeley, CA: University of California Press.

Clarke, A. C. (1952). An examination of the operation of propinquity as a factor in mate selection. *American Sociological Review,* 27, 17–22.

Clark, R. D., & Hatfield, E. (1989). Gender differences in receptivity to sexual offers. *Journal of Psychology and Human Sexuality*, 2, 39–55.

Clark, L. A., & Watson, D. (1988). Mood and the mundane: Relations between daily life events and self–reported mood. *Journal of Personality and Social Psychology*, 54, 296–308.

Clore, G. L., & Byrne (1974). A reinforcement-affect model of attraction. In T. L. Houston (Ed.) *Foundations of Interpersonal Attraction* (143–170). New York: Academic Press.

Cochran, S. D., & Peplau, L. A., (1985). Value orientation in heterosexual relationships. *Psychology of Women Quarterly*, 9, 477–488.

Cohen, L. L., & Shotland, R. L. (1996). Timing of the first sexual intercourse in a relationship: Expectations, experiences and perceptions of others. *Journal of Sex Research*, 33, 291–299.

Cohen, B., Waugh, G., & Place, K. (1989). At the movies: An unobtrusive study of arousal attraction. *Journal of Social Psychology.* 129, 691–693.

Collins, N. L., & Read, S. J. (1990). Adult attachment: Working models and relationship quality in dating couples. *Journal of Personality and Social Psychology*, 58, 644–663.

Cramer, R. E., Cupp, R. G., Kuhn, J. A. (1993). Male attractiveness: Masculinity with a feminine touch. *Current Psychology Development, Learning, Personality, Social,* 12, 142–150.

Cunningham, M. R. (1986). Measuring the physical in physical attractiveness: Quazi experiments in sociobiology of female facial beauty. *Journal of Personality and Social Psychology,* 50, 925–935.

Curran, J. P., & Lippold, S. (1975). The effects of physical attraction and attitude similarity on attraction in dating dyads. *Journal of Personality*, 43, 528–539.

Curtis, R. C., & Miller, K.(1986). Believing another likes or dislikes you: Behaviors making the beliefs come true. *Journal of Personality and Social Psychology*, 51, 284–290.

Cyranowski, J. M., & Andersen, B. (1998). Schemas, sexuality and romantic attachment. *Journal of Personality and Social Psychology*, 74, 1364–1379.

Darley, J. M., & Berscheid, E. (1967). Increased liking as a result of the anticipation of personal contact. *Human Relations*, 20, 29–40.

Darwin, C. (1871). *The Descent of Man and Selection in Relation to Sex.* New York: D. Appleton.

Darwin, C. (1910). *The Expression of Emotion in Man and Animals.* New York: Appleton.

Davis, S. (1990). Men as success objects and women as sex objects: A study of personal advertisements. *Sex Roles, 23,* 43–50.

Deaux, K. (1972). To err is humanizing: but sex makes a difference. *Representative Research in Social Psychology, 3,* 20–28.

DeLamater, J. D., & Hyde, J. S. (1998). Essentialsim vs. social constructionism in the study of human sexuality. *Journal of Sex Research, 35,* 10–18.

de Munck, V. C. (1998). Lust, love, and arranged marriages in Sri-Lanka. In V. C. de Munck et al. (Eds.) *Romantic Love and Sexual Behavior: Perspective from the Social Sciences.* Westport, CT: Praeger, 285–300.

de Munck, V. (1998). *Romantic Love and Sexual Behavior: Perspective from the Social Sciences.* Westport: CT: Praeger.

de-Raad, B., & Boddema-Winesemius, M. (1992). Factors in the assortment of human mates: Differential preferences in Germany and the Netherlands. *Personality and Individual Differences, 13,* 103–114.

de Rougemont, D. (1940/1983). *Love in the Western World.* New York: Pantheon.

Desrochers, S. (1995). What types of men are most attractive and most repulsive to women? *Sex Roles, 32,* 375–391.

Dicks, H. V. (1967). *Marital Tensions.* New York: Basic Books, 37.

Dietch, J. (1978). Love, sex-roles and psychological health. *Journal of Personality Assessment, 42,* 626–634.

Dinnerstein, D. (1976). *The Mermaid and the Minotaur: Sexual Arrangements and Human Malaise.* New York: Harper and Row.

Dion, K. (1972). Physical attractiveness and evaluations of children's transgressions. *Journal of Personality and Social Psychology, 24,* 207–213.

Dion, K. K., Berscheid, E., & Walster, E. (1972). What is beautiful is good. *Journal of Personality and Social Psychology, 24,* 285–290.

Dion, K. L., & Dion, K. K. (1973). Correlates of romantic love. *Journal of Consulting and Clinical Psychology, 41,* 51–56.

Dion, K. K., & Dion, K. L. (1975). Self-esteem and romantic love. *Journal of Personality, 43,* 39–57.

Dion, K. K. & Dion, K. L. (1985). Personality, gender and the phenomenology of romantic love. In P. Shaver (Ed.) *Self, Situation and Social Behavior: Review of Personality and Social Psychology, 6,* 209–238. Beverly Hills: Sage.

Dion, K. L. & Dion, K. K. (1987). Belief in a just world and physical attractiveness stereotyping. *Journal of Personality and Social Psychology, 52,* 775–780.

Dittes, J. E. (1959). Attractiveness of groups as function of self-esteem and acceptance by group. *Journal of Abnormal and Social Psychology, 59,* 114–140.

Drigonas, S. M., Rusbult, C. E., Wieselquist, J. & Whitton, S. W. (August, 1997). Close partner as sculptor of the ideal self: Behavioral affirmation and the Michelangelo phenomenon. Paper presented at the annual convention of the American Psychological Association: Chicago.

Drigotas, S. M. (1993). Similarity revisited: A comparison of similarity-attraction versus dissimilarity-repulsion. *British Journal of Social Psychology*, 32, 365–377.

Driscoll, R., Davis, K. W., & Lipetz, M. E. (1971). Parental interference and romantic love. *Journal of Personality and Social Psychology*, 24, 1–10.

Dryer, D. C., & Horowitz, L. M. (1997). When do opposites attract? Interpersonal complementarity versus similarity. *Journal of Personality and Social Psychology*, 72, 592–603.

Dutton, D. G., & Aron, A. P. (1974). Some evidence for heightened sexual attraction under conditions of high anxiety. *Journal of Personality and Social Psychology*, 30, 510–517.

Eagly, A. H. (1987). *Sex Differences in Social Behavior: A Social Role Interpretation.* Hillsdale, N. J: Erlbaum.

Ellis, B. J. (1992). The evolution of sexual attraction: Evaluative Mechanisms in women. In J. H. Barkow, L. Cosmedes, & Tooby (Eds.) *The Adapted Mind: Evolutionary Psychology and the Generation of Culture.* New York: Oxford University Press, 267–288.

Erikson, E. H. (1959). Identity and the life cycle. *Psychological Issues*, 1, no.1.

Fairbairn, W. R. D. (1952). *An Object-Relations Theory of Personality.* New York: Basic Books.

Fairbairn, W. R. D. (1952/1992). Schizoid factors in the personality. In *Psychoanalytic Studies of Personality.* New York: Routledge, 3–27.

Feingold, A. (1988). Matching for attractiveness in romantic partners and same sex friends: A metaanalysis and theoretical critique. *Psychological Bulletin*, 104, 226–235.

Feingold, A. (1990). Gender differences in effects of physical attractiveness on romantic attraction: A comparison across five research paradigms. *Journal of Personality and Social Psychology*, 59, 981–993.

Feingold, A. (1992). Gender differences in mate selection preferences: A test of the parental investment model. *Psychological Bulletin*, 112, 125–139.

Feldman, S. S., Gowen, L. K., & Fisher, L. (1998). Family relationships and gender as predictors of romantic intimacy in young adults. *Journal of Research on Adolescence*, 8, 263–286.

Felmlee, D. H. (1995). Fatal attractions: Affection and Disaffection in intimate relationships. *Journal of Social and Personal Relationships*, 12, 295–311.

Felmlee, D., Sprecher, S., & Bassin, E. (1990). The dissolution of intimate relationships: A hazard model. *Social Psychology Quarterly*, 53; 13–30.

Festinger, L. (1951). Architecture and group membership. *Journal of Social Issues*, 7, 152–163.

Fisher, H. E. (1992). *Anatomy of Love.* New York: Norton.

Fisher, H. E. (1998). Lust, attraction and attachment in mammalian reproduction. *Human Nature*, 9, 23–52.

Foa, E. B., & Foa, U. G. (1980). Resource theory: Interpersonal behavior as exchange. In K. J. Gergen, M. S. Greenberg & R. H. Willis (Eds.) *Social Exchange: Advances in Theory and Research.* New York: Plenum, 77–94.

Folkes, V. S. (1982). Forming relationships and the matching hypothesis. *Personality and Social Psychology Bulletin*, 8, 631–636.

Foster, C. A., Witcher, B. S., Campbell, W. K., & Green, J. D. (1998). Arousal and attraction: Evidence for automatic and controlled processes. *Journal of Personality and Social Psychology*, 74, 86–101.

Framo, J. (1990). Integrating families of origin into couple therapy. In R. Chasin, H. Grunebaum and Herzig, M. (Ed.) *One Couple Four Realities: Multiple Perspectives on Couple Therapy.* New York: Guilford Press, 49–82.

Freud, S. (1905/1962). *Three Essays on the Theory of Sexuality.* New York: Basic Books.

Freud, S. (1910/1957). Leonardo da Vinci: A study in psychosexuality. *Standard Edition.* Vol. XI. London: Hogarth Press.

Freud, S. (1914/1957). On Narcissism: An Introduction. *Standard Edition.* Part XIV: 73–102. London: Hogarth Press.

Freud, S. (1917/1963). *Introduction Lectures on Psychoanalysis*, Part III. London: Hogarth Press.

Freud, S. (1921). Group Psychology and the analysis of the Ego. *Standard Edition.* 18, 65–143. London: Hogarth Press, 1955.

Freud, A. (1946). *The Ego and the Mechanisms of Defense.* New York: International Universities Press.

Frieze, I. H, Olson, J. E. & Russell, J. (1991). Attractiveness and income for men and women in management. *Journal of Applied Social Psychology*, 21, 1039–1057.

Fromm, E. (1956). *The Art of Loving.* New York: Harper and Row.

Galton, F. (1884). The measurement of character. *Fortnightly Review*, 36, 179–185.

Geiselman, R. E., Haight, N. A., & Kimata, L. G. (1984). Context effects in the perceived physical attractiveness of faces. *Journal of Experimental Social Psychology*, 20, 409–424.

Gergen, M. M., & Gergen, K. J. (1992). Attributions, accounts and close relationships: Close calls and relational resolutions, in J. H. Harvey, T. L. Orbuch & A. L. Weber (Eds.) *Attributions, Accounts and Close Relationships.* New York: Springer.

Gillen, B. (1981). Physical attractiveness. A determinant of two types of goodness. *Personality and Social Psychology Bulletin*, 7, 277–281.

Givelber, F. (1990). Object relations and the couple. In R. Chasin, H. Grunebaum and Herzig, M. (Ed.) *One Couple Four Realities: Multiple Perspectives on Couple Therapy.* New York: Guilford Press, 171–190.

Goffman, E. (1952). On cooling the mark out: some aspects of adaptation to failure. *Psychiatry*, 15, 451–463.

Goldner, V. (1998). Theorizing gender and sexual subjectivity: Modern and Post Modern perspectives. Paper presented at the Israeli Association of Psychotherapy, Israel: November.

Goldner, V. (1998a). Violence and victimization in intimate relationships: A feminist Intersubjective Perspective. Paper presented at the Israeli Association of Psychotherapy, Israel: November.

Goodwin, R. (1990). Sex differences among partner preferences. Are the sexes really very similar? *Sex Roles*, 23, 501–513.

Gouaux, C. (1971). Induced affective states and interpersonal attraction. *Journal of Personality and Social Psychology*, 20, 37–43.

Green, B. L., & Kenrick, D. T. (1994). The attractiveness of gender-typed traits at different relationship levels: Androgynous characteristics may be desirable after all. *Personality and Social Psychology Bulletin*, 20, 244–253.

Green, S. K., & Sandos, P. (1983). Perceptions of male and female initiators of relationships. *Sex Roles*, 9, 849–852.

Greenlees, I. A., & McGrew, W. C. (1994). Sex and age differences in preferences and tactics of mate attraction: Analysis of published advertisements. *Ethology and Sociobiology*, 15, 59–72.

Grube, J., Kleinhesselink, R., & Kearney, K. (1982). Male self-acceptance and attraction toward women. *Personality and Social Psychology Bulletin*, 8, 107–112.

Grush, J. E., & Yehl, J. G. (1979). Marital roles, sex differences and interpersonal attraction. *Journal of Personality and Social Psychology*, 37, 116–123.

Guthrie, E. R. (1938). *The Psychology of Human Conflict*. New York: Harper.

Hadjistavropoulos, T., & Genest, M. (1994). The underestimation of the role of physical attractiveness in dating preferences: Ignorance or taboo? *Canadian Journal of Behavioral Science*, 26, 298–318.

Hartfield, E., & Rapson, R. L. (1992). Similarity and attraction in intimate relationships. *Communication Monographs*, 59, 209–212.

Hartfield, E., & Rapson, R. L. (1993). *Love Sex and Intimacy: Their Biology, Psychology and History*. New York: Harper Collins.

Hartfield, E., & Sprecher, S. (1986). *Mirror, Mirror . . . The Importance of Looks in Everyday Life*. Albany: State University of New York Press.

Hartz, A. J. (1996). Psycho-socionomics: Attractiveness research from a societal perspective. *Journal of Social Behavior and Personality*. 11, 683–694.

Hazan, C., & Shaver, P. (1987). Romantic love conceptualized as an attachment process. *Journal of Personality and Social Psychology*, 52, 511–524.

Hendrick, S. S. (1981). Self–disclosure and marital satisfaction. *Journal of Personality and Social Psychology*, 40, 1150–1159.

Hendrix, H. (1988). *Getting the Love You Want*. New York: Henry Holt.

Hendrix, H. (1992). *Keeping the Love You Find*. New York: Pocket Books.

Hensley, W. E. (1994). Height as a basis for interpersonal attraction. *Adolescence*, 29, 469–474.

Hinsz, V. B. (1989). Facial resemblance in engaged and married couples. *Journal of Social and Personal Relationships*, 6, 223–229.

Homans, G. (1961). *Social Behavior: Its Elementary Forms*. New York: Harcourt Brace.

Hopcke, R. H. (1992). "The male soul figure." A talk presented at the Men's Center Forum. The Men's Center Foundation. Berkeley, California.

Horney, K. (1922/1973). On the genesis of the castration complex in women. In J. P. Miller (Ed.) *Psychoanalysis and Women*. New York: Brunner/Mazel.

Horney, K. (1967). *Feminine Psychology*. New York: Norton.

Hoyt, L. L., & Hudson, J. W. (1981). Personal characteristics important in mate preference among college students. *Social Behavior and Personality*, 9, 93–96.

Hrdy, S. B. (1988). Empathy, polyandry, and the myth of the coy female. In R. Bleier (Ed.), *Feminist Approaches to Science*. New York: Pergamon.

Hubbard, R. (1990). *The Politics of Women's Biology*. New Brunswick, NJ: Rutgers University Press.

Hyde, J. S. (1981). How large are the cognitive gender differences? A Metaanalysis. *American Psychologist*, 36, 892–901.

Hyde, J. S. (1984). How large are gender differences in aggression? A developmental metaanalysis. *Developmental Psychology*, 20, 722–736.

Hyde, J. S. (1990). Metaanalysis and the psychology of gender differences. *Signs: Journal of Women in Culture and Society*, 16, 55–73.

Hyde, J. S. (August 1993). "Sex, love and psychology." Paper presented at the annual convention of the American Psychological Association. Toronto, Canada.

Hyde, J. S., & Linn, M. C. (1986). *The Psychology of Gender: Advances through Metaanalysis*. Baltimore: Johns Hopkins University Press.

Hyde, J. S., & Lynn, M. C. (1988). Gender differences in verbal ability: A Metaanalysis. *Psychological Bulletin*, 104, 53–69.

Ickees, W. (1993). Traditional gender roles: Do they make, and then break, our relationships? *Journal of Social Issues*, 49, 71–86.

Izard, C. E. (1960). Personality similarity and friendship. *Journal of Abnormal and Social Psychology*, 61, 47–51.

Jackson, L. A., & Ervin, K. S. (1992). Height stereotypes of women and men: The liability of shortness for both sexes. *Journal of Social Psychology*, 132, 433–445.

Jacobson, N., & Christensen, A. (1996). *Integrative Couple Therapy*. New York: Norton.

Jensen-Campbell, L. A., Grazino, W. G., & West, S. G. (1995). Dominance, prosocial orientation and female preference: Do nice guys really finish last? *Journal of Personality and Social Psychology*, 68, 427–440.

Jones, D. (1995). Sexual selection, physical attractiveness and facial neoteny: Cross cultural evidence and implications. *Current Anthropology*, 36, 723–748.

Jones, E. (1964). *Ingratiation*. New York: Appleton Century Crofts.

Jones, E., Bell, L., & Aronson, E. (1971). The reciprocation of attraction from similar and dissimilar others: A study in person perception and evaluation. In C. G. McClintock (Ed.) *Experimental Social Psychology*. New York: Holt Rinehart, 142–183.

Johnson, D. E., & Pittenger, J. B. (1984). Attribution, the attractiveness stereotype, and the elderly. *Developmental Psychology*, 20, 1168–1172.

Josselson, R. E. (1992). *The Space Between Us*. San Francisco: Jossey-Bass.

Jung, C. G. (1964). *Man and his Symbols*. New York: Dell

Kacerguis, M. A., & Adams, G. R., (1980). Erikson's stage resolution: The relationship between identity and intimacy. *Journal of Youth and Adolescence*, 9, 117–126.

Kalick, S. M. & Hamilton, T. E. (1986). The matching hypothesis reexamined. *Journal of Personality and Social Psychology*, 51, 673–682.

Kaplan, M. F. (1981). State disposition in social judgment. *Bulletin of the Psychonomic Society*, 18, 27–29.

Karraker, K. H., Vogel, D. A., & Evans, S. (1987). Responses of students and pregnant women to newborn physical attractiveness. Paper presented at the annual convention of the American Psychological Association. New York.

Kelley, H. H., Berscheid, E., Christensen, A., Harvey, J. H., & Huston, T. L. (1983). Analyzing close relationships. In H. H. Kelley, E. Berscheid, A. Christensen, J. H. Harvey (Eds.) *Close Relationships*. San Francisco: Freeman, 20–67.

Keller, M. C., & Young, R. K. (1996). Mate assortment in dating and married couples. *Personality and Individual Differences*, 21, 217–221.

Kellerman, J., Lewis, J., & Lard, J. D., (1989). Looking and loving: The effects of mutual gaze on feelings of romantic love. *Journal of Research in Personality*. 23, 145–161.

Kenrick, D. T., Groth, G. E., Trost, M. R., & Sadalla, E. (1993). Integrating evolutionary and social exchange perspectives on relationships: Effects of gender, self-appraisal and involvement level on mate selection criteria. *Journal of Personality and Social Psychology*, 64, 951–969.

Kenrick, D. T., & Keefe, R. C., (1992). Age preferences in mates reflect sex differences in human reproductive strategies. *Behavioral and Brain Sciences*, 15, 75–113.

Kerckoff, A. C. (1974). The social context of interpersonal attraction. In T. L. Huston *Foundations of Interpersonal Attraction*. New York: Academic Press, 61–78.

Kernberg, O. (1974). Barriers to falling and remaining in love. *Journal of the American Psychoanalytic Association*, 22, 486–511.

Kernberg, O. (1980). Love, the couple, and the group: A psychoanalytic frame. *Psychoanalytic Quarterly*, 129, 78–108.

Kiesler, S. B., & Baral, R. Z. (1970). The search for a romantic partner: The effects of self-esteem and physical attractiveness on romantic behavior. In K. Gergen and D. Marlow (Eds.) *Personality and Social Behavior*. Reading, MA: Addison-Wesley, 155–165.

Kirkpatrick, L. A. (1998). Evolution, pair-bonding and reproductive strategies: A reconceptualization of adult attachment. In J. A. Simpson et al. (Eds.) *Attachment Theory and Close Relationships*. New York: Guilford Press, 353–393.

Klein, G. S. (1976). *Psychoanalytic Theory*. New York: International University Press.

Klein, M. (1959). *The Psychoanalysis of Children*. London: Hogarth.

Kleinke, C. L., & Staneski, R. A. (1980). First impressions of female bust size. *Journal of Social Psychology*, 110, 123–134.

Knee, C. R., (1998). Implicit theories of relationships: Assessment and prediction of romantic relationship initiation, coping and longevity. *Journal of Personality and Social Psychology*, 74, 360–370.

Kohut, H. (1971). *The Analysis of the Self.* New York: International Universities Press.

Kohut, H. (1977). *The Restoration of the Self.* New York: International Universities Press.

Krueger, R. F., & Caspi, A. (1993). Personality, arousal, and pleasure: A test of competing models of interpersonal attraction. *Personality and Individual Differences*, 14, 105–111.

Kruglanski, A., E. & Mayseless, O. (1987). Motivational effects in the social comparison of opinions. *Journal of Personality and Social Psychology*, 53, 834–842.

Lahm, H., Weismann, U., & Keller, K. (1998). Subjective determinants of attraction: Self-perceived causes of the rise and decline of liking, love and being in love. *Personal Relationships*, 5, 91–104.

Larson, J. H. (1992). "You're my one and only": Premarital counseling for unrealistic beliefs about mate selection. *American Journal of Family Therapy*, 20, 242, 253.

Lasswell, M., & Lobsenz, N. (1980). *Styles of Loving: Why You Love the Way You Do*. New York: Ballantine.

Lavrakas, P. J. (1975). Female preferences for male physique. *Journal of Research in Personality*. 9, 324–334.

Lee, J. A. (1998). Ideologies of lovestyle and sexstyle. In V. C. de Munck et al. (Eds.) *Romantic Love and Sexual Behavior*: Perspectives from the social sciences. Westport, CT: Praeger, 33–76.

Leigh, B. C., & Aramburu, B. (1996). The role of alcohol and gender choices and judgements about hypothetical sexual encounters. *Journal of Applied Social Psychology*, 26, 20–30.

Levinger, G., & Breedlove, J. (1966). Interpersonal attraction and agreement: A study of marriage partners. *Journal of Personality and Social Psychology*, 3, 367–372.

Levy, M. B., & Davis, K. E. (1988). Love styles and attachment styles compared: Their relations to each other and to various relationship characteristics. *Journal of Social and Personal Relationships*, 5, 439–472.

Lewis, R. A. (1973). A longitudinal test of the developmental framework for premarital dyadic formation. *Journal of Marriage and the Family*, 35, 16–25.

Lindholm, C. (1998). The future of love. In V. C. de Munck et al. (Eds.) *Romantic Love and Sexual Behavior: Perspectives from the Social Sciences*. Westport, CT: Praeger, 17–32.

Lock, K. D., & Horowitz, L. M. (1990). Satisfaction in interpersonal interactions as a function of similarity in level of dysphoria. *Journal of Personality and Social Psychology*, 58, 823–831.

Lot, A. J., Lot, B. E., Reed, T., & Crow, T. (1960). Personality trait description of differently liked persons. *Journal of Personality and Social Psychology*, 16, 284–290.

Low, N. (1990). Women in couples: How their experience of relationships differs from men's. In R. Chasin, H. Grunebaum and Herzig, M. (Ed.) *One Couple Four Realities: Multiple Perspectives on Couple Therapy*. New York: Guilford Press, 249–268.

Lumpert, A. (1997). *The Evolution of Love*. Westport, CT: Praeger.

Lykken, D. T., & Tellegen, A. (1993). Is human mating adventitious or the result of lawful choice? A twin study of mate selection. *Journal of Personality and Social Psychology*, 65, 56–68.

Lynn, M., & Shurgot, B. A. (1984). Responses to lonely hearts advertisements: Effects of reported physical attractiveness, physique and coloration. *Personality and Social*

Psychology Bulletin, 10, 349–357.

Macerguis, M. A., & Adams, G. R. (1980). Erikson's stage resolution: The relationship between identity and intimacy. *Journal of Youth and Adolescence*, 9, 117–126.

MacLean, P. D. (1973). *The Triune Concept of the Brain and Behavior*. Toronto: Toronto University Press.

Mahler, M. (1974). Symbiosis and Individuation: The psychological birth of the human infant. *The Psychological Study of the Child*, 29, 98–106.

Mahler, M. S., Pine, F., & Bergman, A. (1975). *The Psychological Birth of the Human Infant*. New York: Basic Books.

Major, B., Carrington, P. I., & Carnevale, P. I. D. (1984). Physical attractiveness and self-esteem: Attributions for praise from other-sex evaluator. *Personality and Social Psychology Bulletin*, 10, 43–50.

Margolin, L., & White, G. L. (1987). The continuing role of physical attractiveness in marriage. *Journal of Marriage and the Family*, 49, 21–28.

Marioles, N. S., Strickert, D. P., & Hammer, A. L. (1996). Attraction, satisfaction, and psychological types of couples. *Journal of Psychological Type*, 36, 16–27.

Marks, G., & Miller, N. (1982). Target attractiveness as a mediator of assumed attitude similarity. *Personality and Social Psychology Bulletin*, 8, 728–735.

Martin, C. L. (1987). A ratio measure of sex stereotyping. *Journal of Personality and Social Psychology*, 52, 489–499.

Maslow, A. (1970). *Motivation and Personality*. New York: Harper and Row.

May, J. L., & Hamilton, P. A. (1980). Effects of musically evoked affect on women's interpersonal attraction and perceptual judgment of physical attractiveness of men. *Motivation and Emotion*, 4, 217–228.

May, R. (1969). *Love and Will*. New York: Dell.

Maybach, K. L., & Gold, S. R. (1994). Hyperfemininity and attraction to macho and non-macho men. *Journal of Sex Research*, 31, 91–98.

Mehrabian, A. (1989). Marital choice and compatibility as a function of their trait similarity-dissimilarity. *Psychological Reports*, 65, 1202.

Meissner, W. W. (1978). The conceptualization of marriage and family dynamic from psychoanalytic perspective. In Paolino, T., & McCrady, B. (Eds.) *Marriage and Marital Therapy: Psychoanalytic, Behavioral and Systems Therapy Perspectives*. New York: Brunner/Mazel, 25–88.

Merikangas, K. R., Weissman, M. M., Prusoff, B. A., & John, K. (1988). Assortative mating and affective disorders: Psychopathology in offspring. *Psychiatry*, 51, 48–57.

Mickelson, K. D., Kessler, R. C., & Shaver, P. R. (1997). Adult attachment in a nationally representative sample, *Journal of Personality and Social Psychology*, 73, 1092–1106.

Miller, J. B. (1976). *Toward a New Psychology of Women*. Boston: Beacon Press.

Mita, T. H., Dermer, M., & Knight, J. (1977). Reversed facial images and the mere-exposure hypothesis. *Journal of Personality and Social Psychology*, 35, 397–601.

Mittelman, B. (1944). Complementary neurotic reactions in intimate relationships. *Psychoanalytic Quarterly*, 13, 479–491.

Money, J. (1986). *Lovemaps: Clinical Concepts Of Sexual/Erotic Health and Pathology, Paraphilia and Gender Transposition in Childhood, Adolescence and Maturity.* New York: Irvington.

Moore, M. M. (1985). Nonverbal courtship patterns in women: Context and consequences. *Ethology and Sociobiology,* 6, 237–247.

Moreland, R. L., & Beach, S. R. (1992). Exposure effects in the classroom: the development of affinity among students. *Journal of Experimental Social Psychology,* 28, 255–276.

Morrow, G. D., & O'Sullivan, C. (1998). Romantic ideals as comparison levels: Implications for satisfaction and commitment in romantic involvements. In V. C. de Munck, et al., (Eds.) *Romantic Love and Sexual Behavior: Perspectives from the Social Sciences.* Westport, CT: Praeger, 171–199.

Muehlenhard, C. L., & Hollabaugh, I. C. (1988). Do women sometimes say no when they mean yes? The prevalence and correlates of women's token resistance to sex. *Journal of Personality and Social Psychology,* 54, 872–879.

Mulder, M. B. (1990). Kipsigis women's preferences for men: Evidence for female choice in mammals? *Behavioral Ecology and Sociobiology,* 27, 255–264.

Murray, H. A. (1943). *Thematic Apperception Test Manual.* Cambridge, MA: Harvard University Press.

Murray, S. L., Holmes, J. G., & Griffin, D. W. (1996). The self-fulfilling nature of positive illusions in romantic relationships: Love is not blind, but prescient. *Journal of Personality and Social Psychology,* 71, 1155–1180.

Murstein, B. I. (1976). *Who Will Marry Whom.* New York: Springer.

Nagoshi, C. T., Johnson, R. C., & Ahern, F. M. (1987). Phenotype assortative mating vs. social homogamy among Japanese and Chinese parents. *Behavior Genetics,* 17, 477–485.

Nathan, S. G. (1981). Cross cultural perspective on penis envy. *Psychiatry,* 44, 39–44.

Neimeyer, G. J. (1984). Cognitive complexity and marital satisfaction. *Journal of Social and Clinical Psychology,* 2, 258–263.

Nevid, J. S. (1984). Sex differences in factors of romantic attraction. *Sex Roles,* 11, 401–411.

Newcomb, T. M. (1961). *The Acquaintance Process.* New York: Holt Reinhart.

Nowicki. S. Jr., & Menheim, S. (1991). Interpersonal complementarity and time of interaction in female relationships. *Journal of Research in Personality,* 25, 322–333.

Ogden, T. H. (1979). On projective identification. *International Journal of Psychoanalysis,* 60, 357–373.

Orive, R. (1988). Social projective and social comparison of opinions. *Journal of Personality and Social Psychology,* 54, 953–964.

Park, B., & Rothbart, M. (1982). Perceptions of outgroup homogeneity and levels of social categorization. *Journal of Personality and Social Psychology,* 42, 1051–1068.

Parnas, J. (1988). Assortative mating in schizophrenia. *Psychiatry,* 51, 58–64.

Patterson, C. E., & Pettijohn, T. F. (1982). Age and human mate selection. *Psychological Reports,* 51, 70.

Peck, S. (1978). *The Road Less Traveled.* NY: Simon and Schuster.

Pennebaker, J. W., Dyer, M. A., Caulkins, R. S., Litowitz, D. L., Ackerman, P. L., Anderson, D. B., & McGraw, K. M. (1979). Don't the girls get prettier at closing time: A country and western application to psychology. *Personality and Social Psychology Bulletin,* 5, 122–125.

Perper, T. (1989). Theories and observations on sexual selection and female choice in human beings. Special Issue: *Human Sexuality and Biocultural Perspective.*

Phillips, K., Fulker, D. W., Carey, G., & Nagoshi, C. T. (1988). Direct marital assortment for cognitive and personality variables. *Behavior Genetics,* 18, 347–356.

Pierce, C. A. (1996). Body height and romantic attraction: A metaanalytic test of the male-taller norm. *Social Behavior and Personality,* 24, 143–149.

Pierce, C. A., Byrne, D., & Aguinis, H. (1996). Attraction in organizations: A model of workplace romance. *Journal of Organizational Behavior,* 17, 5–32.

Pines, A. M. (1996). *Couple Burnout.* New York: Routledge.

Pines, A. M. (1997). Fatal attraction or wise unconscious choices: The relationship between causes for entering and breaking intimate relationships. *Personal Relationship Issues,* 1997, 4, 1–6.

Pines, A. M. (1998). *Romantic Jealousy.* New York: Routledge.

Pines, A. M. (1998a) Gender and culture in romantic attraction. Paper presented at the 24th International Congress of Applied Psychology. San Francisco, CA. August.

Pines, A. M. (1998b). A prospective study of personality and gender differences in romantic attraction. *Personality and Individual Differences,* 25, 147–157.

Pines, A. M. (1998c). *Psychology of Gender.* (Hebrew) Tel-Aviv: Open University Press.

Pines, A. M. (1999). How people choose whom to fall in love with (and why this question is important for psychotherapists). American Psychological Association: Boston.

Pines, A. M. & Aronson, E. (1988). *Career Burnout: Causes and Cures.* New York: Free Press.

Plato. *The Symposium.* Ed. B. Jowett. New York: Tudor Publishing, 1956, 315–318.

Pleck, J. (1977). The work-family role system. *Social Problems,* 24, 417–427.

Rank, O. (1945). *Will Therapy and Truth and Reality.* New York: Knopf.

Rabin, C. (1995). *Partners as Friends.* New York: Routledge.

Reader, N., & English, H. B. (1947). Personality factors in adolescent female friendships. *Journal of Consulting Psychology,* 11, 212–220.

Regan, P. C. (1996). Of lust and love: beliefs about the role of sexual desire in romantic relationships. *Personal Relationships,* 5, 139–157.

Regan, P. (1998). Minimum mate selection standards as a function of perceived mate value, relationship context, and gender. *Journal of Psychology and Human Sexuality,* 10, 53–73.

Reik, T. (1957). *Of Love and Lust.* New York: Grove Press.

Reik, T. (1964). *The Need to be Loved.* New York: Bantam.

Reis, H. T., Nezlek, J., & Wheeler, L. (1980). Physical attractiveness in social interaction, *Journal of Personality and Social Psychology,* 38, 604–617.

Rich, A. (1976). *Of Woman Born*. New York: Norton.

Richard, L. S., Wakefield, J. A., & Lewak, R. (1990). Similarity of personality variables as predictor of marital satisfaction: Minnesota Multiple Personality Inventory (MMPI) item analysis. *Personality and Individual Differences*, 11, 39–43.

Rindfuss, R. R., & Stephen, E. H. (1990). Marital noncohabitation: Separation does not make the heart grow fonder. *Journal of Marriage and the Family*, 52, 259–27.

Robinson, E. A., & Price, M. G. (1980). Pleasurable behavior in marital interaction. An observational study. *Journal of Consulting and Clinical Psychology*, 48, 117–118.

Rodin, J. (1987). Who is memorable to whom. A study of cognitive disregard. *Social Cognition*, 5, 144–165.

Rose, S., & Frieze, I. H. (1989). Young singles' scripts for a first date. *Gender and Society*, 3, 258–268.

Rozin, P., Millman, L., & Nemeroff, C. (1986). Operation of the laws of sympathetic magic in disgust and other domains. *Journal of Personality and Social Psychology*, 50, 703–712.

Rubin, L. B. (1983). *Intimate Strangers: Men and Women Together*. New York: Harper and Row.

Rubin, Z. (1973). *Liking and Loving*. New York: Holt Reinhart.

Rubin, Z., Peplau, L. A., & Hill, C. T. (1981). Loving and leaving: Sex differences in romantic attachments. *Sex Roles,* 7, 821–835.

Rushton, P. (1988). Genetic similarity, mate choice, and fecundity in humans. *Ethology and Sociobiology*, 9, 329–334.

Rytting, M., Ware, R. & Hopkins, P. (1992). Type and the ideal mate: Romantic attraction or type bias? *Journal of Psychological Types*, 24, 3–12.

Sadalla, E. K., Kenrick, D. T., & Vershure, B. (1987). Dominance and heterosexual attraction. *Journal of Personality and Social Psychology*, 52, 730–738.

Schachter, S. (1964). The interaction of cognitive and physiological determinants of emotional states. In L. Berkowitz (Ed.) *Advances in Experimental Social Psychology*. New York: Academic Press.

Schafer, R. B., & Keith, P. M. (1990). Matching by weight in married couples: A life cycle perspective. *Journal of Social Psychology*, 130, 657–664.

Schmitt, D. P., & Buss, D. M. (1996). Strategic self-promotion and competitor derogation: Sex and context effects on the perceived effectiveness of mate attraction tactics. *Journal of Personality and Social Psychology*, 70, 1185–1204.

Segal, M. W. (1974). Alphabet and attraction: Unobtrusive measure of the effect of propinquity in a field setting. *Journal of Personality and Social Psychology*, 30, 654–657.

Shaikh, T., & Suresh, K. (1994). Attitudinal similarity and affiliation needs as determinants of interpersonal attraction. *Journal of Social Psychology*, 134, 257–259.

Shaver, P. R., & Brennan, K. A. (1992). Attachment styles and the "Big Five" personality traits: Their connection with each other and with romantic relationship outcomes. *Personality and Social Psychology Bulletin*, 18, 536–545.

Shaver, P. R., & Clark, C. L. (1994). The psychodynamics of adult romantic attachment. In J. M. Masling and R. F. Bornstein (Eds.) *Empirical Perspectives on Object Relations Theories*. Washington, D. C.: American Psychological Association, 105–156.

Shaver, P. R., & Hazan, C. (1993). Adult romantic attachment: Theory and evidence. In D. Perlman & W. Jones (Eds.) *Advances in Personal Relationships* Vol. 4. London: Jessica Kingsley, 29–70.

Shaver, P. R., Hazan, C. & Bradshaw, D. (1988). Love as attachment: The integration of three behavioral systems. In R. J. Sternberg & M. Barnes (Eds.) *The Psychology of Love*. New Haven, CT: Yale University Press.

Shaver, P. R., Schwartz, J., Kirson, D., & O'Connor, C. (1978). Emotion knowledge: Further exploration of the prototype approach. *Journal of Personality and Social Psychology*, 52, 1061–1086.

Shefer, J. (1971). Mate selection among second-generation Kibbutz adolescents and adults: Incest avoidance and negative imprinting. *Archives of Sexual behavior*, 1, 293–307.

Sheppard, J. A., & Strathman, A. J. (1989). Attractiveness and height: The role of status in dating preferences, frequency of dating, and perception of attractiveness. *Personality and Social Psychology Bulletin*, 15, 617–627.

Sigall, H., & Aronson, E. (1969). Liking for an evaluator as a function of her physical attractiveness and nature of the evaluation. *Journal of Experimental Social Psychology*, 5, 93–100.

Silverstein, B., Carpman, S., Perlick, D., & Purdue, L. (1990). Nontraditional sex-role aspirations, gender identity, conflict and disordered eating among college women. *Sex Roles*, 23, 687–695.

Simpson, J. A., Roles, W. S. & Nelligan, J. S. (1992). Support seeking and support giving within couples in an anxiety-provoking situation: The role of attachment styles. *Journal of Personality and Social Psychology*, 62, 434–446.

Singh, D. (1993). Adaptive significance of female physical attractiveness: role of waist-to-hip ratio. *Journal of Personality and Social Psychology*, 65, 293–307

Singh, D. (1994). Body fat distribution and perception of desirable female body shape. *International Journal of Eating Disorder*, 16, 289–294.

Shapiro, J. P. (1988). Relationships between dimensions of depressive experience and evaluative beliefs about people in general. *Personality and Social Psychology Bulletin*, 14, 388–400.

Singh, R., & Tan, L. S. (1992). Attitudes and attraction: A test of the similarity-attraction and dissimilarity-repulsion hypothesis. *British Journal of Social Psychology*, 31, 227–238.

Skrypneck, B. J., & Snyder, M. (1982). On the self-perpetuating nature of stereotypes about women and men. *Journal of Experimental Social Psychology*, 18, 277–291.

Small, M. F. (1992). The evolution of female sexuality and mate selection in humans. *Human Nature*, 3, 133–156.

Smith, E. R., Becker, M. A., Byrne, D., Przybyla, D. P. (1993). Sexual attitudes of males and females as predictors of interpersonal attraction and marital compatibility. *Journal of Applied Social Psychology*, 23, 1011–1034.

Smith, J. E., Waldorf, V. A., & Trembath, D. L. (1990). "Single male looking for thin, very attractive . . . " *Sex Roles*, 23, 675–685.

Snyder, M. (1993). When belief creates reality: The self fulfilling impact of first impressions on social interaction. In A. M. Pines & C. Maslach (Eds.) *Experiencing Social Psychology*. (3rd Ed.) New York: McGraw-Hill.

Snyder, C. R., & Fromkin, H. L. (1980). *Uniqueness: The Human Pursuit of Difference.* New York: Plenum.

Sperling, M. (1987). Ego identity and desperate love, *Journal of Personality Assessment*, 51, 600–605.

Solomon, Z. (1986). Self acceptance and the selection of a marital partner: An assessment of the SVR model of Murstein. *Social Behavior and Personality*, 14, 1–6.

Sperling, M. (1987). Ego identity and desperate love. *Journal of Personality Assessment*, 51, 600–605.

Sprecher, S., Cate, R., & Levin, L. (1998). Parental divorce and young people's beliefs about love. *Journal of Divorce and Remarriage*, 28, 107–120.

Sprecher, S., & Duck, S. (1994). Sweet Talk: The importance of perceived communication for romantic and friendship attraction experienced during a get-acquainted date. *Personality and Social Psychology Bulletin*, 20, 391–400.

Sprecher, S., Sullivan, Q., & Hartfield, E. (1994). Male selection preferences: Gender differences examined in a national sample. *Journal of Personality and Social Psychology*, 66, 1074–1080.

Stein, H., Jacobs, N. J., Ferguson, K. S., Allen, J. G., & Fonagy, P. (1998). What do adult attachment scales measure? *Bulletin of the Menninger Clinic*, 62, 33–82.

Steinman, A., & Fox, D. J. (1970). Attitudes toward women's family role. *Family Coordination*, 19, 363–368

Stephan, W. A., Berscheid, E., & Walster, E. (1971). Sexual arousal and interpersonal perception. *Journal of Personality and Social Psychology*, 20, 93–101.

Stephen, T. (1987). Taking communication seriously? A reply to Murstein. *Journal of Marriage and the Family*, 49, 937–938.

Sternberg, R. J. (1986). A triangular theory of love. *Psychological Review*, 73, 119–135.

Suman, H. C. (1992). Toward choosing a mate: Perceived dimensions of mate selection. *Journal of Personality and Clinical Studies*, 8, 143–146.

Surra, C. A., & Hyston, T. L. (1987). Mate selection as a social transition. In D. Perlman and S. Duck (Eds.) *Intimate relationships: Development, Dynamic and Deterioration.* Newbury Park, CA: Sage, 88–120.

Tavris, C. (1992). *The Mismeasure of Women.* New York: Simon and Schuster.

Taylor, M., & Vandenberg, S. G. (1988). Assortative mating for IQ and personality due to propinquity and personal preference. *Behavior Genetics*, 18, 339–345.

Tennov, D. (1979). *Love and Limerence: The Experience of Being in Love.* New York: Stein and Day.

Thelen, T. (1988). Effect of late familiarization on human mating preferences. *Social Biology*, 35, 251–601.

Thibaut, J. W., & Kelley, H. H. (1959). *The Social Psychology of Groups.* New York: Wiley.

Tooke, W., & Camire, L. (1991). Patterns of deception in interpersonal and intrasexual mating strategies. *Ethology and Sociobiology,* 12, 345–364.

Townsend, J. M. (1995). Sex without emotional involvement: An evolutionary interpretation of sex differences. *Archives of Sexual Behavior,* 24, 173–206.

Townsend, J. M., & Levy, G. D. (1990). Effects of potential partners' physical attractiveness and socioeconomic status on sexuality and partner selection: Sex differences in reported preferences of university students. *Archives of Sexual Behavior,* 19, 149–164.

Townsend, J. M., & Wasserman, T. (1998). Sexual attractiveness: Sex differences in assessment and criteria. *Evolution and Human Behavior,* 19, 171–191.

Trievers, R. (1972). Parental investment and sexual selection. In B. Campbell (Ed.) *Sexual Selection and the Descent of Man 1871–1971.* Chicago: Adline-Atherton, 136–179.

Trost, M., & Alberts, J. K. (1998). An evolutionary view on understanding sex effects in communicating attraction. In D. J. Canary et al (Eds.) *Sex Differences and Similarities in Communication: Critical Essays and Empirical Investigations of Sex and Gender in Interaction.* LEA's communication series. Mahwah NJ: Lawrence Erlbaum, 233–255.

Unger, R. K. (1975). *Sex Stereotypes Revisited: Psychological Approaches to Women's Studies.* New York: Harper and Row.

Umberson, D., & Houghs, M. (1987). The impact of physical attractiveness on achievement and psychological well–being. *Social Psychology Quarterly,* 50, 227–236.

Valins, S. (1966). Cognitive effects of false heart rate feedback. *Journal of Personality and Social Psychology,* 4, 400–408.

Veitch, R., & Griffitt, W. (1976). Good News Bad News: Affective and interpersonal effects. *Journal of Applied Social Psychology,* 6, 69–75.

Walster, E. (1965). The effect of self-esteem on romantic liking. *Journal of Experimental Social Psychology,* 1, 184–197.

Walster, E., Aronson, V., Abrahams, D., & Rottman, L. (1966). The importance of physical attractiveness in dating behavior. *Journal of Personality and Social Psychology,* 4, 508–516.

Walster E., & Berscheid, E . (1971). Adrenaline makes the heart grow fonder. *Psychology Today,* June, 47–62.

Walster-Hartfield, E., & Walster, G. W., (1981). *A New Look at Love.* Reading, MA: Addison-Wesley.

Walster, E., Walster, G. W., Piliavin, J., & Schmidt, L. (1973). "Playing hard to get": Understanding an elusive phenomenon. *Journal of Personality and Social Psychology,* 26, 113–121.

Watts, A. (1985). Divine Madness. In John Welwood (Ed.) *Challenge of the Heart.* Boston: Shambhala.

Weiderman, M. W., & Allgeier, E. R. (1992). Gender differences in mate selection criteria: Sociobiological or socioeconomic explanation? *Ethology and Sociobiology*, 13, 115–124.

Weinberg, H. (1997). On two psychodynamic approaches to love, couple relationships, and marital therapy. *Sihot* ("Conversations", in Hebrew), 11, 93–99.

White, G. L. (1980). Physical attractiveness and courtship progress. *Journal of Personality and Social Psychology*, 39, 660–668.

White, G. L., & Shapiro, D. (1989). Don't I know you? Antecedents and social consequences of perceived similarity. *Journal of Experimental Social Psychology*, 23, 75–92.

White, G. L., Fishbein, S., & Rutstein, J. (1981). Passionate love: the misattribution of arousal. *Journal of Personality and Social Psychology*, 41, 56–62.

Whitehouse, J. (1981). The role of the initial attracting quality in marriage: Virtues and Vices. *Journal of Marital and Family Therapy*, 7, 61–67.

Wilson, W. (1989). Brief resolution of the issue of similarity versus complementarity in mate selection using height preference as a model. *Psychological Reports*, 65, 387–393.

Winch, R. (1958). *Mate Selection: A Study of Complementary Needs*. New York: Harper and Row.

Winnicott, D. W. (1976). Ego distortion in terms of true and false self. In D. W. Winnicott (Ed.) *The Maturational Process and the Facilitating Environment*. London: Hogarth Press, 140–152.

Winnicott, D. W. (1965). *The Family and Individual Development*. New York: Basic Books.

Wright, R. A., & Contrada, R. J. (1986). Dating selectivity and interpersonal attractiveness: Toward a better understanding of the "elusive phenomenon." *Social and Personal Relationships*, 3, 131–148.

Yalom, I. D. (1980). *Existential Psychotherapy*. New York: Basic Books.

Yarab, P. E., Sensibaugh, C. C., & Algeier, E. R. (1998). More than just sex: Gender differences in the incidence of self-defined unfaithful behavior in heterosexual dating relationships. *Journal of Psychology and Human Sexuality*, 10, 45–57.

Zajonc, R. B. (1968). Attitudinal effects of mere exposure. *Journal of Personality and Social Psychology*. Monograph Supplement 9, 2, 1–27.

Zajonc, R. B., Adelman, P. K., Murphy S. T., & Niedenthal, P. M. (1987). Convergence in physical appearance of spouses. *Motivation and Emotion*, 11, 333–5.

Zana, J. J., & Pack, S. J. (1975). On the self-fulfilling nature of apparent sex differences in behavior. *Journal of Experimental Social Psychology*, 11, 583–591.

Ziv, A. (1993). *Psychology: The Science of Understanding Human Beings*. (Hebrew) Tel-Aviv: Am Oved.

Photo Permissions

We have made every reasonable effort to identify and locate copyright owners of materials. If any information is found to be incomplete, we will gladly make whatever additional permissions acknowledgments might be necessary.

FIGURE 2. BAL 179901 *Cupidon,* 1891 (oil on canvas) by William-Adolphe Bouguereau (1825–1905). Roy Miles Esq./Bridgeman Art Library, London/New York.

FIGURE 5. Sustris, Lambert. *Venus Awaits the Return of Mars.* Louvre, Paris, France. Reprinted by permission of Cameraphoto/Art Resource, NY.

FIGURE 6. Marilyn Monroe, courtesy of CORBIS/Hulton-Deutsch Collection.

FIGURE 7. Giraudon/Art Resource, NY S0031146 34062 B&W Print. Falconet, Etienne. *Pygmalion Admiring his Statue (Pygmalion and Galatea).* Musee des Artes Decoratifs, Paris, France.

FIGURE 9. Prince Charles and Princess Diana, courtesy of Corel.

FIGURE 12. BEN44372 *Primavera*: Detail of Cupid, by Sandro Botticelli (1444/5–1520). Galleria degli Uffizi, Florence, Italy/Bridgeman Art Library, London/New York.

Index